*Julie Dannenbaum's
Creative Cooking
School*

JULIE DANNENBAUM'S CREATIVE COOKING SCHOOL

*

Illustrations by Tom Funk

The McCall Publishing Company

NEW YORK

Published simultaneously in Canada by
Doubleday Canada Ltd., Toronto.

Library of Congress Catalog Card Number: 77–154247
ISBN 0–8415–0099–1

The McCall Publishing Company
230 Park Avenue, New York, N.Y. 10017

Printed in the United States of America
Design by Tere LoPrete

CONTENTS

Julie Dannenbaum's Creative Cooking School

INTRODUCTION

The question I'm most often asked is, How did you get interested in running a cooking school?

The answer goes back to my childhood, for I grew up in a family of cooks and teachers.

My mother, an excellent cook, believed in letting me do anything I was ready for—and willing to clean up after. I could hardly reach the stove when I was turning out towering layer cakes. Under her tutelage, I learned how to smoke ham and bacon, how to make cottage cheese, even how to candy violets.

Home was fifty-six acres in central Pennsylvania, where we grew everything: apples to zucchini. In June my brothers and I roamed the woods picking wild strawberries, which Mother served with a pitcher of cream almost too thick to pour; I remember the marvelous taste whenever I see *fraises des bois* on the menu in France, where in springtime you can still get the tiny, flavorful berries and the thick, thick cream. Our cellar was full of foods "put up" from our garden—vegetables, relishes, jams, fruits, brandied and plain—and always there was hard cider. We baked bread twice a week, and we churned our own butter. I can't remember a meal Mother couldn't stretch for last-minute guests she or my father invited to our table.

Mother taught me to love cooking. My grandfather, who was a chef on the German Line, and my great uncle, a baker, taught me to respect it as both art and career. My professor-father was sure I'd become a home economics teacher, and at his urging, I enrolled at Penn State.

I stuck out a year and a half in home ec, then I switched courses, but my interest in *food* never wavered. I cooked for family and friends, entertaining frequently. As soon after World War II as European travel was possible again, I took my first lessons at Le Cordon Bleu in Paris. When Dione Lucas came on television a few years after that, I locked my kids in their playroom and sat glued to the set, entranced with her technique. I commuted to New York to take lessons from her, earned her diploma, and eventually became associated with her in the Egg Basket restaurant, where she taught me how to turn out an omelette in thirty seconds. I learned a lot from other teachers as well—among them, Ann Roe Robbins, Michael Field, James Beard, and in Paris, Simone Beck. Then, ten years before I opened my own cooking school, I began to plan how it would be.

I waited until the timing was right. My children obligingly reached their teens just when Americans started to become wildly interested in food and cooking. And I was ready to move, with the wholehearted backing of my family, especially my cooperative husband.

At first, in 1965, I taught two courses in my home, starting with twelve students. By the end of the year, I had eighty names on a waiting list, and I decided to open a real school.

I leased the first floor of a building in Philadelphia's Germantown and began remodeling it to provide a completely equipped demonstration kitchen. A long work counter down the center of the room has twenty-four feet of chopping blocks, cooking tops with ovens below, a deep double sink, and a built-in marble slab for pastry-making. The wall behind is lined with pegboard for hanging pots, pans, and whisks, and with shelves for supplies. A scalloped canopy over the counter shields fans and lights.

My contractor enrolled in the first class—and helped launch the Creative Cooking School, in October, 1966, with champagne toasts.

In each class, I teach a complete meal—at least four recipes, more often five or six. I feel the old classics are great if you have the time. But I'm realistic: no one wants to spend endless hours in the kitchen; everyone wants to be free when guests arrive—yet still serve them a meal they'll remember.

The first step in cooking a successful dinner is to organize a menu that you can manage. In my classes I point out everything that can be done ahead; that way, the students see how to plan their time. There are similar pointers in this book, so you'll know what can be done a week, a day, or a few hours ahead of a party.

But you should consider, when planning a menu, not only your own time but that of the year, for two reasons. First, foods that are in season, fresh foods, are almost always best to cook with (so make the most of strawberries and asparagus in the springtime, green apples and oranges in the fall). Second, heavier foods are more appealing in cold weather; lighter foods belong on summer menus (so chocolate, lemon, and banana desserts are especially good in the winter, while in the summer peaches and berries, which are plentiful then, and sun-ripened and juicy with flavor, are better). My own favorite menu is one I teach in midwinter: Lobster Bisque (see p. 46), Selle d'Agneau (see p. 102), French Green Salad (see p. 194), and for dessert, Poires au Vin Rouge (see p. 226).

Back to your time: good equipment saves it, and saves drudgery too. Without good sharp knives and a decent-size cutting block, chopping vegetables is much more of a chore than it need be. Heavy pots and pans are easier to cook with and worth the investment; you'll be happiest with professional kinds and sizes. In many of the recipes that follow there are notes about special pieces of equipment I've found particularly useful. Many of the recipes include serving and garnishing directions (no Creative Cooking class is over until each dish is properly garnished and ready for presentation); where needed, there are carving directions too, and here again, I must stress the importance of proper equipment: nothing is more dangerous than trying to carve a roast on a slippery platter or on a board that is too small; nothing is more difficult than carving with a dull knife.

For the benefit of beginners, the recipe directions in this book are detailed: I've tried to include explanations and extra information, along with answers to all the questions I've ever been asked. (This material is set off in separate paragraphs, each identified by a dot [•].) I've already answered one question: How did you get interested in running a cooking school? Anticipating another, also frequently asked—What keeps you interested?—I felt at first, and after five years of teaching, still feel, most rewarded when beginners report back to me about a triumphant dinner, a glorious party. I hope that in the recipes that follow, every other possible question is answered, and that as a result of this book, I'll hear about other good dinners, other successful parties.

DO IT MY WAY

The best way to learn to cook is to cook: stand yourself in front of the stove and start right in.

Watching a teacher may inspire you, but the lesson won't really sink in until you try it yourself. If your first effort is a disaster, great! You'll learn more from your mistakes than from your successes. I remember trying to make Hollandaise Sauce when I was a child. Time after time, I'd watched my mother and grandmother make it, always with success. But mine curdled. By the time I got it right, I'd learned a lot about working with eggs. If you want to cook, you mustn't be intimidated by a few failures.

Anyone who can read, and who has the intelligence to follow a recipe, can become a competent cook, even a good one. Really fine cooks are blessed with innate ability to season food, to plan menus, and to think up new ideas, but experience can certainly help to fill the instinct gap.

Don't bore yourself with so-called beginner recipes when you start to cook. It is just as easy to teach yourself to make a soufflé as a white sauce—in fact, white sauce is the foundation for a soufflé. I teach soufflés or crêpes in my first lesson. My theory at the Creative Cooking School is that students learning to make interesting and elegant dishes pick up all of the basics of cooking along the way, and because my students are always making something new and exciting, they never have time to lose their original enthusiasm.

After five lessons, they have learned how to make soufflés, crêpes, mayonnaise, basic brown sauce, velouté sauce, and Hollandaise, as well as how to roast a piece of meat, poach fish, and cook vegetables. They have also learned how to prepare five fantastic dinner party menus, and most important, how to prepare them all either easily or with enough ease to present them to guests in a relaxed manner that belies earlier arduous efforts.

Certain cooking techniques—those for beating egg whites and for deglazing pans, for example—are called for again and again in the recipes that follow. My students learn these techniques—the best I've developed, or culled from the many teachers with whom I've studied—in their first five lessons. Each teacher has his or her own methods. Mine may not suit you, but before you decide, do it my way.

Blanching

This means giving food a quick bath in boiling water. Do it to bacon, for example, to remove its saltiness, to cabbage and onions to weaken their taste, or to peaches, tomatoes, and almonds to loosen their skins.

Bouquet garni

Bouquets garnis are small packages of herbs used for flavoring soups, sauces, and casseroles; they are removed prior to serving. I use 1 rib of celery, 1 bay leaf, ¼ teaspoon of dried thyme, and 1 tablespoon of parsley for a bouquet garni. I make a celery sandwich by laying the herbs on half the celery, folding the other half over, and tying with a string, one end of which I leave long and tie to the handle of the pot or casserole so the bouquet garni will be easy to remove.

Bread crumbs

Save bread that's beginning to go stale and use it to make your own excellent dry bread crumbs. Put slices—1 slice will yield ½ cup of crumbs—on a baking sheet and place in a 300° oven for 15 to 20 minutes, or until the bread is very dry and hard, then break it into pieces and put them in a blender. I store dry crumbs in a covered jar on my shelf and use as needed. To make fresh, or soft, bread crumbs, grate bread in a hand grater or tear it apart with your fingers.

Butter

I feel that unsalted butter gives pastries a richer flavor than does salted butter. In some areas of the country unsalted butter is more expensive than salted, perhaps because it is more perishable (salt in butter helps to preserve it, so that it will keep longer in the store—and in a home refrigerator too). Some of my recipes specify unsalted butter; in those that don't specify, salted is assumed.

Cooking in a covered casserole

Because the lid of a covered casserole dish gets as hot as the sides of the dish, steam rising from the cooking surface escapes rather than condensing. The escaping steam can change the consistency of a sauce or cooking liquid, often undesirably. To prevent this—to maintain the consistency, that is—cover the casserole with foil before putting the lid on. The dead air space between the foil and the lid will then insulate the lid, making it cool enough to condense the steam.

Cooking over high heat

Learn to cook on high heat—it saves time, and that's important today. To do it successfully, you must use heavy-bottomed pans. And you must be attentive—*never* turn your back on a pan on high heat. To avoid scorching or burning food, toss it or move it around in the pan with a wooden spatula. The way to save any mixture that suddenly gets too hot is simply to lift the pan off the heat. Don't waste time turning a knob or pushing a button.

Custards

Custards and dishes of similar consistency—vegetable rings, molds, and mousses—tend to separate and become watery if overcooked. Those that bake in hot-water baths begin to shrink away from the sides of the dish when they're done. Another test for doneness: insert a knife in the custard; if the knife comes out clean, the custard is done.

Deep frying

Generally I use solid vegetable shortening for deep frying because it gives off less odor than other kinds of fat. When frying, never add too much food to the pan at once or the temperature of the fat will drop.

Deglazing pans

After you brown meat, salvage the juices and brown bits in the pan for added flavor in your sauce. Remove the meat from the pan and pour off the excess fat—usually, this is all but about 1 tablespoon. To deglaze with wine, stock, or water, add about ¼ cup liquid to the pan, boil it up over heat, and scrape up the brown bits with a wooden spatula. To deglaze with brandy, flame the pan (see Flaming), and when the flames have died down, scrape up the brown bits they have loosened.

Deveining shrimp

Peel off shrimp shells with your fingers. Fingers are usually faster for most jobs, and never mind the gadgets. For deveining, use a small sharp knife to make a shallow slit along the back of the shrimp, then remove the vein.

Discoloring

White sauces or custard mixtures that contain egg yolk or white wine are allergic to aluminum pans. If you whisk them smooth in aluminum, you'll see them turn gray before your eyes. Use enamel-on-iron or stainless steel. The chef's professional-weight tin-lined copper saucepan is perfect for sauce-making.

Eggs

HARD-COOKING: Bring eggs to room temperature, slip them gently into boiling water, wait until boiling resumes, then set a timer for exactly 12 minutes. Early in the cooking time, turn the eggs over to help keep the yolks in the center. When the 12 minutes are up, plunge the eggs into cold water and chill rapidly to prevent the yolks from turning green around the edges, which is harmless, but unsightly. Crack and shell the eggs under cold running water.

BEATING EGG WHITES: Eggs are easier to separate when they're cold from a refrigerator. However, always let egg whites warm to room temperature before beating them. To beat as much air as possible into egg whites, use a piano-wire balloon whisk, and keeping the tip of it in the bowl at all times, swing it round and round—use wrist muscles, not shoulder muscles; or use a rotary beater and move the beater all over the bottom of the bowl. If an electric mixer is used to beat the egg whites, the whites must be watched closely when they start to get stiff, for it's easy to over-beat with an electric mixer. You'll get much more volume (desirable for soufflés) if you beat egg whites in an unlined copper bowl (this is due to the physical reaction caused by the steel of the beater coming into contact with the copper). Clean the bowl with 1 tablespoon of coarse salt and 1 tablespoon of vinegar—rub it out with paper towels. Rinse with *hot* water. Dry thoroughly. The bowl—and the beaters too—must be completely free of grease, for a speck of it, or of egg yolk, which is fatty, in the whites will prevent them from beating up properly. Egg whites are "stiff" when most of them can be scooped onto a whisk or beater at once. Whites should form peaks, but not be dry. If your recipe calls for salt and cream of tartar (cream of tartar helps stabilize beaten egg whites), add them when the egg whites begin to foam.

BLENDING IN EGG WHITES: First, stir a big spoonful of beaten egg whites into your base to lighten it; you don't have to be too careful about this for egg whites are not as fragile as you've probably been led to believe. Then add the remaining egg whites and fold in (see Folding) quickly and lightly. Do not overmix; it is always better to leave a few fluffs showing than to risk deflating the egg whites.

MAKING MERINGUE: Use an electric mixer and a large bowl to make meringue. Be sure that the bowl and beaters are clean—no grease—and that the egg whites are room temperature. When the whites start to foam, add cream of tartar and continue beating until soft peaks form. Add sugar, 1 tablespoon at a time, beating constantly, and continue beating until the mixture looks like marshmallow. It is ready when you can pinch it between your fingers and it doesn't feel grainy.

ENRICHING SAUCES WITH EGG YOLKS: Beat the egg yolks with a fork. Then, to avoid curdling the sauce when adding the yolks, warm the yolks gradually by stirring a little hot sauce into them. Stir the warm yolk mixture into the sauce. Do not boil a sauce after you've added egg yolks— it may curdle. Do not add egg yolks to sauces that will be cooled and reheated before serving.

Flaming

Heat brandy or liquor in a small long-handled pan just until finger warm. Ignite it—keep your head back—and pour it, flaming, into the pan or over the dish to be flamed, then shake the pan or dish until the flames die.

Folding

This technique is used to combine a fairly delicate substance with a heavier base. Pour the ingredient to be folded in over the original mixture and, using a large rubber spatula, cut down through the center of the mixture to the bottom of the bowl, across the bottom, up a side, over to the center, then down again. Keep turning the bowl as you fold.

Freezing foods

When freezing prepared or partly prepared foods (pastry, soups and sauces, desserts, etc.), make sure they are properly wrapped. I generally use aluminum foil to wrap solid pieces of food and special freezer jars for soups and sauces. I bag desserts in huge plastic bags. I try to move foods out of my freezer within 2 months.

Herbs

I much prefer fresh herbs, but they're not always available. If I can't get fresh tarragon, thyme, basil, or rosemary, I find that substituting 1 teaspoon of the dried herb for 1 tablespoon of the fresh is satisfactory and, if not otherwise specified, assume the herbs in my recipes are dried. However, I *always* use fresh parsley, garlic, and dill, which are readily available and which have a flavor far superior to that of the dried and frozen herbs.

Mushrooms

CLEANING: Never soak mushrooms. Wipe them clean with paper towels dipped in acidulated water—water with a little lemon juice (1 tablespoon to 1 quart of water) in it—or dip them quickly in acidulated water, then dry them with paper towels.

SLICING: To keep the distinctive mushroom shape, trim the stems, then slice the mushrooms vertically from top to stem.

FLUTING MUSHROOM CAPS: Cut off the stems of the mushrooms even with the caps—don't twist the stems out, or the caps will collapse—then with a small curved knife or a lemon stripper, cut grooves that spiral out from the center of each cap to the edges, all around.

SAUTÉING: Melt butter—use 1 tablespoon for ¼ pound of mushrooms—in a skillet, and when it is hot and foaming, add mushrooms, squeeze on a few drops of lemon juice, sprinkle with salt and freshly cracked black pepper, and toss over high heat for about three minutes.

Pastry bags and tubes

Invest in a professional pastry bag—one that's big and washable—and a few plain, rose, and star tubes in various sizes. When using a pastry bag, fit on the proper tube, then fold the top of the bag down over your left hand (if you're right-handed), making a cuff, and fill the bag—no more than ¾ full—by scooping whipped cream, batter, or whatever into it with a large rubber spatula, pushing the spatula against the thumb of your left hand. Then unfold the cuff and make 3 pleats to close the top of the bag, twisting it to force the contents down to the tube. Hold the tube close to the surface you want to decorate and squeeze the bag from the top (most amateurs have trouble because they squeeze the tube near the tip rather than from the top of the bag). Practice using the pastry tube by filling the bag with vegetable shortening and piping it out. Fill the bag over and over again, until you learn how to make attractive rosettes

or cream puffs all the same size. To clean a pastry bag, wash it in soap and warm water or drop it in a washing machine. After washing, just stand it up and allow it to dry thoroughly.

Poaching

Poaching means very gentle simmering in liquid—that is, the liquid should not bubble, just move a bit.

Reheating French-fried appetizers

Set cake racks on a baking sheet, cover the racks with brown paper, lay the appetizers on the paper, and place in a 350° oven for a few minutes.

Rolling up cake or vegetable rolls

When the cake or vegetable is ready to be turned out of the pan, tear off 2 sheets of waxed paper 6 inches longer than the pan and lay them out, overlapping lengthwise, on a counter or board. (Dust the paper with sugar or confectioners' sugar if the recipe so directs.) Invert the pan over the waxed paper, lift it off, and peel off the waxed-paper liner if one was used in baking. Roll up, using the overlapping sheets of waxed paper as an aid. After the first fold, you can align the edges of the overlapping sheets of paper so you have a double thickness of paper to help you as you continue rolling. Cakes should be rolled warm to set their shape, unrolled for filling, and then rerolled. Vegetable rolls may be filled warm or cool.

Salt

Coarse salt (sea salt or kosher salt) seems saltier than table salt to me. When you rub coarse salt on the exterior of roasts or steaks, an attractive crust will form. Many chefs use coarse salt exclusively. The crystals take longer to dissolve than do those of table salt, which makes coarse salt ideal for salad dressings.

Seasoning cold food

It's important to overseason any food that will be served very cold, for chilling deadens flavor. There are no hard and fast rules on how much to overseason—just use a little more salt, vanilla, herb, or whatever than you normally would.

Skimming fat from sauces and stock

Excess fat makes sauces and stock look, and sometimes taste, greasy. The easiest way to remove it—if you have the time—is to chill the sauce or stock; the fat will rise to the top and solidify, and you can lift it off. Or you can tilt the cooking vessel and spoon off the excess fat. If stock or sauce must be absolutely fat-free, finish skimming with a paper towel: lay it on the surface to pick up remaining fat.

Soufflé dishes

A soufflé collar provides both space and support for a soufflé to puff up properly. To make a collar for a soufflé dish, cut a length of waxed paper long enough to go around the dish with some overlap, fold the paper in half lengthwise, place it around the dish, and tie it on with string so it stands 3 to 4 inches above the dish. If you butter or oil a soufflé dish,

butter or oil the collar too. I find that hot soufflés rise better when the dish and collar are not greased. However, we use both greased and ungreased dishes at the Creative Cooking School. If I grease the dish for a hot soufflé, I usually use butter, because it adds flavor. But because oil is less likely than butter to stick, I recommend oil for cold soufflés, mousses, and any dish that is to be unmolded.

Tomatoes

PEELING: Spear a tomato on a fork, twirl it in the flame of a gas range for a few seconds, and the skin will loosen. The skin will also loosen if the tomato is blanched—that is, plunged into boiling water for about 30 seconds.

SEEDING: Cut each tomato in half crosswise, hold a half in the palm of your hand and squeeze out the seeds.

SLICING: For salads, slice tomatoes from stem to bottom. They'll lose the least juice that way.

Unmolding

To make unmolding easier, molds should be oiled before they're filled. Custards and vegetable molds baked in hot-water baths should be removed from the baths and let stand for 5 minutes—to collect themselves —before unmolding. To loosen either baked or chilled molds, run a small knife around the edge—around the center edge too, if it's a ring mold— using a sawing, up-and-down motion. To unmold, place a serving platter over the mold, invert the platter and mold, give both a shake, and lift off the mold.

Vegetables

REFRESHING: As soon as fresh vegetables have boiled to the tender-crisp stage, drain them and plunge them immediately into cold water. This stops the cooking, and it helps set the color—refreshing the vegetables. Vegetables may be cooked in the morning, refreshed, drained, and covered, and stored in a refrigerator, then reheated at night with butter and seasonings.

SLICING: Use a *mandoline* to slice vegetables. It's speedy, and you'll get nice even slices, which will cook uniformly. The instrument has an adjustable blade so you can make thin or thicker slices. (There is also a ridged blade available for making Waffled Potatoes [see p. 186].)

Whipping cream

I whip heavy cream in a large metal bowl set in a bowl of ice, and I prefer to use a piano-wire balloon whisk rather than the hand-held electric or rotary beaters some cooks like. Cream whipped over ice (and sweetened with confectioners' sugar) is less likely to turn into butter and will not separate on standing. This means you can assemble a whipped-cream dessert in the morning for dinner that night. Confectioners' sugar (preferable to granulated) for sweetening should be added when the cream is mounding softly.

APPETIZERS

Nearly every country has its own infinite variety of tempting appetizers. In France it is hors d'oeuvres; in Scandinavia, smorgasbord; in Italy, antipasto; in Russia, zakuska; and so on. In America hors d'oeuvres, cocktail canapés especially, and other appetizers add the touches that transform an ordinary meal into a party and are, for a host or hostess, a delicious way to show off creative talent—which does not mean one should forget that the prime function of an appetizer is to pique the palate.

I do not enjoy satiating my guests with appetizers unless I'm giving a party and they are the mainstay of the menu. Many times I serve only one—Pâté (see p. 17), for example, or Mushrooms à la Grecque (see p. 25)—as a first course at the table or on small plates in the living room.

Casually served, finger foods, such as Crudités (see p. 25)—with thick Greek mayonnaise, Skordalia, for indulgent guests, coarse salt for abstemious ones—are a perfect preamble to a rich dinner. More and more, raw vegetables are the "in" appetizer, for—face it—appetizers in the main are eaten by people who don't need them.

For the "little something to nibble on" that guests expect with cocktails, many party givers have adopted the Continental custom of passing salted almonds along with a variety of olives. (Just sauté blanched almonds in 2 tablespoons of oil, drain on paper towels, and while the almonds are hot, sprinkle them with coarse salt.) Others fill a basket with flaky home-baked Parmesan Sticks (see p. 30).

For cocktail parties it's fun to have as large as possible an assortment of appetizers. Certainly there should be enough so that guests won't have to go on to a dinner. Such a party can end with omelettes and coffee for those who stay late.

Recipes for a variety of party appetizers, all my favorites, are in this chapter, and all of them are geared for advance preparation; most can be made days or even weeks ahead. I've included such perennial pleasers as Quiche Lorraine (see p. 35)—students of mine say that this quiche is the most delectable they've ever tasted—but my fun comes from ferreting out new dishes like Anchovy Rolls (see p. 23) and Roquefort Mousse (see p. 40). All the pâtés must be prepared in advance, ready to be sliced or scooped out and spread on French bread or toast triangles. Terrines improve if made beforehand and served a few days later.

Of course, the grandest appetizer of all is fresh caviar. Serve it in the tin buried in ice and accompany it with hot toast, lemon, and if you must, chopped onion. It will disappear quickly. I've been told that the taste for caviar, like that for olives, is an acquired one; but when caviar and olives are both served, notice that the caviar almost always disappears first.

When serving appetizers, make them look as good as they taste. The recipes suggest garnishes and serving ideas. Put your imagination to work too; but guard against overdecorated appetizers, and remember that all garnishes should be edible. Interesting platters, divided dishes, chafing dishes, all add festive touches to appetizers, which should, ideally, be clean-tasting, even a little sharp, to titillate the palate. If dinner is to follow, they should complement the rest of the meal.

PÂTÉ

This recipe makes about 2 cups of smooth pâté, delicately flavored. It can be chilled in a crock or a small loaf pan, served in the crock or unmolded from the loaf pan and sprinkled with chopped parsley. Provide thin slices of whole wheat bread, Melba toast, or thick pieces of French bread to spread it on.

1 *lb. chicken livers*
1¼ *cups unsalted butter*
1½ *cups finely chopped Bermuda onion*
1 *teaspoon salt*
½ *teaspoon freshly cracked black pepper*
2 *tablespoons brandy*

¼ *cup dairy sour cream*
1 *teaspoon Spice Parisienne or allspice*
1 *tablespoon Benedictine*
1 *tablespoon lemon juice*
2 *tablespoons chopped black truffles, or crushed pistachios*

1. Wash chicken livers and dry with paper towels. Melt ¼ cup of butter in a large skillet over high heat, and when foaming subsides, add chicken livers. Sauté quickly over high heat.

• Many people feel compelled to move the chicken livers around in the pan. Don't. Let them hit the pan, take on color, and get a little crusty on the bottom. Then turn them over all at once and brown the other sides.

2. When turning the livers, add chopped onion, and if necessary, a little more butter. Cook until onion is wilted. This whole process takes about 15 minutes. The livers should still be pink inside.

3. Remove from heat. Add salt and pepper and flame with brandy that has been put in a little copper pan with a long handle, heated to luke-warm, and ignited with a match.

4. After flames subside, stir in sour cream, spice, and Benedictine.

5. Purée mixture in a blender, then work it through a fine sieve to make it smooth. Set mixture in refrigerator to chill for at least 30 minutes.

6. Beat 1 cup butter in electric mixer until it is light and creamy. Add cooled liver and continue beating until smooth.

• If liver mixture isn't chilled when it is added to creamed butter, the result will be oily in texture.

7. Taste for seasoning.

• As much as another teaspoon of salt may be needed.
• All foods prepared to be served cold should be slightly overseasoned. Cold foods require more salt than hot foods.

8. Stir in lemon juice and truffles, or pistachios, and mix well.

• Unused truffles from an opened can of them can be transferred to a small jar, and with the addition of truffle juice and enough Madeira or brandy to cover, stored in a refrigerator. They will keep indefinitely.

9. Pour pâté into a crock or loaf pan, cover, and chill in refrigerator until firm—at least 2 hours, preferably overnight.

• This pâté keeps in the refrigerator for 4 to 5 days. Be sure it's covered, since chicken livers tend to darken. The best way is to put a little melted butter, liquid aspic (see p. 243), or buttered wax paper over the top, then cover with a tight lid.
• Let the pâté stand at room temperature for 20 minutes before serving it.
• The pâté can be frozen, but for no longer than 1 month. Frozen pâté should be thawed in a refrigerator for 24 hours, then let stand at room temperature for 20 minutes before it is served. *Makes 6 to 8 servings.*

PYRAMID OF CHEESE BALLS

2 cups grated Gruyère cheese
2 rounded tablespoons flour
4 stiffly beaten egg whites
¾ cup bread crumbs (see p. 7)
½ teaspoon salt
¼ teaspoon freshly cracked white pepper
Fat for deep frying
½ cup grated Parmesan cheese

1. Mix Gruyère cheese, flour, and egg whites together and roll mixture, which will be wet, into balls the size of marbles.

•If the balls are made larger they can be served as a first course, or as a luncheon or supper dish with a hot tomato sauce (see p. 250).
• Sharp Cheddar, or any hard, sharp cheese, can be substituted for the Gruyère. Hard cheese is easier to grate.
• For a more piquant flavor, add 1 tablespoon chopped chives or 1 teaspoon freshly grated onion to the cheese mixture.

2. Coat the balls with bread crumbs seasoned with salt and pepper and chill for 15 minutes.
3. Heat fat to 375° in a large heavy saucepan, a deep fryer, or an electric skillet.

• Fat should be at least 2 inches deep. In my classes, we use solid shortening for deep frying.

4. Drop balls into hot fat, 4 or 5 at a time. Brown on all sides, remove with a slotted spoon, and drain on paper towels.

• The reason for frying only 4 or 5 balls at a time is to hold the temperature of the fat. Dump in a dozen chilled balls at once, and temperature plunges.

5. Place a paper doily on a round serving platter, pile balls in a pyramid, and sprinkle them with Parmesan cheese.

• Cheese balls are best when eaten as soon as they are fried. If necessary, they can be held for 15 minutes in a low (150–200°) oven, or they can be frozen, or prepared in the morning and reheated at cocktail time. To reheat, set cake racks on a baking sheet, cover with brown paper, and lay cheese balls on the paper; place in a 350° oven for a few minutes.
Makes 6 to 8 servings, or about 24 balls.

Hors d'Oeuvres Variés

I like to assemble these when I have omelette parties. Guests like them; they're interesting to serve; and they take the place of a salad. Ideally you should have a collection of *raviers*, the small oblong plates used in Europe for serving hors d'oeuvres. The food can be prepared and arranged in the dishes—be aware of colors when doing the arranging—early in the day, covered with plastic wraps, and refrigerated until serving time. For many hors d'oeuvres, the longer the time spent marinating, the better the taste seems to be.

There is no *recipe*, and the following suggestions do not always give measures by the teaspoonful. Use judgment, some imagination—and what happens to be on hand in the refrigerator.

• Ripe avocado, peeled and cut in thin slices, arranged alternately with pink grapefruit sections, and dressed with Vinaigrette Sauce (see p. 252).
• Genoa salami, rolled into cigarette shapes, garnished with chopped black olives, and dressed with good French olive oil.
• Carrots, finely shredded, mixed with white raisins (2 tablespoons for 4 carrots), and dressed with Vinaigrette Sauce.
• Red radishes, sliced as thinly as possible and mixed with enough sour cream (about 2 tablespoons for 1 bunch of radishes) to hold them together. Season with chopped chives (1 tablespoon per bunch), salt (½ teaspoon per bunch), and freshly cracked white pepper (¼ teaspoon per bunch).
• Celery, finely minced, then mixed with drained chopped anchovies (1 2-oz. can for 4 ribs of celery) and a little Vinaigrette Sauce.
• Cherry tomatoes (with their stems on), washed in ice water just before serving, then sprinkled with coarse salt.
• Swiss cheese, diced, then mixed with caraway seeds (1 tablespoon per ½ lb. of cheese) and enough mustard mayonnaise to bind. (To make mustard mayonnaise, stir about 2 teaspoons Dijon mustard into 2 tablespoons mayonnaise [see p. 251].)
• Cauliflower, divided into flowerets and mixed with sour cream (about 3 tablespoons for a small head) and curry powder, to taste (I use about a teaspoonful for a small head).

Shrimp Pâté

This pâté has a bland, delicate taste, which is enhanced if the pâté is prepared a day ahead of when it's to be served. It is good as a first course and can be beautifully presented.

2¼ lbs. raw shrimp, in shells
1 teaspoon peppercorns
2 teaspoons salt
2 cups unsalted butter
½ teaspoon mace
½ teaspoon chili powder
2 tablespoons finely
   chopped parsley

2 tablespoons finely chopped
   fresh tarragon, or 2 teaspoons dried
1 tablespoon Pernod, or anisette
1 tablespoon lemon juice

1. Put shrimp (in shells) in a pot with enough cold water to cover; add peppercorns and salt, and bring to a boil; then reduce heat and cook until the shrimp turn pink (this should take less than 5 minutes). Take pot off heat and let shrimp cool in the liquid. When they are cool enough to handle, remove shells and devein the shrimp.

2. Put shrimp through a food mill, using the finest blade, or chop finely. Set aside.

3. Beat butter with an electric mixer (use the flat whip if the mixer is a heavy-duty one) until it is very creamy; then beat in the shrimp, a little at a time.

• This step can be done by hand, but the result will not be as creamy.

4. Season with more salt, if desired, the mace, chili powder, parsley, and tarragon and beat until mixture is as smooth as possible. Thin with Pernod, or anisette, and lemon juice.

5. Pack the pâté into a crock or a loaf pan and chill it at least 2 hours, preferably overnight.

• Serve from the crock, with toast fingers, crackers, Melba toast, or whole wheat bread. Or for an elegant first course, unmold the pâté from loaf pan, cut it in slices, and serve them on a bed of greens and garnished with thin slices of lemon or with lemon twists (made by cutting thin lemon slices from the center to the edge, then turning the ends to make a twist). *Makes 8 servings.*

OYSTERS BIENVILLE

These are typically New Orleans. The sauce can be made ahead of time, and baking the oysters takes only minutes. The rock salt keeps the oysters *hot*—a fine serving secret.

4 scallions
6 tablespoons butter

2 tablespoons flour
⅔ cup fish stock (see p. 242),

or bottled clam juice
⅓ cup finely chopped mushrooms
1 egg yolk
⅓ cup dry white wine
¼ teaspoon salt

¼ teaspoon freshly cracked
white pepper
6 cups rock salt, about
2 dozen oysters on half shell
½ cup bread crumbs (see p. 7)
½ cup grated Parmesan cheese

1. Chop scallions very, very fine, the white part plus three-quarters of the green. Sauté in 2 tablespoons of butter in saucepan over high heat until just wilted. Do not let them burn: keep moving them around with a wooden spatula.

2. Remove pan from heat and stir in flour. Return to high heat and cook for 1 or 2 minutes, to remove the raw flour taste, stirring constantly with a wooden spatula to keep the mixture from burning or browning.

• This butter-flour paste is called a roux. Thorough blending of it helps ensure a smooth, lumpless sauce.

3. Remove pan from heat and add fish stock, all at once. Whisk vigorously to make a smooth mixture.

• I always switch from a wooden spatula to a whisk when I add the liquid. Working with the whisk virtually guarantees smoothness.

4. Squeeze mushrooms in the corner of a clean towel to remove excess juice, then stir into stock.

5. Using the whisk, beat the egg yolk with wine. Remove sauce from heat and stir a few spoonfuls of the hot sauce into the egg-wine mixture, then very gradually stir this egg-wine enriched sauce back into the rest of the sauce.

6. Season with salt and pepper and cook over low heat for 5 to 10 minutes, stirring constantly.

• The recipe can be made the day before up to this point. Plastic wrap pressed on the surface of the sauce will keep a skin from forming when it's refrigerated. Reheat the sauce, stirring, when ready to bake the oysters.

7. Fill an ovenproof serving dish with a layer of rock salt and place it in a 400° oven for 20 minutes, or until it is very hot.

8. Place oysters, on half shell, on the hot rock salt. Return dish to oven and bake for about 3 minutes. Meanwhile melt remaining 4 tablespoons of butter.

9. Remove dish from oven, spoon some of the sauce over each oyster, sprinkle with bread crumbs and grated Parmesan cheese. Dribble generously with melted butter and return to oven for 2 to 3 minutes, or until oysters are lightly browned. *Makes 4 servings as a first course, 6 to 8 servings for cocktails.*

ANCHOVY ROLLS

8 *slices bread*	*¾ cup milk*
½ cup butter	*1 egg*
3 *tablespoons Dijon mustard,*	*¾ cup bread crumbs (see p. 7)*
about	*Fat for deep frying*
2 *2-oz. cans flat anchovy fillets*	

1. Remove crusts from bread and cut into fingers. Roll bread as thinly as possible with a rolling pin.

• Regular store-bought white bread, the light fluffy kind, is best here.

2. Melt butter and brush each bread strip with it and Dijon mustard. Use enough mustard so it can really be tasted.
3. Put anchovy fillets in a sieve, run cold water over them, shake off excess, and lay them on paper towels to dry thoroughly.
4. Lay an anchovy fillet on each finger of bread. Roll up tightly and fasten with a toothpick. Dip rolls into a mixture of milk and beaten egg, then roll in bread crumbs.
5. Heat fat (2″ deep) in saucepan or electric frying pan to 375° and fry anchovy rolls, a few at a time, until brown. Remove with a slotted spoon and drain on paper towels. Serve hot.

• If too many are fried together, they become soggy, as the temperature of the fat drops.
• The anchovy rolls can be fried in the morning and reheated before serving. Or they can be frozen. To reheat, set cake racks on a baking sheet, cover with brown paper, and lay rolls on paper; place in a 350° oven for a few minutes. ***Makes 8 servings.***

EGGS MIMOSA

10 *hard-cooked eggs*	*1 cup heavy cream*
8 *oz. black caviar*	*1 bunch watercress*
1 *cup mayonnaise (see*	
p. 251)	

1. Allow 1 egg per person. Shell eggs and cut them in half, crosswise. Cut a slice off the bottom of each half to make it stand up. Remove yolks and set them aside.

• To shell eggs, tap them all over to crack the shell, then peel under running water.

2. Arrange egg whites on a serving dish and fill cavities with caviar, mounding it somewhat.

3. Combine mayonnaise, homemade preferably, with heavy cream whipped to the same consistency. Pour over eggs and caviar, masking them completely.

4. Push reserved yolks through a sieve and sprinkle over masked eggs to resemble mimosa. Garnish with watercress.

• The caviar-filled eggs can be prepared and arranged on a platter in advance. Cover with plastic wrap and store in refrigerator. Add mayonnaise mixture, yolks, and garnish just before serving. *Makes 10 servings.*

GINGER SAUSAGE ROUNDS

1½ lbs. bulk pork sausage
1 medium clove minced garlic
1 tablespoon finely chopped candied ginger

3 separated eggs
Fat for deep frying

1. Mix sausage, garlic, candied ginger, and egg yolks together in a bowl. Beat egg whites until fairly stiff and fold them into sausage mixture.

• There is no salt in this recipe, since most sausage is highly seasoned; if using sausage that is not, sprinkle sausage balls with salt after frying.
• If desired, ¾ lb. ground veal and ¾ lb. finely ground beef may be substituted for the pork sausage. Season meat with 1 teaspoon salt and ½ teaspoon freshly cracked black pepper.

2. Heat fat (2″ deep) in a saucepan or electric skillet to 375° and drop sausage mixture from a teaspoon into fat. Don't add too many teaspoonfuls at a time: doing so will lower too much the temperature of the fat, which must be hot to produce crisp sausage balls. Fry for about 5 minutes, or until brown. Remove with a slotted spoon and drain on paper towels. Serve very hot.

• Ginger sausage rounds can be fried in the morning and reheated, or they can be fried and then frozen. To reheat, set cake racks on a baking sheet, cover with brown paper, lay balls on the paper, and place in a 350° oven for several minutes. *Makes 8 to 10 servings, or about 36 rounds.*

CRUDITÉS WITH SKORDALIA

Skordalia is Greek mayonnaise. It's one of the best dips I know to set out with a colorful assortment of neatly trimmed raw vegetables, arranged on a bed of ice.

Crudités

Scrub and chill and arrange on a bed of crushed ice any or all of the following:

Celery ribs, trimmed neatly
Green and/or red peppers,
   seeded and cut into strips
Baby turnips, thinly sliced
Zucchini, sliced or cubed
Cauliflower flowerets
Carrots, sticks or curls
Eggplant, cubed

White and/or red radishes
Cucumber sticks
Baby pattypan squash, sliced
Black olives
Cherry tomatoes
Raw snowpeas
Fennel, sliced

Skordalia

2 cups mayonnaise (see
  p. 251)
3 medium cloves chopped
  garlic
5 tablespoons bread crumbs
  (see p. 7)

¼ cup ground almonds
2 tablespoons chopped pars-
  ley

1. Stir garlic, bread crumbs, ground almonds, and chopped parsley into bowl of mayonnaise. If not seasoned enough, add salt and freshly cracked white pepper, to taste.
2. Chill 2 hours before serving. ***Makes 2½ cups.***

MUSHROOMS À LA GRECQUE

1 lb. large, firm white mush-
  rooms
2 tablespoons lemon juice,
  plus juice to clean mush-
  rooms

¾ cup dry white wine
1 small bay leaf
2 teaspoons minced shallot
⅓ cup olive oil
¼ teaspoon thyme

6 coriander seeds
¼ teaspoon chervil, or 1 teaspoon chopped fresh parsley
½ teaspoon salt
¼ teaspoon freshly cracked white pepper
1 tablespoon chopped parsley for garnish
1 lemon for garnish

1. Dip mushrooms quickly in cold water mixed with a little lemon juice (about 1 tablespoon to 1 quart of water) and wipe them with paper towels. Trim off ends of stems and cut mushrooms vertically, through cap and stem, in very thin slices.

• Never soak mushrooms. Cleaning them in lemon water helps keep them white. If mushrooms are small, they can be left whole, or quartered.

2. Put mushrooms into an enameled saucepan with all remaining ingredients except garnishes. Bring to a rolling boil and boil for 5 minutes, covered.

3. Drain mushrooms, reserving the liquid, and put them in an earthenware or enameled serving dish.

4. Boil reserved liquid to reduce it by one-third. Strain it and pour over mushrooms. If desired, store in refrigerator, covered.

5. Bring mushrooms to room temperature and garnish with chopped parsley and very thin overlapping slices of lemon before serving. *Makes 6 servings.*

GRACE ZIA CHU'S SHRIMP TOAST

Grace Zia Chu is a noted teacher of Chinese cuisine and my favorite Chinese cooking instructor. This recipe is a slight variation from her original. My proportions are a little different, and I use ginger root and scallions.

½ lb. raw shrimp, in shells
6 water chestnuts
1 egg
1 teaspoon salt
1 tablespoon chopped scallion, white part only
1 teaspoon dry sherry
1 tablespoon cornstarch
1 teaspoon minced ginger root
¼ teaspoon sugar
6 slices 2-day-old homestyle bread
1½ cups peanut oil

1. Shell and devein raw shrimp. Wash and drain. Chop them fine along with water chestnuts.

2. Beat egg slightly and mix in shrimp-water-chestnut mixture, salt, scallion, sherry, cornstarch, ginger root, and sugar.

3. Trim crusts from bread, and cut each slice into 4 triangles. Spread shrimp mixture over each triangle.

4. Heat peanut oil (2" deep) to temperature of 375° on fat thermometer. Lower bread triangles into oil, shrimp side down, and fry about 1 minute; then turn, and fry other side. Fry only a few triangles at a time. Drain on paper towels and serve immediately.

• Shrimp toast can be fried ahead of time, refrigerated or frozen, and reheated. If frozen, it can be reheated without thawing. To reheat, set cake racks on a baking sheet, cover with brown paper, and lay toast triangles on paper; place in a 350° oven for a few minutes; if the toast has been frozen, heat it a little longer—5 to 6 minutes. *Makes 6 servings.*

BOUREKAKIA

To make Bourekakia—a favorite of Ann Roe Robbins, the well-known New York cooking authority—you will need two possibly unfamiliar ingredients: feta cheese, a strong-flavored Greek goat cheese, best if bought in brine (but be sure to rinse it before using), and filo dough, a pastry as thin as onionskin, which is available in Greek or Armenian grocery stores. The pastry comes in sheets, rolled up in plastic wrap, and it can be stored in the freezer. It is very fragile and dries out rapidly; when it does, it breaks into little bits. Work with it one sheet at a time, keeping the remaining sheets covered with a damp, not wet, towel. If filo dough is not available, substitute commercial strudel leaves and handle them the same way. This appetizer is irresistible with drinks.

½ cup coarsely mashed feta cheese
6 oz. cream cheese
2 eggs
¼ teaspoon freshly grated nutmeg

½ cup melted butter
6 to 8 sheets filo dough, each about 11" × 15"

1. Beat both cheeses, eggs, and nutmeg together until smooth.

2. Lay a sheet of filo dough on a slightly damp towel and brush it all over with melted butter. With a knife, cut it into strips 2 to 3 inches wide and about 8 inches long. Place a scant teaspoonful of the cheese mixture near one end of each pastry strip. Fold end of strip over cheese, then fold sides in, one over the other, to enclose cheese. Brush folded-over surface with butter and roll up to make a neat little package of pastry with cheese filling inside.

• Work fast. And keep pastry surfaces brushed with butter, partly to prevent their drying out, partly to get a flaky, butter-rich pastry.

3. Bake in a 350° oven for 20 minutes, or until puffed and brown. Serve warm.

• Bourekakia can be prepared 2 days in advance and stored in a refrigerator on a lightly covered tray. Or they can be frozen, then baked, according to the preceding directions, just before you are ready to serve.
• Sometimes I add 2 tablespoons of tarragon or parsley to the filling.
Makes 8 to 10 servings, or about 36 appetizers.

Pâté Maison

Almost every restaurant in France has a pâté it's proud of. In general, this is a rough country pâté, the kind diners get when they order the "house pâté."

2 lbs. calves' liver	¼ teaspoon dried thyme
1½ lbs. veal	¼ cup cognac
2 large eggs	½ lb. blanched bacon
2 teaspoons salt	1 tablespoon roughly chopped
2 teaspoons freshly cracked	truffle
black pepper	6 chicken livers, marinated 1
3 tablespoons dairy sour	hour in 3 tablespoons
cream	cognac
1 large clove very finely	1 cup aspic (see p. 243)
minced garlic	
1 tablespoon finely chopped	
shallots	

1. Grind the liver twice, using the finest blade on the meat grinder; since the veal must also be finely ground, grind it twice too, with the same blade. Then, in a large bowl, mix together liver, veal, eggs, salt, pepper (2 teaspoons is correct), sour cream, garlic, shallots, and thyme.

• I mix the ingredients with my hands—it's the fastest, most thorough way.

2. Heat cognac to lukewarm, ignite, and pour it, flaming, over the meat mixture. Let it burn out. Blend well.
3. Line a pâté mold (or a 9-by-5-by-3-inch loaf pan) with overlapping strips of blanched bacon. Let bacon hang over sides of pan.

• To blanch bacon: put bacon strips in cold water in a saucepan, bring to a boil, boil 1 minute, drain in a sieve.

4. Fill lined mold with half the liver-veal mixture. Sprinkle chopped truffle down the middle lengthwise and arrange the marinated chicken livers in a row over them. Add rest of the liver-veal mixture and fold bacon ends over the top to cover completely.

5. Wrap the mold completely in heavy-duty aluminum foil and place in a pan of boiling water reaching three-quarters up the mold. Bake on the middle shelf of a 325° oven for 2 hours. Remove from oven.

6. Weight pâté down with a brick and chill overnight in refrigerator.

• The pâté may ooze, so it's a good idea to leave the mold in the second pan (emptied of water) when refrigerating it. Weighting it down makes the pâté compact, and easier to slice.

7. Serve pâté (which is excellent with French bread) chilled and cut in thin slices. Garnish it with chopped aspic.

• This pâté can be stored in the refrigerator for 1 week or frozen for up to 1 month. *Makes 12 to 16 servings.*

LIPTAUER CHEESE

The classic accompaniment is icicle radishes, but red radishes, cucumber sticks, celery, and finocchio can all be used. The best bread to serve with this dish is thinly sliced caraway rye.

16 oz. cream cheese	*1 tablespoon paprika*
½ cup unsalted butter	*1 cup finely chopped onion*
½ cup creamed cottage cheese	*1 2-oz. can flat anchovy fillets,*
2 tablespoons heavy cream	*chopped*
1 tablespoon anisette	*1 3½-oz. jar capers*
2 teaspoons caraway seeds	*2 bunches white radishes*

1. With electric mixer, beat cream cheese and butter until very light and creamy. Add cottage cheese and whip until fluffy. Thin with heavy cream and flavor with anisette. Add caraway seeds and mix well.

2. Mound cheese decoratively on a serving plate. Use a spatula to smooth the surface and to make decorative indentations around the sides. Dust top with paprika, preferably medium-sweet Hungarian.

• This recipe may be made up early in the morning and refrigerated until evening; just be sure to cover it. Take it out of the refrigerator about ½ hour before serving time.

3. When serving, set out small dishes containing chopped onion, chopped anchovies, and drained capers as condiments for the Liptauer cheese. Also set out icy-cold white radishes. *Makes 8 to 10 servings.*

PARMESAN STICKS

> *1 recipe of all-purpose puff*   *1 egg white*
> *pastry (recipe follows)*   *4 tablespoons paprika*
> *¾ cup Parmesan cheese*

1. Make puff pastry the day before it is to be shaped and baked. Refrigerating it overnight gives the pastry a chance to rest, thus making it easier to handle.

2. Cut the chilled pastry in half from fold to fold. (It's easier to roll out half at a time.) Roll each half on a lightly floured board sprinkled, about ⅛-inch thick, with the grated cheese.

3. Prick pastry all over with a fork and brush it with slightly beaten egg white. Sprinkle with more cheese and a little paprika. Press the cheese into the pastry with a rolling pin.

4. With a pastry wheel, cut pastry into strips ¾ of an inch wide and 5 to 6 inches long.

5. Dampen a baking sheet with water, or line it with baking parchment. Place pastry strips on baking sheet, twisting them if desired, and chill in refrigerator for 30 minutes.

6. Place baking sheet on the middle shelf of a preheated 400° oven and bake the sticks for about 10 minutes. Reduce heat to 300° and bake another 10 minutes, or until crisp. *Makes 12 to 16 servings, or 50 to 60 sticks.*

All-Purpose Puff Pastry

This is puff pastry made the Scandinavian way, which always works, even on the hottest day.

1¾ cups loosely packed flour, plus flour to dust on dough and rolling surface

½ teaspoon salt
1 cup chilled unsalted butter

1. Place 1¾ cups of flour in a bowl and stir in salt.

• If salted butter is used instead of unsalted, add only ¼ teaspoon salt.

2. Cut butter into chips the size of almonds.

3. Turn the chips over in the flour to coat, then with a pastry blender, cut them into the flour. The mixture should look like small peas.

4. Sprinkle the mixture with iced water (use about 5 tablespoons) and stir it with a large fork until it holds together in big chunks.

• Be sure there's ice in the water. It's important to have everything cold or chilled when making puff pastry.
• The amount of water needed will depend on the weather: on dry days more will be required than on humid ones.

5. With your hand, scoop the mixture together and shape it into a dough ball.

6. Dust the ball with flour, wrap it in waxed paper, and refrigerate it for 30 minutes to 1 hour.

7. Place chilled ball on lightly floured marble or on a lightly floured pastry board and roll it out to make a rectangle approximately 8 inches wide by 16 inches long.

• With the first rolling, the dough will look raggedy and will probably be sticky. Use a little flour, if necessary, to keep it from sticking to the marble or board and to the rolling pin.

8. Fold the rectangle into thirds (like a business letter), give it a quarter turn (folds will be on right and left), then roll it into a rectangle and fold it into thirds again.

• This is called a *turn*. Each turn consists of 2 rollings, and the dough must be turned 3 times in all—that is, rolled and folded a total of 6 times. Each turn will make the dough smoother, so on the next you'll be able to make the rectangle more exact. Try to be as precise as possible.
• A pastry scraper will help you take dough up from the marble or board, to fold in thirds.

9. Wrap dough in waxed paper and chill in refrigerator for at least ½ hour.

• To keep count of the turns, mark the dough with one finger after the first, two fingers after the second, three after the third.

10. Repeat steps 7, 8, and 9, then repeat steps 7 and 8, wrap dough in waxed paper again, and allow it to rest overnight in a refrigerator before the final shaping and baking.

• The dough can be frozen after the third turn. Wrap it in plastic wrap or foil. Remove it from the freezer the day before it is to be used and thaw it in a refrigerator.

11. Roll out dough and cut it as recipe directs.

• Scraps left over can be stacked on top of each other or bunched together, then rolled out and used.

12. Place dough on a baking sheet that has been dampened with cold water, chill in a refrigerator (the dough should always come to a hot oven from the chill of a refrigerator), then bake in a preheated 400° oven for 5 to 10 minutes. *Makes enough for 1 dozen 3-inch tart shells, 1 9-inch tart shell, 24 Piroshki, or 50 to 60 Parmesan Sticks.*

PIROSHKI

Piroshki, little meat turnovers, come from Imperial Russia, where they were usually served with clear borscht. This recipe is for bite-size ones, to serve with cocktails. Any kind of pastry, including plain piecrust, can be used, but puff pastry is best.

1 recipe of all-purpose puff pastry (see p. 30)	*2 chopped hard-cooked eggs*
¾ cup chopped onion	*½ teaspoon salt*
2 tablespoons butter	*¼ teaspoon freshly cracked black pepper*
½ lb. beef, ground twice	*1½ tablespoons dairy sour cream, about*
1 tablespoon chopped parsley	*1 egg white*
2 tablespoons chopped fresh dill	

1. Prepare puff pastry the day before the Piroshki are to be made. It must rest in a refrigerator overnight before final rolling and shaping.

2. Cook onion in butter until transparent, but do not let it brown. Add ground beef and cook until beef is no longer pink. Do not overcook.

• Instead of ground beef, ground veal, chicken, tongue, pork, or ham can be used. The meat should be raw, not leftover.

3. Mix in parsley, dill, hard-cooked eggs, salt, and pepper, and enough sour cream to hold the mixture together.

4. Halve the pastry (after its three turns and overnight chilling); cut through the folds. Roll out one half at a time, rolling it as thin as possible. Cut into rounds with a 2-inch cutter.

• If puff pastry is too thick, the little turnovers will open up when baked.

5. Brush edges of pastry circles with egg white, lightly beaten. Put a scant teaspoonful of filling on each circle. Fold over and seal edges together.

• Don't fill the turnovers too full—it makes the edges difficult to seal. Pinch edges together with fork tines to seal them, pressing all around the edges with determination.

6. Place Piroshki on a damp baking sheet and chill in refrigerator for at least ½ hour, or until ready to bake.

• Piroshki can be made ahead and frozen unbaked. Bake them a few minutes longer if they are still frozen when put in the oven.

7. When ready to bake, move Piroshki from refrigerator to a pre-heated 400° oven for 15 to 20 minutes, or until light brown. Serve hot. *Makes 8 to 10 servings, or about 24 Piroshki.*

BLINI WITH CAVIAR

Blini are Russian crêpes made with yeast. Usually they contain buck-wheat flour, although authentic Russian blini can be made with all-white flour too.

½ package active dry yeast	1 cup melted, unsalted
½ teaspoon salt	butter
1 separated egg	8 oz. red or black caviar
1½ cups lukewarm milk	2 cups dairy sour cream
1½ cups flour	1¾ cups chopped onion or 1
½ cup buckwheat flour	cup chopped fresh chives

1. Soften yeast in 2 tablespoons of lukewarm water; stir in salt.
2. In a large bowl, beat egg yolk into milk; add the yeast mixture. Add flour and buckwheat flour and beat until batter is smooth. Cover bowl with a cloth and let it stand in a warm place for 2 hours while batter rises.
3. Beat egg white until it forms soft peaks; fold into batter.
4. Drop batter by tablespoonfuls onto a greased griddle or frying pan; cook until the blini are brown on the bottom and little bubbles show on top; turn and brown other side.

• The griddle is hot enough when a drop of cold water will dance on it.
• If the griddle is well seasoned, it won't need greasing each time it's used. Moisten a wadded paper towel with oil and keep it handy to wipe the surface should blini begin to stick.
• Keep finished blini warm in a 200° oven while cooking the rest.

5. Pour hot butter over blini and serve (allow 2 blini per serving) with caviar, very cold sour cream, and chopped onion or chives. *Makes 15 servings or 30 blini, 3 inches in diameter.*

QUICHE LORRAINE

A 9-inch quiche can be cut into quarters or sixths and served as a main dish for luncheon or supper. Cut in eighths, it can be served as an hors d'oeuvre or first course. Cut into very thin wedges (it will make 16 to 20), it can be served at a cocktail party. In this event keep the wedges in the original pie shape on a serving platter and let the guests help themselves.

1 lb. bacon	2 eggs
¼ cup fine bread crumbs (see p. 7)	2 egg yolks
	2 teaspoons Dijon mustard
6 tablespoons freshly grated Parmesan cheese	1 teaspoon salt
	¼ teaspoon freshly cracked white pepper, or cayenne pepper
1 9″ partly baked pâte brisée shell (recipe follows)	
½ cup shredded Gruyère cheese	1½ cups half-and-half, or milk, or light or heavy cream

1. Cut bacon in little pieces and fry it slowly until crisp. Drain bacon on paper towels and reserve the fat.

• Another way to cook the bacon is in a baking pan, in a 350° oven.

2. Mix bread crumbs with 2 tablespoons Parmesan cheese and sprinkle into partly baked pâte brisée shell.

• The partly baked pastry shell insures a crisp crust. The fine bread crumbs help to seal the shell and prevent sogginess.

3. Sprinkle bacon bits over bread-crumb mixture, reserving a little bacon for garnish. Sprinkle Gruyère cheese over bacon.

• Instead of Gruyère cheese, Swiss or Cheddar may be used.

4. Whisk eggs and egg yolks in a bowl until blended but not frothy. Add mustard, remaining Parmesan cheese, and salt and pepper. Stir in ¼ cup of the reserved bacon fat (it should be liquid, but not hot).

5. Stir in half-and-half and pour the custard mixture over bacon and cheese in the pastry shell.

6. Bake in a 350° oven for about 15 minutes, or until custard is set. To test whether custard is set, insert a silver knife into it; if the custard is set, none will stick to the knife when it's pulled out.

• If quiche is to be baked ahead—but not frozen—and reheated before serving, bake it only 10 minutes and reheat in a 350° oven for 10 minutes. If it is to be frozen, bake it completely and either heat it or let it come to room temperature before serving.

7. Garnish with reserved bacon bits. *Makes 8 servings.*

Pâte Brisée Shell

This flaky, buttery crust is ideal for quiches, tarts, and turnovers.

2 cups loosely packed flour, 1 teaspoon salt
plus flour to dust on rolling ½ cup chilled unsalted butter
surface ¼ cup vegetable shortening

1. Place 2 cups of flour in a bowl and stir in salt.

• Lightly salted butter can be used instead of sweet butter. If this is done, use only ½ teaspoon of salt.

2. Cut in butter and shortening with a pastry blender or work them in with fingertips, lifting some up and letting it fall off your fingers. Work quickly (so the mixture stays cool), until the mixture looks like small peas.

• Adding vegetable shortening to the butter makes the pastry flakier.

3. Add just enough iced water (3 to 4 tablespoons), 1 tablespoon at a time, to hold the mixture together in a dough ball.

• Sprinkle the water on the flour mixture while tossing it with a fork to distribute the water as evenly as possible. With cupped hand, try to gather the mixture into a dough ball. If it is still crumbly, add another tablespoon of water. The amount of water needed will depend on the humidity of the day. Use as little as possible to make a manageable dough, for too much water makes pastry tough.

4. Wrap the dough ball in waxed paper and chill it at least ½ hour.

• The dough can be wrapped in foil or plastic wrap and frozen. Or it can be kept in a refrigerator for up to 2 days. Defrost frozen dough in a refrigerator before using.

5. Flatten the ball on a lightly floured pastry board or a lightly floured marble surface and roll it in all directions with a lightly floured pin. Keep turning the dough to roll it into an even circle. Dust the board (or marble) and the pin with more flour, if necessary, to keep dough from sticking.

• The dough can be rerolled if it doesn't come out right. If it cracks, paste it together with a little beaten egg white or water.

6. Using a pastry scraper, roll the dough around the rolling pin, then unroll it over a 9-inch pan or flan ring.

• French quiches and tarts, unlike American ones, come to the table out of the pan. The filling is supported by straight-sided crust, which is shaped in a flan ring that is removed after the shell is baked.

7. Ease the dough into the pan or ring, using care not to stretch it.

8. Trim off excess dough by pushing the rolling pin over the top of the pan or ring; then press the dough over the top edge of the pan or ring to attach it and keep it from shrinking away from pan or ring during baking.

9. With a fork, prick the dough—not all the way through—all over the bottom.

10. Chill in a refrigerator for about 20 minutes before baking.

• At this stage the dough can be frozen. Defrost it in a refrigerator before baking.

11. Before baking, line the shaped dough with waxed paper and fill it with dried beans or rice, the weight of which will prevent it from puffing up while it bakes.

12. For tarts, bake for ½ hour in a preheated 350° oven; then remove beans, waxed paper, and flan ring, reduce heat to 325°, and bake another 20 to 25 minutes, or until pastry is a pale gold color. Remove from oven and cool on a rack at room temperature. For quiches, bake in a preheated 375° oven for 20 to 25 minutes, or until pastry is set, then remove beans, waxed paper, and flan ring, add filling, and continue baking as recipe directs.

• Partly baked pâte brisée shells can be refrigerated or frozen. **Makes 1 9-inch shell.**

ONION QUICHE

5 cups chopped onions	2 egg yolks
¼ cup butter	½ teaspoon freshly grated
2 eggs	nutmeg

½ teaspoon sugar
1 teaspoon salt
¼ teaspoon freshly cracked
white pepper
1½ cups half-and-half
¼ cup fine bread crumbs
(see p. 7)

1 9" partly baked pâte brisée
shell (see p. 36)
2 to 3 tablespoons chopped
parsley or chopped chives

1. Sauté chopped onion in butter until transparent but not brown.
2. Whisk eggs and egg yolks in a bowl until blended but not frothy. Add nutmeg, sugar, salt, and pepper. Stir in the half-and-half and slightly cooled onions.
3. Sprinkle bread crumbs into partly baked pâte brisée shell and pour in custard.
4. Bake in a 350° oven for about 20 minutes, or until custard is set. Custard is set when a silver knife, inserted into custard, comes out clean.
5. Sprinkle top with chopped parsley or chopped chives. **Makes 8 servings**.

SPINACH QUICHE

1½ 10-oz. pkgs. frozen
chopped spinach
2 eggs
2 egg yolks
1 teaspoon salt
½ teaspoon freshly cracked
black pepper
½ teaspoon freshly grated
nutmeg

2 tablespoons finely grated
onion
2 cups dairy sour cream
¼ cup fine bread crumbs (see
p. 7)
1 9" partly baked pâte brisée
shell (see p. 36)

1. Thaw spinach, drain it well, and squeeze out any excess moisture.
2. Whisk eggs and egg yolks in a bowl until blended but not frothy. Stir in salt, pepper, nutmeg, onion, and sour cream. Fold in spinach.
3. Sprinkle bread crumbs into the partly baked pâte brisée shell and pour in filling.
4. Bake in a 350° oven for about 20 minutes, or until custard is set— that is, until a silver knife inserted in it comes out clean. **Makes 8 servings.**

CRAB QUICHE

2 eggs
2 egg yolks
2 cups half-and-half

½ teaspoon salt
¼ teaspoon freshly cracked
white pepper

¼ teaspoon freshly grated
   nutmeg
1½ lbs. crab meat
¼ cup fine bread crumbs (see
   p. 7)

1 partly baked 9" pâte brisée
   shell (see p. 36)
2 tablespoons chopped parsley

1. Whisk eggs and egg yolks in a bowl until blended but not frothy. Stir in half-and-half, salt, pepper, and nutmeg.

2. Pick over crab meat to remove bits of shell and membrane.

• Use any grade of crab meat. The finest quality is not necessary in this recipe.

3. Sprinkle bread crumbs into partly baked pâte brisée shell and arrange crab meat over crumbs. Pour custard mixture over crab meat.

4. Bake in a 350° oven for about 20 minutes, or until custard is set. (Custard is set when a silver knife can be inserted in it and pulled out clean.)

5. Sprinkle top with chopped parsley just before serving. *Makes 8 servings.*

SMOKED SALMON QUICHE

This quiche must be served as soon as it comes from the oven. If it stands, the salmon toughens.

2 eggs
2 egg yolks
2 cups half-and-half
¼ teaspoon salt
¼ teaspoon freshly cracked
   black pepper
¼ teaspoon freshly grated
   nutmeg

¼ cup fine bread crumbs (see
   p. 7)
1 partly baked 9" pâte brisée
   shell (see p. 36)
1 lb. thinly sliced smoked
   salmon
2 tablespoons chopped fresh
   chives, or chopped parsley

1. Whisk eggs and egg yolks in a bowl until blended but not frothy. Stir in half-and-half, salt, pepper, and nutmeg.

• A little more salt may be needed, but add it cautiously—smoked salmon can be very salty.

2. Sprinkle bread crumbs into partly baked pâte brisée shell and cover with salmon slices. Pour custard mixture over salmon.

3. Bake in a 350° oven for 20 minutes, or until custard is set. When custard is done, a silver knife will come out clean after being inserted in it.

4. Sprinkle top with chopped fresh chives or chopped parsley. *Serve at once. Makes 8 servings.*

Roquefort Mousse

Serve with drinks or as a separate course, with salad.

1½ cups unsalted butter	¼ teaspoon cayenne pepper
1¼ lbs. Roquefort cheese	1 tablespoon vegetable oil
3 tablespoons cognac	
1 tablespoon finely chopped parsley	

1. In mixer, beat butter until light and creamy. Bit by bit, beat in the Roquefort cheese, and continue beating for at least 10 minutes, or until mixture is very, very fluffy. Add cognac, parsley, and cayenne pepper and blend well.

2. Brush a 5-cup loaf mold with oil (don't use too much oil, and be sure to oil the corners) and pour the soft mixture into the mold. Pack it down. Chill mold in refrigerator for at least 2 hours—overnight is better —so flavors blend.

• The mousse can be stored for several days in the refrigerator, or it can be frozen.

3. When ready to serve, run a knife around edges of pan and unmold on a platter. Serve with Melba toast or commercially made water biscuits. *Makes 16 servings.*

Stuffed Edam or Gouda Cheese

This spread is best when made the day before it is to be served and re-frigerated until serving time. It can also be frozen. Please take note that it is highly seasoned; if you prefer milder foods, I suggest cutting back on the cayenne pepper. Serve it with unsalted warm crackers. I like English water biscuits, or stoned wheat thins.

2 lbs. Edam or Gouda cheese	¾ teaspoon cayenne pepper,
1½ cups unsalted butter	about
3 tablespoons cognac	

1. Bring cheese and butter to room temperature. Cut the top off the cheese and hollow it out, leaving the shell about ½ inch thick.

2. Chop all the cheese that has been scooped out, including the top.

3. Put chopped cheese into mixer bowl along with cognac and ¼ teaspoon of cayenne pepper. Beat until the mixture is very creamy. This will

take about 10 minutes. If a heavy-duty mixer is used, beat with the flat whip.

4. Beat in butter, a little at a time, and continue beating until mixture is extremely creamy.

5. Taste for seasoning, and add more cayenne pepper to taste and perhaps a little salt.

6. Use a large rubber spatula to put mixture into a pastry bag fitted with a large star tube. Squeeze mixture into the cheese shell, making a decorative rosette on top.

7. Sprinkle with ½ teaspoon more of cayenne pepper. *Makes 16 servings.*

SOUP

Soup-making as an art—and it is an art—was almost lost after the advent of the tin can.

Yet nothing is more gratifying than homemade soup ladled from a beautiful tureen into warmed or chilled bowls. Whether it is steaming hot or icy cold, bisque or chowder, clear or thick, soup is unquestionably one of the highlights of a meal.

A heavy soup bolsters an otherwise light entrée. A light soup sharpens the appetite at once. Or soup—served with chunks of French bread and a pot of unsalted butter, a good green salad, and fruit and cheese for dessert—can be the main course, and an excellent way to appease appetites.

Fine soup satisfies the most exacting tastes. It introduces the ability of the cook immediately; it establishes the foundation of the entire meal. Making it demands time, and care in the preparation of basic stocks, but making fine soup can be one of the most individual and creatively satisfying forms of cookery.

Garnishes are essential to soups, and their variety is almost limitless: a light sprinkling of chopped fresh herbs or parsley, of croutons, or of grated cheese, dollops of salted whipped cream or of sour cream, baked custard cut in diamonds or rounds, delicate quenelles, tiny profiteroles, or dumplings, thin slices of lemon, chopped egg, fancy cut vegetables, thin strips cut from crêpes—these are but a few suggestions. Ice cubes may be dropped into some cold soups at the last moment, and shredded or grated fresh vegetables added to cream soups to accent the color and flavor.

Conventions change, but it is difficult to imagine a time when soup will not play an important role in every civilized menu.

POTAGE PAYSANNE

This is my favorite soup. It freezes beautifully, and it is the perfect gift to take to someone who appreciates good soup. It is great as a main course or before a light supper.

8 large, peeled baking potatoes	1 small parsnip
4 large, peeled yellow onions	2 medium cloves garlic
2 small carrots	1 bay leaf
6 ribs of celery	2 tablespoons salt
4 leeks, white part only	1 teaspoon freshly cracked white pepper
3 tomatoes, unpeeled, but with stem ends removed	1 cup frozen unsalted butter
2 peeled turnips	2 sprigs fresh chervil, optional
6 large mushrooms	2 lbs. fresh spinach, washed and trimmed of stems

1. Cut the first 9 vegetables into medium-size pieces, splitting the leeks lengthwise and holding them under running water to rinse away the sand.

• Don't omit the turnips, whether a lover of them or not, for they combine with the other vegetables to add subtle flavor.

2. Put the cut vegetables into a large heavy saucepan and add enough cold water to cover. Add the garlic and other seasonings.

• The garlic doesn't have to be peeled; just lay the cloves on a chopping board, cover with the flat of a heavy knife, and lean on the knife. This will crush the garlic just enough.

3. Place the frozen butter on top of the vegetables, and add the fresh chervil if it's available. Don't substitute dried chervil. Cover the pan with a tight-fitting lid, and cook over medium heat about 45 minutes, or until vegetables are tender but not mushy.

4. Remove from heat and stir in spinach, stirring until spinach is wilted. This takes only a few minutes.

• Watercress, lettuce, or sorrel may be substituted for the spinach if desired.

5. Purée the mixture through a food mill, using the medium disk, or a coarse sieve. Do not put it in a blender; if blended, this soup comes out an entirely different product.

6. Taste, and, if desired, add more salt. Serve hot.

• A little hot cream may be added to thin the soup and give it added richness. *Makes 12 to 16 generous servings.*

MINESTRONE ALLA MILANESE

There are as many different kinds of minestrone in Italy as there are vegetable soups in America. Every province has its own. This one, from Milan, is sometimes served cool (not cold), even though it is a thick soup. Genoa flavors minestrone with pesto, a rich paste of fresh basil, pine nuts, garlic, and olive oil pounded together with a mortar and pestle or worked in a blender; the pesto is added to the soup by the teaspoonful. Some minestrones are greener than others; some have more meat in them; some more vegetables. This one has only vegetables, including *cannellini* (white kidney beans). Serve it with bread sticks or good Italian bread.

½ *lb. cubed salt pork*
1½ *cups chopped onions*
¾ *cup chopped carrots*
½ *cup chopped celery*
2 *20-oz. cans* cannellini *(white kidney beans), rinsed and drained*
2 *cups sliced zucchini*
1 *cup shredded cabbage*
1 *cup tomatoes, peeled, seeded, and diced*
2 *tablespoons tomato paste*
2½ *cups cubed baking potatoes*
2 *quarts chicken stock (see p. 241)*

3 *cloves chopped garlic*
1 *tablespoon chopped parsley*
2 *teaspoons salt*
½ *teaspoon freshly cracked black pepper*
1 *tablespoon chopped fresh basil, or 1 teaspoon dried basil*
½ *lb. fresh green peas, shelled*
¾ *cup elbow macaroni or other pasta*
1 *cup freshly grated Parmesan cheese*

1. Put the salt pork in a deep soup kettle and try it out—that is, cook the cubes over high heat until they are very crisp.

2. Add all remaining ingredients except pasta, peas, and cheese and bring to a boil. Cover, reduce heat, and simmer about 1 hour, or until vegetables are barely tender.

3. Add pasta, peas, and ½ cup of cheese and simmer another 30 minutes.

4. Taste for seasoning and add more salt if desired. Serve hot, or at room temperature, in bowls garnished with the remaining Parmesan cheese, freshly grated. *Makes 12 to 16 servings.*

CHESTNUT SOUP

Every time I serve chestnut soup my guests rave. Nobody knows what it is.

Instead of garnishing it with parsley, I sometimes add a dollop of salted whipped cream; this makes it pretty rich, but many people like it. Other times I use chopped roasted chestnuts as a garnish.

¾ cup unsalted butter
1 cup diced celery
½ cup diced carrots
1½ cups diced onions
1 teaspoon salt
4 lbs. skinned fresh chest-
nuts, or 3 10-oz. cans
cooked chestnuts, or 3 15-
oz. cans unsweetened
chestnut purée

2 quarts strong chicken stock
(see p. 241)
2 egg yolks
¼ cup dry Madeira
2 cups light cream
2 tablespoons chopped
parsley

1. Melt ½ cup of the butter in a large saucepan until it is hot and bubbly. Add the vegetables and salt. Stir over heat until vegetables are wilted. Do not let them brown.

2. Add chestnuts and chicken stock.

• To skin chestnuts, use a small, sharp knife and cut a strip off one side of the chestnut shell, then coat shell with a little oil; bake nuts in a 350° oven 20 to 30 minutes, until both shells and inner brown skins can be removed easily. Or put chestnuts into cold water, bring them to a boil, and boil 1 minute. The shells and inner skin are easiest to remove while the nuts are still warm.

• If canned chestnuts are used, be sure they're the water-pack variety (chestnuts also come packed in sugar syrup, for use in desserts) and add the liquid along with the nuts.

• If substituting canned purée, be sure it is unsweetened.

3. Cover pan, bring to boil, then reduce heat to a simmer, and cook 45 minutes to 1 hour, or until chestnuts and vegetables are soft.

4. Purée the vegetables and broth through a food mill, using the fine disk, or through a sieve. (Don't use a blender to purée this soup. It makes the texture too fine.)

5. Return ingredients to saucepan, set it over medium heat, and add remaining butter 1 teaspoon at a time, whisking it in.

6. Beat egg yolks in a small bowl, beat in Madeira and cream. Gradually add enough of the hot ingredients to the cream-egg mixture to warm it.

• Warming the mixture gradually helps prevent curdling.

7. Stir warmed mixture into the saucepan and heat until piping hot, *but do not boil.* Serve hot, garnished with chopped parsley.

• If chopped roasted chestnuts are used instead of parsley, bake about one dozen chestnuts in a 350° oven for 20 to 30 minutes, or until soft. Skin, then chop finely. Sprinkle with salt and add a teaspoonful to each serving. *Makes 8 servings.*

LOBSTER BISQUE

This is a French recipe for making bisque, a very elegant, very rich soup.

1 quart fish stock (see p. 242)	*3 tablespoons dry Madeira*
2 small uncooked lobsters	*½ cup light cream*
¾ cup unsalted butter	*1 tablespoon finely chopped*
¼ cup flour	*parsley*
1 tablespoon tomato paste	*1 cup croutons*
¾ cup heavy cream	

1. Bring fish stock to a boil and add the lobster. Simmer about 20 minutes, or until lobsters turn red. Let them cool in the stock.

2. When the lobsters are cool, carefully remove all the meat from them, dice it, and set it aside. Save the stock.

3. Because the lobsters are small, the shells can be crushed and used to flavor butter. Cut shells in pieces and put them in a blender, along with the tiny legs. Add ½ cup of butter, push it down, and keep starting and stopping the blender, pushing the mixture down frequently. This takes a little work, but it finally goes through. When the mixture is completely ground, force it through a very fine strainer. None of the shells should come through, just the lobster-flavored butter.

4. Melt ¼ cup of butter in saucepan, stir in flour with a wooden spatula, and cook over high heat, stirring about 2 minutes. The flour should cook but not brown. Add tomato paste and remove from heat. Strain in the

fish stock, and whisk it vigorously. Return to high heat and cook, stirring constantly, until mixture comes to a boil. Turn heat to low and simmer *very* slowly for 10 to 15 minutes.

5. Add lobster-flavored butter, bit by bit, beating it in with a whisk.

6. In a small bowl, beat heavy cream over ice until it begins to thicken. Mix in the Madeira and continue beating until mixture is thick. Stir this and light cream carefully into saucepan.

7. Stir in diced lobster meat and heat through, but do not boil. Stir in chopped parsley and serve hot, with croutons. ***Makes 4 to 6 servings.***

MUSHROOM SOUP ROYALE

The combination of dried and fresh mushrooms gives this consommé-type soup a most interesting flavor. The custard garnish is what makes it *royale.*

1 small (about 2-oz.) box dried (not freeze-dried) mushrooms

1½ quarts veal stock (see p. 242), or chicken stock (see p. 241), or a mixture of the two

½ lb. finely diced fresh mushrooms

3 tablespoons butter

¼ cup Calvados

Custard Royale (recipe follows)

2 tablespoons chopped parsley

1. Soak dried mushrooms in cold water to cover for at least 1 hour. Drain, chop, and combine with stock in saucepan. Simmer for 1 hour.

2. Cook the diced fresh mushrooms in butter over low heat for a few minutes, or just long enough to give them a good butter flavor. Add to mixture in saucepan and simmer a few minutes longer.

3. Strain (the soup can be served without straining if desired), stir in Calvados, and serve very hot in soup cups, with a garnish of Custard Royale and chopped parsley.

Custard Royale

1 egg

1 egg yolk

2 tablespoons milk

¼ teaspoon salt

Pinch freshly cracked white pepper

¼ teaspoon freshly grated nutmeg

1. Beat egg and egg yolk in a small bowl, then add milk and seasonings. Pour mixture into a greased 9-inch-by-5-inch loaf pan. The custard mixture should be ⅛ to ¼ inch deep. Set loaf pan in a pan of hot water and

place in a 300° oven. Bake for 20 to 30 minutes, or until custard is set. Custard is set when a silver knife, inserted into custard, comes out clean.

2. Cool, then cut in small fancy shapes with truffle cutters—diamond shapes, rounds, and so on—and use as garnish for soup.

• Place a cutout in each soup cup before filling it with hot soup. The custard will float to the top. ***Makes 6 to 8 servings.***

PUMPKIN SOUP

I feel compelled to serve pumpkin in one form or another at Thanksgiving time. Since pumpkin pie is not one of my favorite foods, we have pumpkin soup. It is a delicious change on a holiday menu.

2 cups pumpkin pulp
3 cups strong chicken stock (see p. 241)
½ cup chopped onion
½ cup chopped celery
2 tablespoons butter
1 teaspoon salt
½ teaspoon freshly cracked white pepper

3 tablespoons honey
½ teaspoon freshly grated nutmeg
1 cup heavy cream
½ cup light rum, about
2 tablespoons chopped parsley, or sliced boiled chestnuts

1. Combine pumpkin pulp, chicken stock, onion, and celery in a saucepan. Bring to a boil, turn heat to simmer, cover, and cook about 20 minutes or until vegetables are barely tender.

• Canned pumpkin pulp can be used, but be sure it's unseasoned.

• To make pumpkin pulp, cut pumpkin in half and remove seeds and stringy fibers, then cut pumpkin in small pieces and peel; cook, covered, in a small amount of boiling salted water 25 to 30 minutes, or until tender; drain and mash. A 2-pound pumpkin makes 2 cups of pulp. The pulp can be frozen in pint containers.

2. Purée the cooked vegetables through a food mill, using the finest disk, or a sieve. Return to saucepan and beat in butter, salt and pepper, honey, and nutmeg. Add the heavy cream and bring just to a boil.

3. Pour into soup bowls and add 1 tablespoon light rum to each serving.

4. Garnish with chopped parsley, or sliced boiled chestnuts (see p. 45).

• For a sweeter soup, drained chopped marrons (about one tablespoonful for each serving) can be used instead. *Makes 6 to 8 servings.*

MANHATTAN CLAM CHOWDER

Just a reminder: Manhattan clam chowder is the one made with tomatoes. New England clam chowder has the milk or cream base.

4 strips diced bacon	*1 teaspoon thyme*
1½ cups chopped onions	*1 tablespoon salt*
2 cups diced potatoes	*½ teaspoon freshly cracked*
1 cup diced celery, rib and leaves	*black pepper*
¾ cup green pepper, seeded and diced	*2 cups chopped clams (48 fresh clams) with juice, or frozen chopped clams*
1 1-lb. can tomatoes	*2 tablespoons chopped parsley*
2 cups tomato juice	
2 cups bottled clam juice	

1. In the bottom of a large soup kettle, try out bacon—that is, fry it until it is almost crisp.

2. To the bacon and bacon fat, add chopped onions. Cook until onions are transparent, stirring constantly. Do not let onions brown.

3. Add potatoes, celery, green pepper, canned tomatoes (break them up slightly with a fork), tomato juice, clam juice, 2 cups of water, thyme, salt, and pepper.

•Some markets have a canned mixture of tomato juice and clam juice. This is a convenient combination, usable here.

4. Bring mixture to a boil, then reduce heat to simmer, cover the kettle, and cook about 1 hour, or until vegetables are tender.

5. Add clams, with their juice, and cook for another 10 minutes. Only 10, so clams will not toughen.

6. Before serving, sprinkle chowder with chopped parsley.

• When serving, I usually pass a basket of thick round crackers, an excellent accompaniment for this soup. ***Makes 10 to 12 servings.***

CREAM OF TURTLE SOUP

This soup is often called boula-boula, or just plain boula. It is simple to make—so simple that even a novice cook can prepare it like a professional—but very elegant.

1 10-oz. pkg. frozen peas	*1 teaspoon salt*
1 2-lb. can turtle soup with meat	*3 to 4 drops Tabasco sauce*
½ cup dry Madeira	*1 cup stiffly whipped heavy cream*

1. Cook peas according to package directions, but use a little less water, and cook for only 5 minutes. Drain, then purée them through a food mill or sieve.

2. Heat the turtle soup, add the puréed peas, and whisk to blend well. Add Madeira and season with ½ teaspoon of salt and 3 or 4 drops of Tabasco. Heat to boiling point and pour into oven-warmed soup bowls, the kind that can take a few seconds under a broiler.

3. Add the remaining ½ teaspoon of salt to stiffly whipped cream and put a spoonful on top of each bowl of soup. Put the bowls under broiler just long enough to brown the whipped cream. It takes only a few seconds. Serve immediately. ***Makes 5 to 6 servings.***

CRÈME DE CRÉCY

There is carrot soup hot, and there is carrot soup cold—and which I serve depends on me and the weather.

3 cups coarsely grated carrots	*1 teaspoon salt*
¼ cup uncooked rice	*½ teaspoon cayenne pepper*
1½ quarts strong chicken stock (see p. 241)	*2 tablespoons chopped parsley for hot soup, or for cold soup, 2 tablespoons chopped parsley or chopped chives or 6 to 8 lemon slices*
1 cup light cream for hot soup, or 1½ cups barely whipped heavy cream for cold soup	

1. Use the coarse side of a 4-sided grater to grate carrots. One bunch should yield about 3 cups.

2. Add carrots and rice to chicken stock and bring to a boil. Reduce heat, cover, and simmer until carrots are barely tender and rice is cooked through.

3. If soup is to be served hot, purée the carrot-rice mixture through a food mill, using the medium disk, then return the mixture to saucepan and add light cream, salt, and cayenne pepper, whisking thoroughly to blend. Heat through, and before serving, garnish with chopped parsley.

If soup is to be served cold, purée the carrot-rice mixture in a blender no more than half full at one time (too much hot mixture will overflow a blender). Chill, and before serving, stir in heavy cream whipped just beyond the foaming stage (but not to the point at which beaters leave a soft mound when lifted). Add salt and cayenne pepper (a few drops of Tabasco sauce can be used instead of cayenne pepper if desired), taste for seasoning. Adjust if necessary; cold foods usually require heavier seasoning than do hot ones. Garnish with chopped parsley or chopped chives, or float a thin slice of lemon on top of each bowl. *Makes 6 to 8 servings.*

CURRIED AVOCADO SOUP

2 tablespoons diced onion

1 tablespoon butter

1 tablespoon curry powder, about

3 cups chicken stock (see p. 241)

3 avocados, peeled and coarsely mashed

1 teaspoon salt

3 to 4 drops Tabasco sauce

2 cups barely whipped heavy cream

6 to 8 lime or lemon slices

2 tablespoons chopped parsley

1. In a saucepan cook onion in butter over high heat until transparent. Stir in curry powder—a scant tablespoon may be enough, depending on how much curry taste you want—and cook, stirring constantly, for 3 minutes to refine the raw curry taste.

2. Pour in chicken stock.

• As an alternative, 2½ cups of chicken stock and ½ cup of dry sherry or other dry white wine can be used.

3. Bring to a boil, remove from heat, add mashed avocados, salt, and Tabasco.

4. Purée through a sieve or a food mill, or in a blender no more than half full at one time (too much hot mixture will overflow a blender). Cover with plastic wrap and chill in refrigerator.

5. When ready to serve, fold in heavy cream whipped just past the foaming stage (but not to the point at which beaters leave a soft mound when lifted).

• If the soup is to be served hot, use less salt and stir in 2 cups of light cream instead of the heavy cream and heat through.

6. Garnish each serving with a slice of lime or lemon and a sprinkling of chopped parsley. *Makes 6 to 8 servings.*

SENEGALESE

¼ cup butter
1½ cups very finely chopped onions
1 medium clove chopped garlic
1 teaspoon curry powder
½ teaspoon salt
¼ teaspoon freshly cracked white pepper
1 10-oz. pkg. frozen peas, thawed

¼ teaspoon ground cardamom seed
2 tablespoons flour
2½ cups chicken stock (see p. 241)
1 cup heavy cream
6 tablespoons finely diced cooked white meat of chicken

1. In a saucepan melt butter and cook onions over high heat until transparent, stirring frequently. Do not let onions brown.
2. Add garlic and cook 1 minute longer. Stir in curry powder and salt and pepper and continue cooking a little longer.
3. Add thawed peas and cardamom. Cover and cook, shaking pan frequently, until peas are tender.
4. Remove cover and smooth in flour. Cook for 2 minutes, stirring constantly.
5. Pour in chicken stock, bring to a boil, and boil 2 minutes.
6. Remove mixture from pan and purée in a blender.

• Fill the blender less than half full (several times if necessary), since too much will overflow.

7. If soup is to be served hot, stir in heavy cream, return to heat, and bring just to a boil. If it's to be served cold, chill the puréed mixture, and before serving, stir in cold heavy cream. Adjust seasoning if necessary; cold foods require heavier seasoning than do hot ones.
8. Garnish each bowl of hot or cold Senegalese with a tablespoonful of finely diced chicken. *Makes 4 to 6 servings.*

PARSLEY SOUP

2 *tablespoons diced onion*	1 *teaspoon salt*
2 *tablespoons butter*	3 *to 4 drops Tabasco sauce*
1½ *cups chopped parsley,*	2 *cups light cream, or 2 cups*
without stems	*barely whipped heavy*
2 *cups chicken stock (see*	*cream*
p. 241)	2 *tablespoons chopped pars-*
½ *cup dry white wine*	*ley*

1. In a saucepan cook onion in butter over high heat for 2 or 3 minutes, or until transparent. Add 1½ cups chopped parsley and cook 3 minutes longer, stirring with a wooden spatula.

• Do not use parsley stems. They give this soup a bitter taste.

2. Pour in chicken stock, cover pan, and simmer for 10 minutes.
3. Add wine, salt, and Tabasco, then purée in a blender no more than half full at one time (to prevent overflowing).
4. If soup is to be served hot, stir in light cream and heat through. If it's to be served cold, chill the puréed mixture, and before serving, fold in heavy cream whipped just past the foaming stage (but not to the point at which beaters leave a soft mound when lifted). Adjust seasoning if necessary.
5. Garnish soup (hot or cold) with chopped parsley. *Makes 4 to 6 servings.*

BILLI-BI

(Cream of Mussel Soup)

3 *quarts mussels*	3 *parsley sprigs*
2 *cups dry white wine*	2 *tablespoons butter*
3 *tablespoons finely chopped*	1 *teaspoon salt*
shallots	¼ *teaspoon cayenne pepper,*
2 *tablespoons chopped celery*	*about*
leaves	2 *cups heavy cream*
½ *cup sliced celery*	

1. Scrub mussels (which in many cities have to be ordered from fish markets in advance) with a stiff brush, using a sharp knife to remove the beards. Scrub thoroughly and rinse in several changes of cold water to remove as much sand as possible. Discard any mussels that are open.

• This is a time-consuming job; it is easier if mussels are soaked in water for an hour before scrubbing.

2. Put the mussels in a deep saucepan, pour in wine, and add shallots, celery leaves and sliced rib, parsley, butter, salt, and ¼ teaspoon of cayenne pepper. Cover and bring to a boil. Let mussels steam over high heat for about 5 minutes, or until they open. Shake pan frequently.

3. Remove mussels. Discard any that haven't opened, and set aside the rest.

4. Strain broth through a sieve lined with a double thickness of dampened cheesecloth. Return broth to pan and reheat. Taste for seasoning; more cayenne pepper may be needed.

5. If soup is to be served hot, add heavy cream and heat just to boiling.

• To further enrich the hot soup, beat 2 egg yolks until frothy, add ¼ cup of the heavy cream to them and warm the mixture by stirring a little broth into it; then stir it and the remaining 1¾ cups of cream into the pan and whisk over heat until the broth thickens slightly.

• If soup is to be served cold, chill the strained broth, and before serving, whip the heavy cream just beyond the foaming stage (but not to the point at which beaters leave a soft mound when lifted) and fold it in. The barely whipped cream gives the soup body. Adjust seasoning if necessary.

6. Add 2 of the set-aside mussels to each bowl of soup.

• Any remaining mussels can be shelled and frozen, to be used later, either in a salad or, with mustard mayonnaise, as appetizers. *Makes 4 to 6 servings.*

GARLIC SOUP

A very unusual cold soup. The flavor secret is in blanching the garlic. This gives the soup its unidentifiable, mysterious essence.

16 small cloves peeled garlic	¼ teaspoon freshly cracked
2 tablespoons butter	white pepper
2 tablespoons olive oil	2 egg yolks
1 quart strong chicken stock	1 cup light cream
(see p. 241)	2 tablespoons chopped
1 teaspoon salt	chives

1. Put the garlic cloves in a small pan and blanch them by covering them with cold water, bringing to a boil, and boiling 1 minute. Drain, then rinse cloves under cold water.

2. Chop garlic very, very fine.

3. Heat butter and olive oil in a heavy saucepan, then add the chopped garlic and cook very gently until it is golden. Don't burn it; don't even let it really brown.

4. Remove pan from heat and pour in chicken stock. Add salt and pepper, return pan to heat, and bring to a boil. Cover, reduce, heat, and simmer for about ½ hour.

5. Remove mixture from heat and strain it through two thicknesses of dampened cheesecloth.

6. Beat egg yolks, gradually add a little of the hot mixture to warm them, then add them, warmed, to the rest of the hot mixture. Place the egg-enriched mixture over low heat and whisk slowly until it thickens slightly. Don't let it boil or soup will curdle.

7. Chill mixture at least 2 hours, and before serving, stir in the light cream.

8. Serve in chilled bowls—I like to set them in crushed ice—and garnish each bowl with chopped chives.

• Hot crackers, unsalted biscuits especially, are my preferred accompaniment for this soup. *Makes 6 servings.*

COLD CREAM OF CUCUMBER SOUP

4 *large cucumbers*	1 *teaspoon salt*
2 *tablespoons butter*	½ *teaspoon freshly cracked*
3 *tablespoons chopped scal-*	*white pepper*
lions, white part only	2 *cups barely whipped heavy*
2 *tablespoons flour*	*cream*
2 *cups chicken stock (see*	
p. 241)	

1. Peel one of the cucumbers, cut off the end, cut 6 thin slices crosswise and set aside for garnish.

2. Peel the other three cucumbers and cut them and what's left of the first cucumber in halves, lengthwise. Scrape out seeds with the tip of a teaspoon, then cut cucumbers into 1-inch pieces.

3. Melt butter in saucepan and cook chopped scallions over high heat for 2 or 3 minutes, or until transparent.

4. Stir in flour and cook, stirring, for 2 minutes.

5. Add pieces of cucumber and continue to cook, stirring constantly, for about 5 minutes or until transparent. Do not let the cucumber pieces brown.

• The cucumber pieces will give off some liquid; nevertheless, they must be watched carefully so that they don't brown.

6. Pour in chicken stock, season with salt and pepper, and bring to a boil, then cover pan, reduce heat to simmer, and simmer for 10 minutes.

7. Purée the mixture in a blender no more than half full (too much hot mixture will overflow a blender), then chill it thoroughly in refrigerator.

8. Before serving, fold in heavy cream whipped just past the foaming stage (but not to the point at which beaters leave a soft mound when lifted), and garnish with the thin cucumber slices.

• Occasionally I top off each serving with tiny sprigs of mint instead. **Makes 6 servings.**

HERB TOAST FINGERS

These fingers are extremely good with soup.

½ cup butter
¼ teaspoon thyme
½ teaspoon salt
¼ teaspoon freshly cracked black pepper
1 tablespoon lemon juice

1 teaspoon chopped parsley
1 small clove chopped garlic
½ teaspoon chopped shallot
12 slices day-old homestyle bread

1. Put all ingredients except bread in a small saucepan or skillet and heat slowly. Stir until well mixed.

2. Trim crusts from bread, cut bread into fingers, and dip them, both sides, in the heated mixture.

3. Place the fingers on a baking sheet and bake them in a preheated 350° oven for about 20 minutes, or until brown, turning them once. Serve hot, warm, or at room temperature.

• The fingers can be frozen up to 1 month and reheated in a warm (200°) oven 10 to 15 minutes. Or they can be stored 2 weeks in plastic bags (to retain crispness). **Makes 12 to 14 servings, or about 36 fingers.**

SEAFOOD

At one time only the gods were permitted to enjoy the marvelous flavor of fish: fish was considered far too exquisite for lowly mortals. Not today, however. Today nutritionists and cooking experts urge everyone to eat fish—for nourishment and for sheer deliciousness.

Fortunately the United States has an abundance of excellent fish and shellfish in its oceans, lakes, rivers, and streams. In many cities it is possible, thanks to jet transportation, to get a variety of fresh fish—in excellent condition—every day. Outside the cities, people rely on local streams and lakes for beautiful freshwater fish. It goes without saying that seafood is available in the frozen, smoked, salted, dried, or canned state all over the country.

The United States has about two hundred commercial species of fin and shellfish, ranging in size from baby whitebait to giant tuna and sea bass, from tiny oyster crabs to the Alaskan king crab, which can weigh as much as fifteen pounds. How sad and boring it is when the housewife limits herself to fried fillets! It's especially so since fish is extremely versatile: it can be baked, broiled, steamed, pan fried, sautéed, poached, deep fried, planked, smoked, and baked en papillote. Further, it cooks very quickly, making it perfect for last-minute meals.

Europeans eat far more fish than do Americans, possibly because they are more deft in its preparation. Most of the recipes on these pages are easy. For example, Trout Meunière (see p. 67), meaning "cooked in the style of the miller's wife," is floured, seasoned with salt and pepper, sautéed until beautifully golden, and served with lemon wedges and chopped parsley. It couldn't be easier to prepare, and it constitutes, providing it is not overcooked, pretty elegant fare when accompanied by green salad and a boiled potato.

There are good American substitutes for seafood called for in European recipes. For example, flounder works very well in all sole recipes. Flounder en Papillote (see p. 61) and Ring Mold of Flounder (see p. 63) are both adapted from recipes originally designating sole.

Baked Lobster Nicholas (see p. 69) is one of my favorites, and it's less trouble than fixing a meat loaf. The lobster is simply split, seasoned with butter and lemon juice, baked until red, and served with lemon wedges and melted butter.

For the best seafood dishes, beware of overcooking, the most common error in the preparation of seafood. And use the freshest fish possible. However, frozen fish need not be shunned, for flash freezing of seafood allows much of its fresh flavor to remain. I find the large bags of flash-frozen shrimp indispensable; they are cleaned, and separated, so that few or many can be cooked.

How to identify fresh fish? The eyes are full, bulging, bright, and clear; the gills are clean and odorless. Scales retain their bright sheen and cling tightly to the skin. Fresh fish should smell like the sea or fresh water.

Most of the fish now seen in the markets is already cleaned and dressed, filleted or steaked. However, there is no need to fear cleaning a fish. It's really quite simple. Wash the fish in cold running water; scrape off the scales from tail to head, using a fish scaler or a knife held at a right angle to the fish; gut the fish by slitting the belly open, starting at the tail end and cutting forward to the head; cut around the pelvic fins, near the head, and remove them (I usually leave the head on, and trim the tail neatly); remove dorsal fins; and wash fish well in cold water to remove any blood. If the fish smells fishy, soak it for a few minutes in cold water and lemon juice. After handling fish, I rub my hands with salt and then rinse in cold water; this usually removes any fish odor.

It's ideal, although not necessary, to have a long narrow fish platter, individual fish plates, and fish forks and knives for serving. When lobster and large crabs are served, it's essential to have large platters, small seafood forks, and lobster crackers (nutcrackers).

FLOUNDER WITH CHAMPAGNE SAUCE

8 flounder fillets, about 7 by 3 by ½ inches

2 teaspoons lemon juice, plus lemon juice to wash fish

½ cup butter, plus butter to grease baking dish and baking paper

1 teaspoon salt

½ teaspoon freshly cracked white pepper

1½ cups thinly sliced white mushrooms

¼ teaspoon freshly cracked black pepper

1 cup champagne

1 tablespoon chopped shallot

2 small bay leaves

6 peppercorns

Champagne Sauce (recipe follows)

2 tablespoons roughly chopped truffle, optional

1. Wash fillets in water acidulated with lemon juice (1 tablespoon to 1 quart) to keep the fish white. Dry the fish with paper towels and fold the fillets in half, skin side inside; the skin side can be identified by its silvery gray color. Brush with ¼ cup melted butter, add white pepper and ½ teaspoon of salt, and place in a buttered baking dish. An oval ovenproof glass dish is ideal. Set aside.

2. Melt the remaining ¼ cup of butter in a skillet. When foaming subsides, add mushrooms, 2 teaspoons lemon juice, black pepper, and remaining ½ teaspoon of salt. Cook over high heat for 3 minutes only, shaking the pan to toss mushrooms.

• White mushrooms are used for this to keep the mixture light and appetizing-looking.

3. Remove from heat, add the champagne (domestic is fine), return to heat, and bring to a boil. Pour mushrooms and champagne over fish in baking dish.

4. At each end of the baking dish put ½ tablespoon chopped shallot, 1 small bay leaf, and 3 peppercorns. Cover dish with buttered brown paper or foil (to keep fish from drying out) and bake in a preheated 350° oven for about 12 minutes, or until just barely done. Time this step carefully. *Do not overcook the fish.*

• To test for doneness, remove fish from oven and touch with a toothpick to see if it flakes.
• If the fish is to be eaten by dieters or if it's being cooked ahead, stop right now and either serve immediately or let fish cool in the liquid, then cover and refrigerate it.

5. When ready to make sauce, remove and strain liquid (there should be 1¼ to 1½ cups) from fish and set liquid aside.

• To remove the liquid, tip the baking dish enough to spoon it out, or take it up with a bulb baster.

6. Before serving, remove fish fillets and mushrooms to ovenproof serving platter, overlapping fillets slightly. If some fish liquid has collected during standing, stir it into the sauce, straining it if necessary. Then "nap" the fillets with sauce—that is, shake the sauce (use a big spoon and make it quiver as if being held by someone with a case of nerves) over the fillets to coat them evenly and completely. Then place the fish under the broiler for a few seconds to brown tops, and if desired, sprinkle chopped truffle down the center of the platter.

• If desired, 1½ cups of white seedless grapes may be heated with the sauce before it is spooned on the fish.

Champagne Sauce

3 tablespoons butter
3 tablespoons flour
1¼ to 1½ cups fish-champagne liquid
2 egg yolks, optional
2 tablespoons heavy cream, optional
2 tablespoons cognac, optional

1. Melt butter in a saucepan (not aluminum; the sauce would turn gray). Stir in flour with a wooden spatula and cook, stirring constantly, for about 2 minutes, but do not let flour brown. Remove from heat, add fish-champagne liquid, and whisk vigorously; return to heat and bring to a boil, whisking constantly.

• If sauce seems too thick, thin with light cream.
• The sauce can be served at this point, or it can be enriched.
• If sauce must wait, float bits of butter over the top. The butter melts and keeps a skin from forming. When reheating the sauce, add a little light cream if needed. Sauces usually thicken when they stand.

2. To enrich sauce: beat egg yolks with a small whisk and beat in heavy cream and cognac; remove a little hot sauce from pan and stir into the egg-cream mixture to warm it; then stir heated mixture into the pan and cook until sauce thickens slightly, but do not let it boil.

3. Taste for seasoning and add salt and pepper if desired. **Makes 8 servings.**

FLOUNDER EN PAPILLOTE

Fish baked in paper is almost guaranteed to be meltingly tender, rich in flavor.

> 8 *pieces baking parchment,*
> 10 *by* 10 *inches*
> 8 *flounder fillets, about* 7 *by*
> 3 *by* ½ *inches*
> *Lemon juice to wash fish*
> ½ *cup melted butter, plus but-*
> *ter to grease baking sheet*
>
> 1 *teaspoon salt*
> ½ *teaspoon freshly cracked*
> *white pepper*
> *Apple and Mushroom Stuffing*
> *(recipe follows)*

1. Fold the parchment—try not to crease it—and cut out 8 wide hearts with a very slight dip in the center. Set aside.
2. Wash fish in water acidulated with lemon juice (1 tablespoon to 1 quart) to keep fish white. Dry fillets and lay them on a tray, skin side up.

• The skin side of fish (or where the skin was) can be identified by its silvery gray color. The flesh side is white.

3. Brush skin side of fish with melted butter, using about ¼ cup, and season with salt and pepper. Set aside while making stuffing.
4. Put a spoonful of stuffing at the broader end of each fillet and fold the other end of the fish over the stuffing to cover it.

5. Brush the parchment hearts with melted butter. Lay a folded fish in the center of the right side of each heart. Brush with butter. Bring left sides of parchment hearts over fish, match edges, and fold them over together in two or three narrow folds to lock the fish inside.

• The fillets can be stuffed in parchment in the morning, stored in a refrigerator, brought to room temperature, and baked just before they are to be served.
• White or brown paper sandwich bags can be substituted for the parchment. Brush the insides of the bags with butter. Place a stuffed and folded fillet in each and close bag.

6. Place the 8 packages on a buttered baking sheet (or an ovenproof serving platter) and bake in a preheated 375° oven for 20 to 25 minutes. Serve en papillote, letting each diner open his own steaming, fragrant package.

Apple and Mushroom Stuffing

1½ cups peeled, cored, and chopped green apples
¼ cup butter
¾ cup thinly sliced mushrooms
2 teaspoons lemon juice
½ teaspoon salt
¼ teaspoon freshly cracked black pepper
½ lb. cooked shrimp, shelled, deveined, and sliced
1 tablespoon chopped fresh dill or parsley
¼ cup dry white wine

1. Cook the apples in 2 tablespoons of butter 4 minutes, or until tender but not mushy.

2. In another pan, sauté mushroom slices in the remaining 2 tablespoons of butter with lemon juice, salt, and pepper. Shake the pan and cook over high heat for 3 minutes.

3. Combine apples, shrimp, and mushrooms. Stir in fresh dill or parsley.

• Don't use stems of dill. Strip off the feathery heads and chop them.

4. Moisten mixture with dry white wine. **Makes 8 servings.**

RING MOLD OF FLOUNDER STUFFED WITH SALMON MOUSSE

The beautiful pink salmon mousse is completely encased in white fish fillets—absolutely elegant!

> 8 *to 10 flounder fillets, about 7 by 3 by ½ inches*
> 1¾ *lbs. fresh salmon, weight after skin and bones are removed*
> *Lemon juice to wash fish*
> 2 *tablespoons vegetable oil to grease mold*
> 2 *egg whites*
> 1 *cup light cream*
> 2 *teaspoons salt*
> 1 *teaspoon freshly cracked white pepper*
>
> 1 *tablespoon chopped fresh tarragon, or 1 teaspoon dry tarragon*
> 2 *tablespoons chopped parsley*
> *Butter to grease baking paper*
> ¾ *lb. fluted, sautéed mushrooms (see p. 11)*
> 8 *slices of truffle*
> 1 *bunch watercress*
> *Hollandaise Sauce (see p. 246), Béarnaise Sauce (see p. 248), or Lemon Butter (see p. 253)*

1. Wash flounder in cold water acidulated with lemon juice (1 tablespoon to 1 quart). Dry and set aside.

2. Brush a 10-inch ring mold with oil. Line the mold with the fillets, overlapping them at least ¼ inch. Lay them skin side up, with narrow ends in the center of the mold. Ends of fillets will overhang both center and outside edges. Set aside.

3. Work salmon through a meat grinder, using the finest blade, or chop it very finely. Put it in mixer and beat in egg whites at high speed, using the flat whip if the mixer is a heavy-duty one.

• The salmon can be beaten in a bowl over ice, using a wooden spatula, if a mixer isn't available.

4. Slowly beat in cream.

5. Season mixture with salt, pepper, tarragon, and parsley. Beat hard and spoon into the fish-lined mold. Bang the mold to make mixture settle, then fold fillet ends over to cover top.

6. Cover mold with buttered brown paper or foil. Set it in a baking pan half filled with boiling water (called a *bain-marie*) and bake in a preheated 350° oven for 25 to 30 minutes, or until done.

• To test for doneness, remove fish from oven and touch fillet tops with a toothpick to see if they flake.

7. Remove from oven and let stand at least 5 minutes before attempting to unmold.

• To unmold, run a little knife around the edge of the mold, then place a serving platter over the mold, turn both platter and mold over, and lift mold off. Blot up any juice with paper towels.

8. Fill the center of unmolded ring with fluted, sautéed mushrooms, decorate the top of the ring with thin rounds of truffle and surround with watercress. To serve, cut in wedges. Pass dish of Hollandaise Sauce, Béarnaise Sauce, or Lemon Butter. *Makes 10 servings.*

Poached Striped Bass with Sauce Gribiche

A fish poacher is handy for cooking a whole fish. It has a rack with handles, so the cooked fish can be lifted out of the court bouillon easily. If you haven't a fish poacher, use a roasting pan—one long enough to accommodate the fish. The fish used in this recipe should be cleaned and split. Ask your fish man to do the work, but not to separate the halves or to remove the head or tail.

> *1 whole striped bass, sea bass, or salmon, 4 to 6 lbs.*
> *Lemon juice to wash fish, if needed*
> *1 recipe court bouillon (see p. 242)*
> *1 head Boston lettuce*
> *Sauce Gribiche (recipe follows)*
> *10 lemon slices*
> *4 tablespoons chopped parsley*

1. Wash the fish well in water and trim the tail neatly.

• If the fish smells fishy, soak it for a few minutes in a mixture of cold water and lemon juice (1 tablespoon to 1 quart).

2. Place the fish in a poacher, or if a poacher isn't available, improvise a hammock for the fish, either by rolling the fish in a few turns of cheesecloth, leaving enough hanging free at the ends to serve as handles, or by

folding foil to the same width as the fish, but 3 inches longer at each end, and poking a few holes in the foil, then laying the fish on it. Lower the fish into cooled court bouillon, cover, and slowly bring to a boil. Reduce heat—the liquid should barely move—and simmer, covered, for 7 minutes per pound, or until done.

• Test for doneness: touch fish with a toothpick—open the cheesecloth if necessary—to see if it flakes. As a further test (for any fish but salmon): poke down alongside the bone; if it looks pink, the fish is not cooked.

3. When fish is done, turn off heat and let fish cool for 15 to 30 minutes in the liquid.

• This helps to firm the flesh. The fish can be served immediately from the liquid, or chilled.

4. To serve: Peel off skin—I use my fingers to do this—then with a long, thin knife, slice straight down to the bone, making slices 1 inch thick (when the bone is reached, turn the knife to work it under the slice). When the top layer has been sliced, remove bones in one piece and slice bottom layer of fish. Lift the slices onto plates lined with a leaf of Boston lettuce, allowing 3 slices per serving.

• If desired, the fish can be sliced straight through, without removing the bones.

5. Spoon a ribbon of Sauce Gribiche over the fish slices. Or serve spoonfuls beside the fish on the plates. Garnish with serrated slices of lemon edged in chopped parsley.

Sauce Gribiche

3 hard-cooked eggs	3 tablespoons wine vinegar
1 teaspoon Dijon mustard	1 tablespoon minced gherkins
½ teaspoon salt	1 tablespoon drained capers
¼ teaspoon freshly cracked white pepper	1 tablespoon chopped parsley
1 cup olive oil	1 teaspoon dried tarragon
	1 teaspoon dried chervil

1. Press yolks of hard-cooked eggs—save the whites—through a sieve into a small bowl, and beat with a wooden spatula until smooth; add mustard and salt and pepper.

2. Using the same technique as in making mayonnaise (see p. 251), beat oil into the egg-yolk mixture with a small whisk, adding a few drops at a time at first, then drizzling it in, a tablespoon at a time, whisking constantly.

3. When sauce begins to thicken, add vinegar, a tablespoon at a time,

alternating with oil. Continue whisking until all the vinegar and oil are used and sauce is thick and creamy.

4. Fold in gherkins, capers, parsley, tarragon, and chervil. Chop egg whites and fold them in. Chill. *Makes 8 to 10 servings.*

ROULADE OF SALMON

A center cut of salmon is not necessary for this recipe. Any firm fish can be substituted, but *don't* try mackerel, shad, or other oily fish.

1½ lbs. fresh salmon, weight after skin and bones are removed

6 eggs, separated

½ cup butter, melted and cooled

½ cup flour

1 teaspoon salt

½ teaspoon freshly cracked white pepper

2 tablespoons chopped parsley

¼ cup chopped fresh dill

3 tablespoons lemon juice

2 tablespoons vegetable oil to grease pan and paper

2 cups dairy sour cream

4 to 6 tablespoons chopped fresh dill

1. Put salmon through a meat grinder, using the finest blade, or chop it very finely. Set aside.

2. Beat egg yolks well and beat in the cooled melted butter. Add flour 1 tablespoon at a time, mixing constantly with a wooden spatula.

3. Add ground fish to egg-yolk mixture, along with salt, pepper, parsley, dill, and lemon juice. Mix well.

4. Beat egg whites until they form soft peaks. Stir a big teaspoonful of whites into salmon mixture to lighten it, then gently fold in remaining beaten whites.

5. Spread mixture in a jelly-roll pan that has been brushed with vegetable oil and then lined with waxed paper that extends 3 inches at each end, but first, brush paper with vegetable oil. Put pan on middle shelf of a preheated 350° oven and bake for 15 minutes.

6. Turn mixture out of pan onto 2 sheets of waxed paper, the top sheet overlapping the bottom by 3 inches. Remove pan and waxed-paper lining and with the aid of the fresh waxed paper, roll the mixture like a jelly roll.

• If it cracks, don't worry. You can always cover it with chopped parsley.

7. Serve warm, with sour cream mixed with chopped fresh dill to taste.

• To reheat a roll made in advance, let it come to room temperature, then put it in a 200° to 250° oven just long enough to warm through. Before serving, pour ½ cup of *hot* melted butter over it. This will moisten it again. ***Makes 8 to 10 servings.***

TROUT MEUNIÈRE

The trout used in this recipe should be cleaned and split—most fish sellers will do the work—but they should not be separated into halves. The heads and tails should remain intact.

6 *trout, about 1 lb. each*	¾ *cup butter*
¼ *cup lemon juice, plus lemon juice to wash fish*	5 *tablespoons finely chopped parsley*
1 *cup flour, about*	2 *lemons, cut into 8 wedges*
1 *teaspoon salt*	1 *tablespoon paprika*
½ *teaspoon freshly cracked white pepper*	

1. Wash the fish in water acidulated with lemon juice (1 tablespoon to 1 quart) and dry them on paper towels.

2. Roll trout in flour, shaking off excess. Sprinkle with salt and pepper.

3. Heat ½ cup of the butter in a skillet until it's hot but not brown. Lay fish in pan and cook over medium high heat for 6 minutes without moving them, then turn carefully and cook 6 minutes on other side. The fish should then be golden brown. Place them on a warm serving dish and keep warm in a low oven.

4. Add the remaining ¼ cup of butter to skillet and heat until it's lightly browned but not burned. Remove skillet from heat, add ¼ cup

parsley and ¼ cup lemon juice, swirl in pan, and pour over fish in platters.

5. Garnish platter with 8 wedges of lemon—4 dipped along the core in remaining chopped parsley, 4 dipped in paprika. *Makes 6 servings.*

WHITEBAIT WITH CAPER MAYONNAISE

In England, where whitebait are very popular, plates are piled high with dozens of these tiny fish, which are only about an inch long. They are fried in deep fat and eaten whole, usually with thin slices of brown bread made into triangular sandwiches with tartar sauce filling. Whitebait cannot be prepared ahead; they must be fried at the last minute. Look for whitebait (sometimes called shiners) during March and April. If you can find them, and if you have a deep fat fryer with a basket, you will be rewarded with a fine eating adventure.

2 lbs. whitebait	*2 cups flour, about*
3 cups vegetable shortening,	*¼ cup drained capers*
for deep frying	*1 cup mayonnaise (see p. 251)*

1. Wash the whitebait and dry them carefully on paper towels. Don't press them; they are fragile.

2. In a deep fat fryer, heat shortening to 375° on a fat thermometer. It should be hot and ready to use before the whitebait is floured.

3. Put flour in a baking tray or pan and roll fish in flour to coat. Flour only as many fish as can be fried at one time.

• If too many are fried at once, they tend to stick together, and they're not very attractive.

4. Put floured fish into a coarse strainer and rap it—I do this against my hand—so that excess flour falls off.

5. *Immediately* put fish into frying basket and plunge into hot fat before the flour dampens. Fry only a moment or until golden. Lift out basket and drain fish immediately on paper towels.

6. Flour and fry the next batch of fish, but first, be sure fat temperature is back to 375°.

7. Serve with caper mayonnaise. To make: stir drained capers into homemade mayonnaise. *Makes 8 servings.*

LOBSTER FLAMBÉ

2 live 1½-lb. lobsters	*2 tablespoons cognac*
2 tablespoons butter	*Melted butter, optional*
2 tablespoons vegetable oil	

1. The lobsters used in this recipe must be split alive. Lay one lobster on a cutting board, head and claws to the left.

• The claws are usually plugged. If not, lay a towel over them. The safe way to pick up a lobster is by grabbing it right behind the head, where the claws join the body. When a lobster is held this way, its pincers can't reach your hand.

2. On the back of the lobster's head, where it joins the body, there is a cross. Plunge the tip of a large sharp knife into this cross. This severs the spinal cord, and the lobster dies immediately.

3. With the same knife, split the lobster lengthwise, through the head, body, and tail, and open it out flat. Remove the sand bag just behind and between the eyes, and the long intestinal vein.

4. To make it easier to fit lobster pieces in a skillet, remove big and little claws.

5. Repeat steps 1–4 for the second lobster.

6. Heat butter and oil in a skillet. When hot, add lobster pieces and shake skillet back and forth over high heat for about 3 minutes.

7. Pour cognac over lobster pieces and ignite. Shake skillet until flames die.

• If using a gas flame, turn it down before adding cognac; then turn it back up and tip the skillet toward it. The cognac will ignite.

8. Cover skillet and cook lobster pieces over high heat until they turn bright red, about 3 to 5 minutes.

• Frozen lobster tails can be prepared the same way. They don't even have to be defrosted. After they have been buttered and flamed, cover and cook until they turn red. The larger frozen tails will take about 10 minutes. You will need 6 ½-lb. lobster tails for 2 servings.

9. Serve with or without melted butter. *Makes 2 servings.*

BAKED LOBSTER NICHOLAS

Nicholas owned a fish market at the seashore where I had a house for years. This is the way he taught me to cook plain lobster. Since then, I've rarely done it any other way.

2 live 2-lb. lobsters	*8 lemon wedges*
½ cup butter	*¼ cup melted butter, about*
¼ cup lemon juice	

1. Split and clean lobsters, following steps 1, 2, and 3 in recipe for Lobster Flambé (see p. 68). Do not detach claws.

2. Lay lobster halves on a baking sheet, cut side up. Dot each half with 2 tablespoons butter and sprinkle with 1 tablespoon lemon juice.

• The lobsters can be split and readied to bake 2 to 3 hours before they are to go in the oven. Keep them on ice or refrigerate them, but be sure to bring them to room temperature before proceeding with the recipe. Don't hold them on ice longer than 2 or 3 hours. The sooner the lobsters are baked after being split, the better they are.

3. Place on the middle shelf of a preheated 350° oven and bake 25 to 30 minutes, or until red.

4. Place lobster halves on a large serving plate, garnish with lemon wedges, and serve with hot melted butter.

• If dinner is delayed, the lobsters can be kept for about 15 minutes in a 200° oven. Pour a little melted butter and lemon juice over the halves to keep them from drying out. *Makes 2 servings.*

COLD LOBSTER MOUSSE

Cardamom seed provides the special, mysterious touch in this recipe, which can, if desired, be prepared a day in advance of when it's to be served.

3 cups (1½ lbs.) finely chopped cooked lobster
½ cup finely minced celery
¼ cup finely minced onion
2 tablespoons lemon juice
¼ cup chopped parsley
½ teaspoon salt
½ teaspoon (scant) freshly cracked pepper
¼ teaspoon ground cardamom seed

1½ cups mayonnaise (see p. 251)
1½ cups heavy cream
2 packages unflavored gelatin
½ cup dry Madeira
Vegetable oil to grease dish or mold
1 small cucumber

1. In a large bowl put lobster, celery, and onion. Sprinkle with lemon juice. Add parsley, salt, pepper, and cardamom. Toss to mix. Fold in mayonnaise and set aside.

• Instead of lobster meat, the same proportion of shrimp or crab meat can be used.

2. Whip cream to the same consistency as the mayonnaise and set aside.

• If cream is whipped too stiffly in making mousses and cold soufflés, it is difficult to mix it smoothly.

3. Sprinkle gelatin in Madeira in a glass measuring cup to soften. Stand the cup in a pan of hot water and stir over heat to dissolve gelatin. Fold it into the cream quickly.

4. Fold the cream-gelatin mixture into the lobster-mayonnaise mixture and pour into an oiled 6- to 8-cup soufflé dish or an oiled ring mold. Cover with waxed paper and put in refrigerator to chill. Chill at least 2 hours before unmolding.

• Before unmolding any soufflé or mousse, run a little knife around the edge with an up and down motion. Place serving dish over mold, invert, give a shake, and lift off mold.

5. Before serving, surround the mousse with a garnish of cucumber ruffles made like this: cut unpeeled cucumber into thin slices; slit them from edge to just beyond the center; hold ends and twist them in opposite directions gently.

• Cherry tomatoes and black olives can be used as an alternate, and very pretty, garnish for the mousse.
• If I've made the mousse in a ring mold and garnished it with cucumber, I like to fill the center with cucumber salad. *Makes 6 to 8 servings.*

CURRIED SHRIMP WITH CONDIMENTS

The fun of serving curry is the presentation of the condiments. On a huge shiny black tray, I set out white Chinese lotus bowls (with matching porcelain spoons) and fill them with the following: grated coconut, currant jelly, chutney, shredded orange rind, bacon bits, chopped green or red pepper (or both), pine nuts, hard-cooked eggs (white chopped, yolks sieved), crystallized ginger, Bombay duck (fish sautéed in bacon fat), currants or raisins plumped in wine, bits of avocado sprinkled with lime juice, bits of banana sprinkled with lemon juice, chopped scallion tops, chopped fresh pineapple, and sometimes crystallized violets or rose petals. Instead of bread, I serve *pappadoms,* Indian curry biscuits, which I fry on a griddle before serving.

2 lbs. large raw shrimp, in shells	¾ cup butter
4 peppercorns	2 cups chopped onions
½ teaspoon salt	½ cup chopped carrots
⅔ cup sliced onions	½ cup chopped celery
1 bay leaf	1 medium apple, unpeeled but cored, then chopped

3 to 4 tablespoons curry
   powder
3 tablespoons flour
1 cup light cream

1 cup coconut milk
Condiments
1 recipe of Saffron Rice (see
   p. 187)

1. Shell—save the shells—and devein raw shrimp and set them aside.

2. Put shrimp shells in a saucepan with 6 cups of water, peppercorns, salt, sliced onion, and bay leaf. Bring to a boil, reduce heat to simmer, and cook for at least ½ hour, longer if there is time. Strain stock and set aside to be used in the curry sauce—and also in the Saffron Rice.

3. In a heavy casserole, melt ¼ cup of the butter and sauté shrimp gently, turning them with a wooden spatula, for about 3 minutes. Remove shrimp and set aside.

4. Add remaining ½ cup of butter to casserole and melt, scraping up brown bits. Add chopped onions, carrots, celery, and apple and cook until onions are transparent.

5. With wooden spatula, smooth curry powder and flour into the vegetable mixture. Cook 1 or 2 minutes for flour-and-curry flavor to develop.

• Curry powder is a blend of spices, usually about a dozen different ones, including coriander, cumin, turmeric, various peppers, cloves, mace, allspice, cardamom, and mustard. In India it is freshly made each time it's used, and it varies with each type of dish: sometimes it is quite mild; other times very pungent. Excellent curry can be bought in gourmet shops; many of the curry powders carried in supermarkets are less strong.

6. Stir in 2 cups of the stock made from shrimp shells and cook about 15 minutes, or until vegetables are tender. Add cream and coconut milk and cook until sauce thickens.

• Unsweetened canned coconut milk can be bought, or the milk can be obtained from fresh coconut by piercing the eye of the coconut with an ice pick or skewer and letting the liquid drain out into a cup. Two coconuts may be needed to get enough milk. If necessary, substitute more cream and add a pinch of sugar.

7. Purée the sauce through a food mill, using the medium disk, or blend it in a blender.

• When hot mixtures are put into a blender, keep it less than half full to avoid overflow.
• If the puréed sauce seems too thick, thin it with a little shrimp stock or cream; if not thick enough, cook it until it is reduced.

8. Taste for seasoning, then combine shrimp and sauce and heat 3 or 4 minutes. Take care not to overcook shrimp.

• Sauce can be made ahead, but don't combine shrimp and sauce until serving time. Refrigerate sauce and sautéed shrimp separately, or freeze them, again separately. At serving time, bring them to room temperature, heat the sauce, and add the shrimp to heat through.

9. Serve in a casserole over a spirit lamp. Surround the dish with condiments and Saffron Rice.

• Curry kills the flavor of wine, so plan on serving ale, beer, iced tea, or hot tea. *Makes 6 to 8 servings.*

SHRIMP À LA KIEV

A friend of mine who spends a lot of time in Asia asked if I could tell him how to make shrimp Kiev. I had never seen a recipe for it. In fact, I had never heard of it. One day Alvin Kerr, a well-known food authority, who had been to Hong Kong recently, told me that shrimp Kiev was frequently served in Hong Kong restaurants. Well, now it's being served in Philadelphia too. I figured out my own way to make it. Fillet of flounder or blowfish can be substituted for shrimp.

12 *large raw shrimp, in shells*	¾ *cup flour*
¼ *cup dry white wine*	2 *beaten eggs*
½ *cup unsalted frozen butter*	1 *tablespoon vegetable oil*
3 *tablespoons lemon juice*	¾ *cup bread crumbs (see*
½ *teaspoon salt*	*p. 7)*
¼ *teaspoon freshly cracked*	2 *cups vegetable shortening*
white pepper	*for deep frying*
2 *tablespoons chopped*	6 *lemon wedges*
chives	

1. Shell the shrimp and slit them lengthwise on the inside curve *but do not cut all the way through.* Lay them out flat, like an open book (this is called butterflying), on waxed paper sprinkled with 2 tablespoons dry white wine. Cover with a second sheet of waxed paper, and pound shrimp flat, using the flat side of a cleaver.

• The larger the shrimp, the easier this is to do. Don't use small shrimp. Sprinkling the waxed paper and shrimp with wine makes it easier to remove the paper when shrimp are pounded.
• Don't worry about the black veins, they're harmless. If you must remove them, do it after shrimp are pounded.

2. Brush flattened shrimp with the remaining 2 tablespoons of wine and lay a thin finger of frozen butter on each shrimp. Sprinkle each with lemon juice, salt, pepper, and chives.

3. Start with the long side and roll shrimp around the butter, tucking in the ends.

• Don't bother fastening these rolls with toothpicks or skewers. Shrimp, like chicken, is very gelatinous and will stick to itself.

4. Coat rolls with flour, shaking off excess, then dip in eggs mixed with oil and roll in bread crumbs. Be sure to coat the ends of the rolls.

5. Lay rolls, seam side down, on a baking sheet and freeze for at least ½ hour, or chill in refrigerator for at least 1 hour.

• Shrimp rolls can be frozen and stored for weeks, wrapped in foil or plastic wrap. Do not thaw before frying. Just take the rolls from the freezer to the hot fat.

6. Before serving, heat shortening in a heavy saucepan or an electric skillet to 375° on a fat thermometer. Fry just 2 rolls at a time. If rolls have come from a refrigerator, fry about 3 minutes; if they are frozen, fry about 5 minutes. Remove from fat with a slotted spoon and drain on paper towels. Serve hot, with lemon wedges.

• It's a good idea to make a few extra shrimp rolls, since one may be troublesome to roll, or one may split open when it's deep fried. *Makes 6 servings of 2 shrimp each.*

Hot Shrimp Mousse

2 *lbs. raw shrimp, in shells*	¼ *cup dry Madeira*
4 *egg whites*	2½ *cups cold heavy cream*
2 *teaspoons salt*	*Oil to grease mold*
½ *teaspoon freshly cracked white pepper*	*Butter to grease baking paper*

1. Shell, wash, and devein shrimp. Cut them and put in a blender with egg whites, salt, pepper, and Madeira. If blender won't hold the entire mixture, blend in several batches. Blend until smooth and fluffy.

2. Transfer mixture to a bowl and either refrigerate for 2 hours or set

the bowl over ice and stir with a wooden spatula until mixture is very cold.

3. Beat in the cream, a little at a time, and when all of it has been added, pour the mixture into an oiled 1½-quart mold.

4. Set the mold in a pan of boiling water, cover top with buttered brown paper or buttered aluminum foil, place in a preheated 350° oven, and bake 35 to 40 minutes, or until set.

• Another way to set the mousse is to put the mold in its pan of boiling water directly over medium heat and cook for 40 minutes.

5. Remove mold from heat and let stand for 5 minutes before unmolding.

• To unmold, run a little knife around the edge with an up and down motion, then place serving platter over mold, invert, shake, and lift off the mold.

6. Serve at once with Beurre Noir (see p. 253), Lemon Butter (see p. 253), or Hollandaise Sauce (see p. 246). *Makes 8 to 10 servings.*

MUSSELS MARINARA

This is the Italian version of steamed mussels, with tomato sauce added.

2 *quarts mussels*	2 *tablespoons chopped parsley*
2 *cups dry white wine*	
½ *cup finely chopped onions*	*Marinara Sauce (recipe follows)*
1 *crumbled bay leaf*	
1 *teaspoon thyme*	

1. Scrub mussels with a stiff brush and remove the beards with a knife. Rinse in several changes of cold water to remove sand. Discard any mussels that are open.

• This is a time-consuming job; it is easier if mussels are soaked in water for an hour before scrubbing.

2. Put mussels in a deep kettle along with wine, onions, bay leaf, thyme, and parsley. Cover the kettle tightly and shake occasionally while steaming mussels over high heat for about 12 minutes, or until they open.

3. Remove from heat, strain off broth, and save it to add to marinara sauce. Discard any mussels that haven't opened.

4. Before serving, combine sauce and mussel broth and pour over mussels in deep soup plates.

Marinara Sauce

3 lbs. fresh, ripe tomatoes
¼ cup olive oil
3 large cloves finely chopped garlic
1½ cups finely chopped onions
1 teaspoon salt
½ teaspoon freshly cracked black pepper

1 tablespoon chopped fresh basil, or 1 teaspoon dry basil
2 tablespoons chopped parsley

1. Peel and chop tomatoes, then set them aside.

• An easy way to peel tomatoes is to plunge them in boiling water, count slowly to 10, and lift them out with a slotted spoon. Skins will slip off easily with the help of a paring knife. Or spear a tomato (through the stem end) on a fork and hold it over a gas flame, turning to heat it all over. In a few seconds the skin pops and will peel off easily.

2. Heat olive oil in saucepan and cook garlic and onions in oil until transparent. Do not let them brown.
3. Add tomatoes, salt, pepper, basil, and parsley. Bring to a boil, then reduce heat and simmer, stirring frequently, for 20 minutes.

• If this mixture gets too thick (it depends on the juiciness of tomatoes), add a little broth from the mussels. *Makes 4 to 6 servings.*

FRUITS DE MER EN CASSEROLE

An elegant make-ahead party casserole that can be frozen, sauce and all. Defrost in refrigerator. To reheat, bring to room temperature and put in a preheated 350° oven for 10 to 15 minutes. *Always undercook any dish you plan to reheat.*

¾ lb. halibut, or any firm, nonoily white fish
2 egg whites
½ cup light cream
1½ teaspoons salt
1 tablespoon chopped parsley
1 teaspoon chopped fresh tarragon, or ⅓ teaspoon dried

1 teaspoon chopped shallot
1 small clove chopped garlic
6 flounder fillets
¼ cup cognac
¼ teaspoon freshly cracked white pepper
12 large raw shrimp, shelled and deveined
½ lb. cleaned and chopped raw shrimp

½ lb. bay scallops
¼ cup melted butter, plus
    butter to grease baking
    dish and baking paper

½ cup fish stock (see p. 242)
Mushroom Sauce (recipe fol-
    lows)
¼ cup chopped parsley

1. Grind halibut, using the finest blade of meat grinder, or chop it very finely. Put it in a mixer bowl with egg whites and beat at high speed for 5 minutes, or until egg whites are completely beaten into the fish.

• If a mixer is not available, beat fish in a bowl over ice, with a wooden spatula.

2. Slowly add cream, a few drops at a time, using the mixer at low speed, then increasing to high.

3. Add 1 teaspoon of the salt, parsley, tarragon, shallot, and garlic and beat them in. Set aside.

4. On a cutting board cut each flounder fillet in half, lengthwise. Pat dry with paper towels and brush the skin side with cognac.

• The skin side can be recognized because it is darker than the flesh side and has a silvery cast to it.

5. Sprinkle flounder with white pepper and remaining salt and spread with the halibut mixture. Lay 1 shrimp on each piece and roll it up. Stand each roll on its end in a buttered baking dish.

6. Over the flounder rolls, scatter the chopped shrimp and the scallops.

• If bay scallops aren't available, use sea scallops. Cut them into quarters or halves, depending on their size.

7. Brush surfaces of rolls generously with melted butter, pour on fish stock, and cover with buttered waxed paper.

8. Place baking dish in a preheated 350° oven and poach the rolls for about 20 minutes, or until done.

• They may take a little longer to cook, depending on the thickness of the flounder. Test rolls for doneness by removing from oven and touching with a fork to see if they flake. If they don't, return to oven for a few minutes more.

9. Pour off excess liquid and use it to thin Mushroom Sauce if it seems too thick. Before serving, pour Mushroom Sauce over the casserole and sprinkle with chopped parsley.

Mushroom Sauce

1 tablespoon dried mush-
    rooms
¾ cup sliced fresh mushrooms

2 tablespoons butter
1 teaspoon lemon juice
½ teaspoon salt

¼ teaspoon freshly cracked
white pepper
1 small clove chopped garlic
1 tablespoon flour

½ teaspoon tomato paste
1¼ cups fish stock (see p. 242)
¼ cup light cream

1. Soak dried (not freeze-dried) mushrooms in water to cover for at least 1 hour. Drain, squeeze out excess moisture, chop, and set aside.

2. Sauté the sliced fresh mushrooms in butter over high heat. Sprinkle them with lemon juice and salt and pepper and shake the pan, tossing the mushrooms as they cook. Cook about 3 minutes.

3. Add garlic and dried mushrooms and cook over high heat for 3 more minutes.

4. Mix in flour and tomato paste thoroughly. Add fish stock and light cream. Bring to a boil, then simmer 10 minutes. *Makes 6 servings.*

CIOPPINO

A West Coast specialty. Frequently called American bouillabaisse.

¼ cup olive oil
6 medium cloves chopped
garlic
1½ cups chopped onions
¾ cup chopped green pepper
1 cup chopped celery
¼ cup chopped parsley
2 cups dry red wine
12 fresh tomatoes, peeled,
seeded, and chopped, or
1 20-oz. can Italian plum
tomatoes
1 teaspoon salt

½ teaspoon freshly cracked
black pepper
¼ teaspoon basil
¼ teaspoon oregano
2 tablespoons tomato paste
1 live 1½-lb. lobster
1 dozen clams, in shells
1 lb. raw shrimp, shelled and
deveined
1 lb. red snapper, cut in
pieces
1 lb. bass, cut in pieces

1. Heat olive oil in a large kettle or saucepan. Stir in garlic, onions, green pepper, celery, and 2 tablespoons of the chopped parsley. Cook, stirring with wooden spatula, until onions are transparent. Do not let vegetables brown.

2. Add wine, tomatoes, salt, pepper, basil, oregano, and tomato paste. Bring to a boil, then cover and simmer for 30 minutes.

3. Split and clean the live lobster, following steps 1, 2, and 3 in recipe for Lobster Flambé (see p. 68). Cut lobster in pieces.

4. Scrub the clams well and rinse them several times in cold water. Throw away any clams with open or damaged shells.

5. After sauce has simmered for 30 minutes, add shrimp, red snapper, bass, lobster, and clams. Cover and bring back to a boil. By the time the clams open, about 5 to 8 minutes, the cioppino is done.

6. Discard clams that do not open.

7. Sprinkle with rest of the chopped parsley and serve in individual bowls. *Makes 4 servings.*

MEATS

To get good meat, make friends with a good butcher. And don't be surprised at the cost of the friendship. Good meat is expensive. If the price of the best quality seems prohibitive, it is far more sensible to eat eggs, poultry, cheese, and fish.

To be sure of obtaining meat of the best quality, buy government-graded prime. Prime is usually reserved for first-class hotels and restaurants, but many meat markets have it for those who will pay the price.

Beef can be judged by looking at the exposed surface. If the beef is good, the surface will be bright red, firm, and fine-textured, with little visible connective tissue. The bones will be porous and pinkish white. The fat will be creamy in color and flaky, and a network of marbling will be visible. Well-aged beef—that which has been hung the proper length of time—may be dark in color or green from mold before trimming; this is normal, and when the meat is trimmed, the inside will be a good red.

Pork is more likely to be of consistent quality than are other meats. Its color should be grayish pink, the flesh should be firm and well marbled (and it should be cooked to an internal temperature of 170° to kill any trichinae). Hams should be short and plump, with smooth, thin skins.

Lamb has pink flesh, which turns dull red when it reaches the mutton stage. Baby lamb has pink fat, but when the animal ages, the fat is white. Nothing is more succulent than lamb cooked just to the pink stage, the way Europeans cook it. Regrettably, most Americans abuse lamb by overcooking it.

Veal is becoming somewhat more popular than it used to be in the United States, but it is still not as popular as it is in Europe. And good veal, which has flesh that is whitish pink, firm, moist, and fine-grained, is still scarce. The lighter the color of veal the more tender the meat. Veal shows no marbling of fat.

Americans should be able to cook meat to perfection, for they have so many aids. With things like temperature-controlled ovens, meat thermometers, larding devices, roasting pans with adjustable racks, practical oven-to-table equipment, and enamel-on-iron casseroles, there is really no excuse for overcooking roasts or making watery stews or coating chunks of meat with pasty gravy.

Many of the meat recipes, for entertaining and for family meals, found in this chapter can be prepared in advance, and some—particularly stew (which should be undercooked if it is to be reheated later)—even improve with standing.

For serving large pieces of meat, whether roasted or braised, a sturdy carving board and a carving set, with knife honed to razor sharpness, are almost imperative.

RIB ROAST OF BEEF

Everyone who appreciates beef has very definite ideas about how to do a rib roast. I certainly do: for one thing, I always buy the first 4 ribs of prime beef, and I never have the bones removed. Bones give the meat beautiful flavor. Here is my method.

> 4 ribs of prime beef, with   2 teaspoons freshly cracked
>   bones   black pepper
> ½ cup coarse salt

1. Bring roast to room temperature and rub salt—the coarse salt makes an attractive crust—and pepper on top of the fat but not over the flesh.

2. Stand the roast on its bones, fatty side up, in a shallow roasting pan, and put it into a preheated 350° oven. Time it—calculate 17 minutes cooking time per pound for a roast that is well done on the outside and very rare inside—so it can be allowed to stand for 15 minutes out of the oven before it is carved. This gives the juices a chance to settle and makes carving easier.

• If using a meat thermometer, insert it so that the point is in the center of the meat, not touching bone. For very rare meat, the temperature should read 125°. Remember, the roast continues to cook after it is taken out of the oven.

• Because I like to taste the beef, I do not make any kind of gravy or brown sauce. I do, however, like the English custom of serving horse-radish sauce—made by simply whipping 1 cup of heavy cream and folding in horseradish, preferably fresh horseradish, to taste—with rib roast. And I always serve roast beef with potatoes. Any kind will do, but I'm partial to Potatoes Dauphinoise (see p. 183).

• If dinner is delayed, do not try to reheat a rib roast. Serve it warm, or cool. It's still wonderful. *Makes 10 to 12 servings.*

ROAST FILLET OF BEEF

If you don't like your beef rare, don't serve a roast fillet of beef. If it's overcooked, it loses all its flavor and juiciness.

1 well-trimmed 5- to 6-lb. fillet of beef
1 tablespoon coarse salt
1 teaspoon freshly cracked black pepper

8 large fluted sautéed mushroom caps (see p. 11)
1 bunch watercress

1. If the fillet is not a long, well-shaped piece of meat, tie it with a string every 2 inches around so that it is. Bring it to room temperature, rub it all over with salt—the coarse salt makes an attractive crust—and pepper and place it on a rack in a shallow roasting pan.

2. Roast in a preheated 425° oven for 35 minutes. This will give a very rare piece of meat.

• If a meat thermometer is used, the temperature should register 125°.

3. Remove from oven and let stand about 15 minutes before carving.

4. Garnish platter with sautéed mushroom caps and watercress.

• Serve plain or with Béarnaise Sauce (see p. 248), Maître d'Hôtel Butter (see p. 253), or Sauce Périgourdine (see p. 250). If serving with Périgourdine, reserve the pan drippings from the beef to add to the sauce for extra enrichment. *Makes 8 servings.*

STEAK AU POIVRE

When I was at Le Cordon Bleu in Paris, a long time ago, the chef did Steak au Poivre. When he put it on the platter to present it with the usual flourishes, he said, "I once knew an American who ate the steak pepper and all!" According to him, the pepper should be scraped off before the steak is eaten. This amused me. What's the point of pounding on the pepper if it's not there to enjoy? If you don't love pepper, don't make Steak au Poivre.

6 *1-inch strip or shell steaks*	2 *teaspoons salt*
¼ cup melted butter	*¼ cup cognac*
¼ cup freshly cracked black pepper, about	1 *bunch watercress*

1. Trim excess fat from the steaks, then brush both sides with melted butter.

2. With the heel of your hand pound freshly cracked black pepper into both sides of each steak, allowing a good teaspoonful for each side. (Remember, it's not Steak au Poivre unless a lot of pepper is used.)

3. Heat a large heavy frying pan to the smoking point. Put in the steaks—not touching—and sear them over high heat for 5 minutes on each side.

• This timing produces a rare steak. Not raw, but rarer than medium rare.

4. Season the steaks with salt and put them on a hot serving platter.

5. Deglaze the frying pan with a little cognac, either by flaming the cognac or by just letting it boil for 1 or 2 minutes. Scrape up the brown bits and pour the sauce over the meat.

• Some cooks, when they deglaze the pan with cognac, add a little heavy cream, then bring the mixture to a boil before pouring it over the meat. I prefer just cognac.

• As an alternative to the pan sauce, try Béarnaise Sauce (see p. 248).

6. Decorate the platter with lots of watercress. Its good peppery flavor goes well with this steak. And make sure there's plenty of robust red wine with which to wash the steak down. (Men will bless you.) **Makes 6 servings.**

STEAK DIANE

Pound steaks thin, then cook them individually in a chafing dish while guests watch the show. The following recipe makes just 1 serving.

1 *10-oz. shell, Delmonico, or sirloin strip steak, cut ¼ or ½ inch thick*	3 *tablespoons butter*
½ teaspoon salt	2 *tablespoons cognac*
¼ teaspoon freshly cracked black pepper	2 *tablespoons dry Madeira*
	2 *tablespoons chopped chives*

1. Place the steak—if using a ½-inch one, first slit it not quite through and open it up (butterfly it, that is)—between two sheets of waxed paper and pound it as thin as possible. Sprinkle with salt and pepper.

2. Melt 2 tablespoons of butter in a heavy pan or chafing dish. When butter is hot and no longer foaming, sear the steak over high heat for 2 minutes on each side.

3. Add cognac, give it a second to warm, then ignite it either with a match or by tipping the chafing dish toward a flame. Shake the dish until flames die.

4. After removing steak to a warm serving plate, make a quick pan sauce by adding Madeira, boiling for 1 or 2 minutes, swirling in 1 tablespoon of butter, and sprinkling with chopped chives. Pour sauce over steak. *Makes 1 serving.*

FILET DE BOEUF EN CROÛTE WITH SAUCE PÉRIGOURDINE

This is a sort of compromise beef Wellington—individual fillets topped with pâté and baked in a crust of rough puff pastry. It's much easier to serve, since there is no carving. Besides, I think it's a sacrilege to take a whole fillet, cook it partially, coat it with duxelles and pâté, wrap it in pastry, and cook it a second time. I prefer my whole fillet (see p. 82), plain or with Béarnaise. Note that fillets made en croûte must be thick if they are to be rare when the pastry is completely baked.

4 1¼- to 1½-inch pieces fillet of beef	1 recipe of rough puff pastry (recipe follows), made 24 hours in advance
1 teaspoon salt	
½ teaspoon freshly cracked black pepper	Flour to dust pastry board
	1 10-oz. can pâté de foie gras
3 tablespoons butter	1 egg yolk
2 tablespoons cognac	Sauce Périgourdine (see p. 250)

1. Trim excess fat from fillets, then salt and pepper them.

2. Heat butter in a heavy skillet, and when foaming subsides, sear fillets—do not let them touch—for 1 minute on each side over high heat.

3. Heat cognac in a small long-handled pan until warm to the touch. Ignite it and pour it, flaming, over the fillets. Shake skillet until flames die.

4. Remove fillets from skillet, set them in a dish in the refrigerator, and chill for at least one-half hour. Reserve pan juices to add to sauce.

• Fillets must be chilled thoroughly before they're wrapped in pastry; if they aren't, the pastry gets soft and sticky. Even more important, chilled meat will stay rare while the pastry bakes.

5. When fillets are chilled, roll out pastry. Cut the folded pastry into 4 equal pieces, roll each piece separately, as thin as possible, on a lightly floured board.

6. Put a slice of pâté de foie gras on each fillet, then lay pastry over the pâté and form it around each fillet. Tuck the pastry around the bottom edge of each fillet, but don't try to cover the whole bottom, for pastry won't bake satisfactorily on the bottom.

7. Place pastry packages in a shallow baking pan, about 2 inches apart, and with a knife, cut 3 slits across the top of each package to let steam escape.

8. Brush pastry with egg yolk thinned with a little water (a mixture called *dorure*), then decorate the top of each package with 2 pastry leaves cut from scraps with a leaf cutter. Mark veins in the leaves with the back of a knife blade and brush leaves with what's left of the egg-yolk mixture.

• The pastry-wrapped fillets can be made in advance of when they're to be baked and either kept in a refrigerator overnight, or frozen for future use. If freezing the fillets, wrap them in plastic wrap or foil, and thaw in refrigerator before baking.

9. Bake in a preheated 450° oven until pastry is a deep golden brown. Check at 20 minutes, and if not brown, bake a few minutes longer.

10. Serve with Sauce Périgourdine. **Makes 4 servings.**

Rough Puff Pastry

This pastry can be used as a crust for meat pies, as well as for Filet de Boeuf en Croûte.

> 1½ cups lightly packed flour, plus flour to dust on rolling surface
>
> ½ teaspoon salt
> ¾ cup chilled butter

1. Place 1½ cups of flour in a bowl and stir in salt.
2. Cut butter into chips the size of almonds.
3. Turn the chips over in the flour to coat them; then with a large fork, stir in just enough iced water (no more than ⅜ cup) so the mixture can be gathered together in a dough ball.

• Don't worry about the lumps of butter. They are supposed to be visible.
• The amount of water needed will depend on the weather, particularly the humidity.

4. Place the ball on lightly floured marble or pastry board, and knead it just enough to get it together.

• Dough should be kept as cool as possible, so work on a marble surface if you have it.

5. Wrap in waxed paper and chill in a refrigerator for at least ½ hour.

6. Roll dough into a rectangle about 8 inches wide by 20 inches long, fold it in thirds (like a business letter), and give it a quarter turn (folds will be at the sides). Then roll it into a rectangle, fold it, and give it a quarter turn again. And again, for a total of 3 rollings and foldings.

• When the dough is rolled, it will be sticky. Use flour on the rolling surface as needed. If dough is too sticky, return it to refrigerator for more chilling. Scrape dough that sticks to rolling pin and press it back onto rolled dough.

• Butter lumps will still be visible during the first rolling. Don't worry about them.

7. Wrap the rolled dough in waxed paper and refrigerate it to chill thoroughly.

• It's better to make the dough a day or more before it's to be used.

• The dough can be wrapped in plastic wrap or foil and frozen. Put it in a refrigerator to thaw a day before it is to be used.

• If more dough is needed, do not double the recipe. Instead, make it twice. *Makes enough to cover a 4-pound piece of meat or a 10-inch pie.*

FRENCH POT ROAST

1 4-lb. rump, chuck, bottom round, or top round of beef	2 cloves chopped garlic
3 cups dry red wine	¼ cup vegetable oil
¼ cup wine vinegar	1 veal knuckle
1 tablespoon salt	18 small white onions
1 teaspoon freshly cracked black pepper	6 medium carrots
1 bay leaf	18 medium mushrooms
½ teaspoon thyme	Lemon juice to clean mushrooms
¼ cup olive oil	2 tablespoons chopped parsley
1½ cups sliced onions	

1. Place beef in the refrigerator for 24 hours in a marinade made by mixing together—use a bowl large enough to hold the beef—2 cups of the wine, the wine vinegar, salt, pepper, bay leaf, thyme, olive oil, sliced onions, and garlic. Turn beef about every 4 hours while it marinates.

2. After 24 hours remove beef from marinade and drain it, reserving the marinade. Dry beef thoroughly with paper towels.

3. Heat oil in a large heavy casserole until almost smoking, then brown meat on all sides over high heat, turning it with wooden spatulas. This takes about 15 minutes. Remove meat and set aside.

4. Put reserved marinade into the casserole and bring it to a boil. Add the remaining cup of wine and the veal knuckle and return meat to casserole. Cover casserole with foil, put on the lid, and put into a preheated 350° oven to cook for 3 hours.

5. While beef cooks, prepare vegetables: Drop the small onions into boiling water for 30 seconds to loosen skins. Peel, then parboil in water to cover for about 15 minutes. Drain and set aside. Peel carrots, cut them into 3 chunks each, and parboil them in water to cover for about 20 minutes. Drain and set aside. Wipe mushrooms with paper towels dipped in acidulated water (1 tablespoon lemon juice to 1 quart water), cut off stems even with caps—don't twist stems out, or caps will lose their shape when cooking—discard stems, and set caps aside.

6. About ½ hour before beef is done, take casserole out of oven and add parboiled onions and carrots, and uncooked mushroom caps. Cover again with the foil and lid and return casserole to oven to finish cooking.

7. After removing the casserole from the oven, put the beef on a carving board and let it stand for 10 or 15 minutes to give the juices a chance to settle.

8. Discard the veal knuckle and bay leaf. Taste the sauce for seasoning.

9. Carve the meat and arrange it on a serving platter, overlapping the slices. Arrange vegetables in piles around the meat. Sprinkle it all with chopped parsley. Pass the sauce separately.

• Braised beef can also be served chilled, molded in aspic, along with its vegetables. Use a loaf pan or ring mold and oil it with 2 tablespoons of vegetable oil. Into the bottom of the mold, spoon a thin layer of aspic made by straining the sauce in which the meat cooked and bringing it to a boil in a saucepan, then adding 1 tablespoon of gelatin softened in ½ cup of red wine, stirring to dissolve, and after setting pan over ice, continuing to stir until the mixture is syrupy and on the point of setting. Arrange the vegetables, plus some cooked peas (for color), over the aspic. Carve the meat and lay slices over the vegetables. Spoon on the remaining aspic and chill until set. Before serving, run a knife around the edge of the mold (use an up-and-down motion), then place a platter over the mold, invert, give a shake, and lift off the mold. *Makes 6 to 8 servings.*

HELENE'S SWEET AND SOUR BEEF

1 4-lb. rump, chuck, top round, bottom round, or sirloin tip of beef	*½ cup butter*
	2½ cups chopped onions
	1 cup red wine vinegar
1 tablespoon salt	*¼ cup sugar*
1 teaspoon freshly cracked black pepper	*1 cup pitted jumbo prunes, plus 8 for garnish*

1. Rub the piece of beef with salt and pepper.

2. Melt ¼ cup of the butter in a heavy casserole. When it's hot and the foaming subsides, brown the meat over high heat on all sides, turning it occasionally with wooden spatulas. Don't prick it with a fork. It will take about 15 minutes to brown well.

3. Remove meat and set aside. In the casserole melt the remaining ¼ cup of butter. Add onions, stirring them with a wooden spatula to coat with butter. Cook, stirring frequently, over high heat, until onions are transparent. Do not let them brown. This takes about 10 minutes.

4. Place meat on top of onions in casserole, add vinegar and sugar, and cover top of casserole with foil. Put lid over the foil. Simmer over low heat for about 3 hours, or until meat is tender. Every ½ hour during cooking, remove lid and foil and baste the meat, spooning sauce from bottom of casserole over meat. Halfway through cooking, turn meat over.

5. One half hour before serving, add 1 cup prunes. Replace foil and lid and continue cooking.

6. Before carving, let the beef rest 15 minutes. Carve and arrange slices on a warm platter. Garnish with remaining prunes and serve with pan juices. *Makes 6 to 8 servings.*

POT ROAST IN BEER

1 4-lb. rump, chuck, bottom round, top round, or sirloin tip of beef	1½ cups sliced onions
	1 cup sliced carrots
	2 cups beer
3 tablespoons sugar	½ cup olive oil
1 tablespoon salt	3 tablespoons vegetable oil
1 teaspoon ground cloves	2 tablespoons chopped parsley, or 1 bunch watercress
6 peppercorns	

1. Put the beef in a bowl and sprinkle with sugar, salt, cloves, peppercorns, sliced onions, and sliced carrots. Pour on beer and olive oil. Marinate the meat in this mixture in the refrigerator for 24 hours, turning it about every 4 hours.

2. Remove beef from marinade, drain it—reserve the marinade—and dry it thoroughly.

3. Heat oil in a large heavy casserole. When it's hot, brown the meat over high heat on all sides, turning it occasionally with wooden spatulas. Don't prick it with a fork. It takes 15 minutes to brown thoroughly.

4. Add ¾ cup of reserved marinade to the casserole, cover top with foil, and put on the lid. Cook over low heat for about 3 hours, or until beef is tender. Halfway through cooking, remove lid and foil and turn beef over. If the pot looks dry, add another ½ cup of marinade. The beef should braise throughout the cooking in a small amount of liquid. Cover again and continue cooking.

5. Let the beef rest 15 minutes before carving. Carve it into slices and arrange on a warm platter. Sprinkle with chopped parsley or garnish platter with a bunch of watercress. Serve with pan juices. *Makes 6 to 8 servings.*

RAGOÛT DE BOEUF

There are two schools of thought on beef for stews. Some people buy the less expensive cuts and cook them longer. Personally, I prefer good top round or sirloin, and I am very careful to get it off the fire before it is overcooked: good beef, cooked too long, tends to be dry. Ragoût de Boeuf, a change from Boeuf Bourguignon, and an ideal make-ahead dish (it freezes beautifully, or can sit in a refrigerator for 2 days before it's reheated and served), is fairly indestructible, but beware of overcooking: if this stew is cooked too long, it's apt to come out not only with dry beef but also with a generally mushy look.

2 tablespoons dried (not freeze-dried) mushrooms
1½ cups beef stock (see p. 240)
3½ lbs. top round or sirloin of beef, cut in 2-inch cubes
3 tablespoons butter
1 tablespoon vegetable oil
5 tablespoons cognac
3 tablespoons minced shallots
1 clove finely chopped garlic
2 teaspoons arrowroot, potato starch, or cornstarch
1½ tablespoons tomato paste
2 cups dry Burgundy wine
Bouquet garni (see p. 7)
1 teaspoon salt
½ teaspoon freshly cracked black pepper
1 ½-inch piece of lemon peel
2 tablespoons fresh fennel leaves or chopped parsley

1. Soak mushrooms in beef stock for at least 1 hour. Remove mushrooms, squeezing them to remove excess moisture, and chop very fine. Set aside. Reserve beef stock for later use.

2. Pat cubes of meat dry with paper towels and brown them thoroughly, a few at a time—do not let the cubes touch each other—in a mixture of hot butter and oil. Use a 4-quart flameproof casserole or Dutch oven set over high heat, and turn the cubes with tongs to brown all sides. Remove browned cubes to a tray while doing others.

• It's a temptation to dump all the meat in at once and move it around with a wooden spatula. Don't, or the pieces won't get brown and crispy, and may end up as a gray, juicy mess.

3. When all the meat is browned, set it aside, pour off excess fat, leaving about 1 tablespoonful, and deglaze the casserole—remove it from heat first—by warming 2 tablespoons of cognac in a small long-handled pan, igniting it, and while it is flaming, pouring it into the casserole. When flames die down, scrape up with a wooden spatula all the brown bits loosened by the cognac; these will add flavor and color to the sauce.

4. Add shallots and garlic to the casserole, return to high heat, and cook for 1 or 2 minutes.

5. Remove from heat and add reserved mushrooms, then stir in arrowroot (or potato starch or cornstarch) and tomato paste and mix together thoroughly.

• I like to use arrowroot or potato starch as a thickener rather than flour because it keeps the sauce clear, and you need only half the amount of arrowroot that you would need of flour.

6. Stir in wine and reserved beef stock, then return meat to casserole and bring to a boil.

7. Add bouquet garni, salt, and pepper, and lay the lemon peel on top.

8. Lay foil over top of casserole, cover with a tight-fitting lid, and set on the middle shelf of a preheated 350° oven to cook for 1½ to 2 hours, or until beef is tender. (Cooking time depends on the quality of the beef.) Three times during cooking, take casserole out of the oven, remove lid and foil, and baste the meat with 1 tablespoon of cognac.

9. Before serving, remove bouquet garni and lemon peel. Garnish with chopped fresh fennel leaves or chopped parsley.

• I like to serve this stew with Rice Pilaf (see p. 186), little boiled parslied potatoes, potatoes mashed in cream, noodles, green noodles, or pasta seashells. *Makes 6 to 8 servings.*

HUNGARIAN GOULASH

6 *tablespoons butter*	1 *tablespoon flour*
3 *lbs. rump, bottom or top round, or sirloin tip of beef, cut in 1-inch cubes*	1 *teaspoon salt*
	½ *teaspoon freshly cracked black pepper*
2 *cups finely chopped onion*	1 *cup tomato purée*
1 *clove finely chopped garlic*	1 *cup beef stock (see p. 240)*
¼ *cup sweet Hungarian paprika*	½ *cup dry red wine*
	1 *cup dairy sour cream*

1. Melt ¼ cup of the butter in a large heavy casserole. Dry meat cubes on paper towels. When butter is hot and no longer foaming, brown the meat over high heat, a few pieces at a time, on all sides. Do not let the pieces touch and do not prick them with a fork—use tongs to turn pieces.

• If the meat is moist, or if it is crowded in the pan, the meat will steam instead of brown

2. Remove meat from casserole. Add remaining 2 tablespoons of butter and stir in onion and garlic. Cook until transparent, stirring with a wooden spatula, but don't let mixture brown.

3. Add paprika, working it in with the wooden spatula.

• It must be sweet Hungarian paprika, not hot paprika. I used the hot kind once, and my mouth was on fire for two weeks.

4. Smooth in flour and continue to cook over high heat for 3 minutes more, stirring.

5. Return meat to the casserole and add salt, pepper, tomato purée, beef stock, and wine. Bring to a boil, cover casserole with foil, and put

the lid on. Set casserole in a preheated 325° oven and cook for 2 hours, or until tender.

6. Before serving, stir in sour cream. Serve from casserole with Spaetzle (see p. 181) or with noodles cooked in boiling water until tender, drained, and dressed with melted butter (½ cup to 2 lbs. of noodles), salt and pepper to taste, and 1 tablespoon of caraway seeds. *Makes 6 to 8 servings.*

HAMBURGERS WITH ICE WATER

Nice little trick here: the ice water keeps the hamburgers very, very moist.

6 tablespoons butter	1 teaspoon salt
¾ cup finely chopped onion	½ teaspoon freshly cracked
2 lbs. lean ground beef	black pepper

1. Melt 2 tablespoons of the butter, stir in chopped onion, and cook over high heat, stirring, until onion is transparent. Do not let it brown.

2. Put beef in a bowl and mix in onion, salt, and pepper.

3. Beat in 1 cup of ice water, 2 tablespoonfuls at a time, with a wooden spatula or with your hand.

4. Scoop up enough beef mixture in a large serving spoon to make a good-size patty; shape it with hands dipped in ice water. Repeat, using the rest of the beef mixture to get 5 more patties.

5. Place patties on a dampened cutting board and smooth with a spatula.

6. Melt the remaining ¼ cup of butter in a large skillet. When it is hot and no longer foaming, sauté patties over high heat for about 2 minutes on each side. *Makes 6 servings.*

HAMBURGERS WITH CAPER BUTTER

They're good enough for company.

2½ lbs. lean ground beef	2 teaspoons salt
¾ cup butter	1 teaspoon freshly cracked
¼ cup capers	black pepper

1. Shape ground sirloin into 8 patties, about ½ inch thick.

2. Cream butter in a mixer (using the flat whip if the mixer is a heavy-duty one) or with a wooden spatula.

3. Drain and wash capers, then add them to the butter, shaping it into 4 balls. Flatten them a little.

• Instead of caper butter, the hamburgers can be stuffed with Lemon Butter (see p. 253) or Maître d'Hôtel Butter (see p. 253).

4. Lay 1 butter ball on each of 4 patties. Cover with remaining 4 patties and pinch edges together to seal.

5. Season the stuffed hamburgers on both sides with salt and pepper.

6. Heat an ungreased skillet to the smoking point. Put the hamburgers in—do not let them touch—and cook over high heat for 3 minutes on each side. *Makes 4 servings.*

BRAISED OXTAILS

4 lbs. oxtails, disjointed	1 teaspoon freshly cracked
¾ cup flour, about	black pepper
¼ cup vegetable oil	2 cups dry red wine
1 cup chopped carrot	1 cup beef stock (see p. 240)
1 cup chopped onion	Bouquet garni (see p. 7)
2 cloves finely chopped garlic	2 tablespoons chopped pars-
2 teaspoons salt	ley

1. Dredge the oxtails (any butcher will disjoint them) in flour, shaking off excess.

2. Heat oil in a large heavy casserole. Brown the oxtails, a few at a time, over high heat. Turn the oxtails to brown them evenly, and don't let them touch.

3. Return all browned oxtails to the casserole and add carrot, onion, garlic, salt, and pepper. Pour on wine and beef stock. Lay the bouquet garni on top.

4. Bring to a boil, cover the casserole with foil to condense the steam, put on lid, and place in a preheated 350° oven for about 3 hours, or until oxtails are tender.

5. Remove from oven, discard bouquet garni, and skim off fat. Taste sauce for seasoning, adding salt and pepper if desired.

6. Sprinkle with chopped parsley and serve from the casserole. Good with little boiled potatoes. *Makes 6 servings.*

LIVER WITH ONION-AND-SOUR-CREAM SAUCE

½ cup butter	1 cup dairy sour cream
1 cup very finely chopped onions	½ teaspoon salt
	¼ teaspoon freshly cracked
¾ cup dry white wine	black pepper
½ cup flour, about	8 ½-inch slices calves' liver

1. Make sauce first. Melt ¼ cup of the butter in a saucepan and add chopped onions. Stir until onions are coated with butter and cook over high heat until transparent. Do not let them brown.

2. Add wine and cook, uncovered, over moderately high heat for 20 minutes, or until wine evaporates. At this point the onions will be soft and deliciously flavored with wine.

3. Remove from heat, and sprinkle 1 tablespoon flour over onions, stirring to blend it in. Fold in sour cream, return to heat, and bring to a boil. Turn heat down and cook over low heat for 2 to 3 minutes. Season with salt and pepper.

• Don't worry about the sour cream curdling; sour cream that is combined with flour won't.

4. Dip liver slices in remaining flour, shaking off excess.

5. Melt remaining ¼ cup of butter in skillet. When it's hot and no longer foaming, sauté liver over high heat, a few slices at a time, for 2 minutes on each side. Don't crowd the pan; don't let slices touch.

6. Arrange slices on a serving platter and pour hot sauce over them. *Makes 6 to 8 servings.*

STUFFED HAM WITH CHAMPAGNE SAUCE AND FROSTED WHITE GRAPES

This unusual recipe for a buffet ham is my very own. Happily my students are wild about the flavor and about how easy it is to serve. Most of all, they like the glamorous look of the handsome ham garnished with frosted white grapes. And note: if you don't want to stuff the ham, the sauce and grape garnish are also elegant on a plain baked ham.

½ a boneless precooked ham, about 8 lbs.	¼ teaspoon freshly cracked white pepper
1½ cups seedless white grapes	2¾ cups champagne
1 beaten egg	2 tablespoons cognac
4 teaspoons fresh tarragon, or 1⅓ teaspoons dried	¼ cup heavy cream
4 tablespoons melted butter	Few drops lemon juice, optional
2 tablespoons bread crumbs (see p. 7)	1 bunch watercress
½ teaspoon salt, about	Frosted White Grapes (recipe follows)

1. With a large knife, dig a hole about 4 inches in diameter and 3 inches deep in the center of the ham, on the flat, or cut, side. Chop the removed ham very fine, discarding any fat.

2. Put chopped ham in a bowl along with ¾ cup of the grapes, the

beaten egg, 1 tablespoon of fresh (or 1 teaspoon of dried) tarragon, 2 tablespoons of the melted butter, the bread crumbs, the salt—add this cautiously—and the pepper. Mix together well, then pack into the ham cavity.

• If there is a little stuffing left over, wrap it in foil and bake it along with the ham. Serve as extra stuffing.
• The ham may be stuffed and readied for the oven the day before it is to be baked.

3. Press a large piece of heavy-duty foil against the stuffed end of the ham and shape it around the sides, down far enough so there is room to tie it on with string. Place ham in baking pan, foil side down. (This position holds the stuffing inside the ham.)

4. Brush exposed ham with 2 tablespoons of melted butter. Pour 1 cup of the champagne over the ham and bake in a preheated 325° oven for 10 minutes per pound. Baste the ham 3 times during baking, using ¼ cup champagne each time.

5. Remove ham from oven (do not remove foil until just before serving) and place it on a carving board. Let it rest while making sauce.

6. To make sauce: pour excess fat from pan, leaving about 1 tablespoonful. To lift the flavorful glaze made by champagne and ham juices, flame the pan with cognac—that is, warm the cognac in a small long-handled pan, ignite, then pour it, flaming, into the baking pan. Shake the pan until flames die. Scrape up the brown bits.

7. Stir in heavy cream and remaining 1 teaspoon of fresh (or ⅓ teaspoon of dried) tarragon, bring to a boil, and boil for 3 minutes.

8. Add remaining cup of champagne and boil again until mixture thickens slightly. Taste for seasoning and add a pinch of salt if needed. A few drops of lemon juice won't come amiss.

9. Add the remaining ¾ cup of grapes and heat through.

10. Don't try to slice the ham straight across—the servings will be too large. Carve slices of the ham off the sides, cutting straight down from the outside edge in to the point at which the stuffing begins (see illustration, p. 96). This method of carving will yield individual-size servings. Spoon stuffing onto each serving. Serve sauce separately in a small bowl. Garnish ham platter with watercress and frosted grapes. *Makes 12 to 16 servings.*

Frosted White Grapes

2 medium bunches seedless white grapes
2 egg whites

1 cup crystallized or granulated sugar

1. Remove grapes from the large stem in little bunches.
2. Beat whites until they form soft peaks. Dip the grapes in egg whites (you can be casual about this, each grape doesn't have to be covered).
3. Lay grapes on waxed paper, sprinkle with sugar and chill.

• The grapes can be made in the morning and refrigerated.
• Frosted grapes can also be served as a dessert—and an elegant one it is, too.

HAM EN CROÛTE

When I describe this to my classes, I call it "ham tied up in pastry ribbon." It makes a sensational package.

1 10-lb. canned ham   *Flour to sprinkle on pastry*
1 cup white raisins   *board*
1 full bottle dry Madeira   *1 beaten egg yolk*
1 recipe of sour-cream pastry *½ cup Dijon mustard*
(recipe follows), chilled

1. The day before the ham is to be baked, remove it from the can and cut little slits all over it with a small sharp knife. Use the knife to poke raisins into the slits. Push some raisins deep into the ham; place others near the surface. The raisins should be distributed through the

ham as evenly as possible; when it is carved, they should form a mosaic design. After adding the raisins, put ham into a large bowl, cover with Madeira, and let soak overnight at room temperature.

2. When ready to bake the ham, remove it from Madeira and dry it thoroughly.

• The Madeira can be saved (store in a refrigerator) and used to soak another ham, or pork or tongue.

3. Roll sour-cream pastry that has chilled for at least 1½ hours about ¼ inch thick on a lightly floured board, then roll out two strips, each 1½ inches wide and 20 to 25 inches long, and a rectangle about 6 inches wide and 10 inches long.

4. Place ham on baking sheet and wrap one long pastry strip around top and sides of ham, lengthwise; tuck the ends securely under the ham. Wrap the second strip around width of ham, again tucking ends under.

5. Brush the pastry all over with beaten egg yolk thinned with a little water. This egg wash, called *dorure*, not only makes the pastry shine but also helps hold the bow to be made next in place. Save some of the wash for the bow.

6. Make bow by pleating the remaining rectangle of pastry in the middle.

7. Lay bow on top of ham, where pastry ribbons cross. Brush bow with the rest of the egg wash. Then place ham in a preheated 350° oven and bake from 45 to 60 minutes, or until pastry crust is done (how long this takes depends on how thick the crust is).

8. Serve with Dijon mustard. *Makes 12 to 16 servings.*

Sour-Cream Pastry

Use sour-cream pastry for Ham en Croûte and for topping meat and fish pies, and for turnovers. It is not recommended for conventional pies.

1½ cups lightly packed flour, plus flour to dust on dough and kneading surface	½ teaspoon salt ¾ cup chilled unsalted butter ½ cup dairy sour cream

1. Place ½ cup of flour in a bowl and stir in salt.

2. Cut butter into chips the size of almonds.

3. Turn the chips over in flour to coat them; then, with a pastry blender, cut them into the flour. The mixture should look like coarse cornmeal.

4. Add sour cream and mix with a fork.

5. Gather together the mixture, which will be soft, with your hand, lay it on a floured board, knead it a few times, then form it into a dough ball, sprinkle it with a little flour, and wrap it in waxed paper.

6. Chill in a refrigerator for 1½ hours or more.

• The dough can be made the day before it is needed, and stored in the refrigerator; it can also be frozen.

• This dough is sometimes a little hard to roll out. To make a nice round circle, don't roll over the edge, just get near the edge. To save steps, keep turning the pastry, moving it instead of walking around the rolling surface. *Makes enough to cover a 4-pound piece of meat or a 10-inch pie.*

BRAISED HAM

1 10- to 12-lb. precooked ham, with bone	*½ teaspoon freshly cracked black pepper*
½ cup butter	*1 bay leaf*
1 cup chopped onions	*2 cups dry Madeira*
1 cup chopped carrots	*1 cup chicken stock (see p. 241)*
1 cup chopped celery	
½ cup chopped mushrooms	*2 tablespoons freshly chopped parsley*
½ teaspoon thyme	

1. Trim excess fat from ham, leaving about ¼ inch covering the meat.

2. Melt butter in heavy casserole—one large enough to hold the ham—and stir in onions, carrots, and celery. Cook over high heat, stirring, until onions are transparent, but do not let vegetables brown.

3. Place ham on the vegetables. Around it sprinkle chopped mushrooms, thyme, and pepper. Put bay leaf on top, then pour on Madeira and chicken stock.

• As an alternative dry white wine can be substituted for the Madeira.

4. Cover casserole with foil and heavy lid. Set in a preheated 350° oven to braise for about 2 hours. Allow 10 minutes per pound.

5. Remove ham to a serving platter and keep warm. Skim off excess fat from liquid in casserole, discard bay leaf, and prepare sauce either by puréeing the vegetables and the liquid in a blender (which should be no more than half full so the hot mixture doesn't overflow) or by working them through a food mill or sieve.

6. Taste sauce for seasoning and adjust if necessary; if the ham is salty, no additional salt will be necessary.

7. Slice ham on serving platter, pour sauce over it, and sprinkle it with chopped parsley. *Makes 12 to 16 servings.*

Hot Ham Mousse

5 tablespoons butter, plus
  butter for baking paper
3 tablespoons flour
1 cup light cream
2 lbs. ham, any kind (leftover,
  precooked, uncooked,
  baked, or boiled)
3 egg whites

¼ cup dry Madeira
1 teaspoon salt
½ teaspoon freshly cracked
  black pepper
1 tablespoon fresh tarragon or
  1 teaspoon dried
1 tablespoon Dijon mustard

1. Make a *panade* (a thickener to be beaten into the ham mixture) by melting 3 tablespoons of butter in a small saucepan, stirring in flour with a wooden spatula, and cooking over high heat 2 minutes, stirring constantly. Do not let it brown. Remove from heat, add cream, and whisk vigorously. Return to high heat and cook, stirring, until mixture comes to a boil and is very thick.

2. Pour *panade* into a small baking dish and refrigerate for 15 minutes, or until set.

3. Melt the remaining 2 tablespoons of butter and butter a ring mold or soufflé dish generously with it. Set aside.

4. Grind ham in a meat grinder, using the finest blade, or chop with a knife.

5. Put ground ham into mixer bowl and beat in egg whites thoroughly (use the flat whip if the mixer is a heavy-duty one). Add Madeira and season with salt, pepper, tarragon, and mustard.

6. Add the chilled *panade*, beating it in, a spoonful at a time, until thoroughly mixed.

7. Spoon the mixture into prepared mold or soufflé dish, cover it with buttered brown paper or foil, and place the mold in a baking pan half filled with boiling water. Bake in a preheated 350° oven for 30 to 35 minutes, or until mixture is firm to the touch.

8. Remove from oven and let stand 5 minutes. Using an up-and-down motion, run a small knife around the edge of the mold to loosen it, then put serving platter over the mold, invert mold and platter, give them a shake, and lift off the mold. **Makes 6 servings.**

Ham Slice with Madeira

2 tablespoons butter
1 1¼-inch slice precooked
  ham

2 tablespoons chopped shallots
2 tablespoons fresh tarragon,

or 2 teaspoons dried
9 tablespoons dry Madeira
½ cup chicken stock (see
p. 241)

1 teaspoon potato starch
2 tablespoons chopped parsley

1. Melt butter in a heavy skillet and sauté ham over high heat for 3 minutes on each side. Remove and set aside.

2. Stir shallots into the butter left in the pan, and cook, stirring with a wooden spatula, until transparent. Do not let the shallots brown. Add tarragon and ½ cup of the Madeira and bring to a boil, scraping up the brown bits. Add chicken stock.

3. Make a smooth mixture of potato starch and the remaining 1 tablespoon of Madeira and stir it into the pan. Bring to a boil.

4. Return ham to pan and cook over medium heat, basting with the pan sauce. After 5 minutes turn ham over and continue basting until it is heated through. Taste for seasoning; add pepper, as well as salt if desired.

5. Remove ham to serving platter, pour sauce over it, and sprinkle with chopped parsley. *Makes 4 servings.*

PORK WITH PISTACHIOS

When buying the pork for this recipe, ask the butcher to remove the chine bone (backbone). Having it out will make carving easier.

1 6-lb. loin of pork
4 cloves garlic, peeled and cut into slivers
¼ cup natural pistachio nuts
1 tablespoon coarse salt
1 teaspoon freshly cracked black pepper

½ to 1 cup dry Madeira
½ cup chicken stock (see p. 241)
1 bunch watercress

1. Trim excess fat from pork, so that there is no more than ¼ inch remaining.

2. With a small sharp knife, make little slits all over the fatty side of the pork. Go deep into the meat with the knife, and using it as a slide, poke a sliver of garlic and a pistachio nut into each slit. When the meat is carved, it will show a mosaic of pistachio nuts.

3. Rub the meat all over with salt and pepper, then put it in a heavy casserole, fatty side up, pour on ½ cup of Madeira, and cover casserole with foil and the lid. Bake in a preheated 350° oven for about 2½ hours or 25 minutes per pound. Halfway through the baking period, take the casserole out of the oven, remove lid and foil, and turn meat over. Add

another ½ cup of Madeira if casserole looks dry. Replace foil and lid and return meat to oven to finish baking with bone ends up.

• If you are using a meat thermometer, the meat will be done when the temperature reaches 170°.

4. When pork is done, put it on a serving platter and keep it warm. Pour off all but 1 tablespoon of the fat from casserole and deglaze with chicken stock—that is, add stock to casserole, place over heat, and stir, scraping up the brown bits. Taste the sauce for seasoning.

5. Carve pork loin between the bones. Garnish platter with watercress and pass sauce separately. *Makes 6 servings.*

PORK CHOPS WITH SAUCE ROBERT

6 ¾-inch loin pork chops   Sauce Robert (see p. 249)
1 teaspoon salt
½ teaspoon freshly cracked
  black pepper

1. Trim excess fat from chops, put it into a large skillet, and cook it over medium-low heat for about 10 minutes, until it melts. This is called rendering. Discard rendered pieces of fat.

2. Season chops with salt and pepper and sauté them in the hot fat over low heat for 15 minutes on each side. Test for doneness by pricking chops near the bone with a fork. If juices run pink, sauté for another 5 minutes.

• Pork chops should always be cooked slowly. When cooked too quickly, over high heat, they toughen.

3. Remove chops to serving platter and keep warm while making sauce.
4. Pour hot sauce over chops before serving. *Makes 6 servings.*

PORK CHOPS IN MUSTARD CREAM

6 ¾-inch loin pork chops   1 tablespoon Dijon mustard
1 teaspoon salt   1¼ cups heavy cream
½ teaspoon freshly cracked   2 tablespoons chopped pars-
  black pepper   ley
2 tablespoons dry red wine

1. Trim excess fat from chops, put it into a large skillet, and cook over medium-low heat for 10 minutes, until fat melts. Discard rendered pieces of fat.

2. Season chops with salt and pepper, then put them into the hot fat and sauté slowly, over low heat, for 15 minutes on each side. Test for doneness by pricking chops near the bone with a fork. If juices run pink, sauté for another 5 minutes.

• Cook pork chops slowly, for when they're cooked too quickly, over high heat, they toughen.

3. Remove chops to serving platter and keep warm. Pour off all but 1 tablespoon of the fat and deglaze the pan with red wine, stirring the juices over high heat with a wooden spatula to lift the brown bits. Stir in mustard and heavy cream and bring to a boil. Cook the mixture over moderately high heat to reduce it and thicken it slightly. Adjust seasoning if necessary. Pour over meat.

4. Sprinkle chops with parsley before serving. **Makes 6 servings.**

BARBECUED SPARERIBS

Try to get ribs that have a lot of meat on them, and ask your butcher to cut them into portions of 2 ribs each.

4 lbs. spareribs	*6 tablespoons lemon juice*
1 cup finely chopped onion	*¼ cup brown sugar*
2 tablespoons vegetable oil	*1½ cups chili sauce*
½ cup vinegar	*½ teaspoon freshly cracked*
2 tablespoons soy sauce	*black pepper*

1. If the butcher hasn't already done it, cut ribs into serving portions of 2 ribs each.

2. Make sauce by mixing all remaining ingredients together in a bowl.

• This sauce can also be used for barbecued chicken. No salt is needed because soy sauce is salty.

3. Lay ribs in a shallow baking pan and pour sauce over them. Bake, uncovered, in a preheated 350° oven for 30 minutes, then take out pan, turn ribs, baste them with sauce, and return them to the oven for another 45 minutes, basting them several times. **Makes 6 to 8 servings.**

SELLE D'AGNEAU

This elegant and costly cut of lamb, called saddle of lamb, must be ordered in advance from most butchers. Ask to have both sides of the loin left still attached to the backbone. The loin should not be cut down the middle; neither should it be boned. The entire saddle, with flaps left on, is what is needed. An 8-lb. saddle is the size I prefer, but the usual 5- to 6-lb. size more than pleases me and will certainly serve up to 8 people. Expensive it is, but happily it goes a long way.

1 saddle of lamb, 8 lbs. preferably
1 tablespoon butter, plus butter to rub on meat
2 teaspoons coarse salt
¼ teaspoon freshly cracked black pepper

½ cup dry red wine
8 large fluted sautéed mushroom caps (see p. 11)
1 bunch watercress
1 lemon

1. Trim any excess fat from underneath the saddle. Roll flaps up underneath, toward the spine. Tie in 4 or 5 places with butcher's cord. Rub lamb with softened butter, coarse salt, and pepper.

2. Place saddle on rack in roasting pan and roast in a preheated 425° oven for 12 minutes per pound, or until a meat thermometer registers 130°. Don't overcook the saddle; it should be served rare.

3. Remove lamb from oven and let stand 5 minutes before carving.

• During this resting period, lamb continues to cook.

4. Make a simple sauce by skimming the excess fat from roasting pan, adding red wine, and boiling for 1 minute to reduce, then scraping up the good brown bits and swirling in 1 tablespoon of butter. Taste for seasoning; it may need a little salt and pepper.

5. Arrange saddle on a carving board with fluted sautéed mushroom caps lined up along the spine. At one end of the board place a bunch of watercress, and in it two fluted lemon cups made by zigzagging around the center of a lemon—cutting at least halfway through—with a small sharp knife, then pulling the lemon halves apart.

6. Carve the meat, using a long, thin ham slicer if you have one, parallel to the spine, in long thin slices, first one side, then the other.

Then turn the saddle over, cut loose the tenderloins (fillet sections), and carve them in long thin slices too. Serve sauce separately, in a bowl. *Makes 6 to 8 servings.*

RACK OF LAMB

A rack of lamb requires very little preparation and makes an extremely successful dinner party entrée. Serve it with Minted Hollandaise (see p. 247) or Béarnaise Sauce (see p. 248), Flageolets (see p. 165), Sautéed Cherry Tomatoes (see p. 189), and Stuffed Mushrooms (see p. 179).

1 rack of lamb, 8 chops
1 tablespoon coarse salt
1 teaspoon freshly cracked
   black pepper

1 clove garlic, peeled and cut
   into slivers

1. Have the butcher trim the rack (or trim it yourself) so that 1½ to 2 inches of bone are exposed on each chop, all gristle and fat is removed, and the chine bone (backbone) at the bottom is taken out. Removing the chine makes the rack easy to carve into chops.
2. Rub the lamb all over with salt—the coarse salt makes an attractive crust—and pepper.
3. Insert the point of a small sharp knife in the fatty side of the meat, and using the knife blade as a slide, push a garlic sliver down into the hole. Repeat with the remaining garlic slivers.
4. Place lamb, fatty side up, on a rack in a baking pan and roast in a preheated 425° oven for 45 minutes, for pink lamb.
5. Before serving, carve between each chop. *Makes 4 servings.*

LAMB CHOPS IN MINT ASPIC

8 1-inch rib lamb chops
3 cups chicken stock (see
   p. 241)
½ teaspoon salt
¼ teaspoon freshly cracked
   black pepper
1 tablespoon tarragon vine-
   gar

1½ tablespoons (1½ envelopes)
   unflavored gelatin
6 tablespoons chopped fresh
   mint leaves
2 egg whites

1. French the bones on the lamb chops—that is, scrape bare the ends (about 1½ inches from the tips). Then trim excess fat from chops.

2. Put the chops in a pan and add 2½ cups chicken stock, salt, pepper, and tarragon vinegar. Bring to a boil, skim off any foam, and simmer, covered, for 25 minutes.

3. Let chops cool in broth; then remove them and chill for 1 hour in refrigerator.

4. Strain broth into a saucepan and set over high heat for 5 minutes.

5. Soften gelatin in the remaining ½ cup of chicken stock and stir into saucepan, then add ¼ cup of the mint leaves and the 2 egg whites and beat with a rotary beater or a whisk over high heat until frothy.

6. Remove pan from heat and let stand 10 minutes, then strain liquid aspic into a bowl through a sieve lined with 2 thicknesses of damp cheesecloth. Taste it for seasoning—more salt and pepper may be necessary—and add the remaining 2 tablespoons of mint leaves.

7. Set bowl of liquid aspic into a bowl of ice and stir until it is thick and syrupy.

8. Remove from ice and pour ⅓ of the aspic, now beginning to set, onto a chilled, very shallow round serving platter. Refrigerate the platter for 10 to 15 minutes, or until aspic is set.

9. Arrange the chilled chops in a circle on the platter of firm aspic, with bones in the center. Spoon another ⅓ of the aspic over chops.

• If aspic in the bowl has set too much, stir it over hot water for a minute.

10. Return chops to refrigerator for another 10 to 15 minutes to set aspic. Bring chops out and spoon remaining ⅓ of the aspic over them. Return to refrigerator to chill ½ hour, or until firm.

• French Potato Salad (see p. 197) is an excellent accompaniment for the chops. *Makes 6 to 8 servings.*

NOISETTES OF LAMB

8 slices of bacon	*2 tablespoons butter*
8 1½-inch loin lamb chops	*1 bunch watercress*
2 teaspoons salt	*Hollandaise Sauce (see p. 246)*
1 teaspoon freshly cracked black pepper	

1. Blanch the bacon slices—that is, put them in a saucepan, cover with cold water, and bring to a boil, then boil 1 minute. Drain in a sieve.

2. Bone lamb chops, then sprinkle them with salt and pepper and wrap a piece of bacon around the edge of each. Tie the bacon on with heavy string.

• Chops can be boned and wrapped in bacon a day ahead of time and stored in the refrigerator. Do not cook them until ready to serve.

3. Melt butter in a heavy skillet, and when it is hot and no longer foaming, sauté boned chops, or noisettes, over high heat, not letting them touch each other. For rare meat, sauté noisettes 3 to 4 minutes on each side (6 to 8 minutes in all); for medium rare, sauté 4 to 5 minutes on each side (8 to 10 minutes in all); and for well-done, sauté 5 to 6½ minutes on each side (10 to 13 minutes in all).

4. Arrange noisettes on a platter and garnish with watercress. Serve with Hollandaise Sauce.

• Minted Hollandaise Sauce (see p. 247) or Béarnaise Sauce (see p. 248) can be used instead, if desired. *Makes 8 servings.*

GIGOT D'AGNEAU PERSILLÉ

This is baby leg of lamb, encrusted with golden bread crumbs and parsley and roasted the French way, until it's pink.

1 *leg of lamb, under 5 lbs.*	10 *tablespoons soft butter*
2 *cloves garlic, 1 cut into slivers, 1 chopped*	½ *cup finely chopped parsley*
¼ *cup olive oil*	½ *teaspoon salt*
1 *tablespoon coarse salt*	1 *bunch watercress*
¾ *teaspoon freshly cracked black pepper*	1 *lemon*
1½ *cups bread crumbs (see p. 7)*	*White paper for frill*

1. Poke slivers of garlic into the meat by inserting point of a small sharp knife in the fatty side and using the knife blade as a slide to push slivers down into the holes.

2. Rub lamb all over with olive oil, coarse salt, and ½ teaspoon pepper, then set it, fatty side up, on a rack in an open roasting pan and roast in a preheated 325° oven for 18 minutes per pound.

3. To make coating, mix bread crumbs, butter, chopped parsley, chopped garlic, ½ teaspoon of salt, and the remaining ¼ teaspoon of pepper in a bowl. Twenty minutes before roasting time is up, remove lamb from oven and press on coating, then return to oven to finish cooking.

• Of course the lamb can be roasted without the coating, but then it won't be *persillé*, French for parslied.

4. Place lamb on a warm serving platter garnished with watercress, and in it, two fluted lemon cups made by using a small sharp knife to notch cuts around the center of a lemon, with each cut going at least

halfway through, then pulling the lemon halves apart. Cover the bone end of the lamb with a paper frill made by folding in half lengthwise a rectangle (use one about 10 inches wide and 15 inches long) of white paper (parchment or shelf paper), and with scissors, making cuts about 3 inches deep at ½-inch intervals along the folded edge, then unfolding the paper, and refolding it—without creasing—inside out to make the frill puffy. Coil the frill to a diameter of about 1½ inches to fit over the bone and fasten it with staples or cellophane tape. Not only does the frill look pretty, it also helps the carver keep his hands clean.

5. To carve the lamb, place it with the bone end to the right and cut 2 or 3 thin slices opposite the thick meaty portion, then turn the leg to rest on the cut surface, cut a wedge shape at the base of the bulge, and carve thin slices, from right to left, down the leg bone. Slide knife along leg bone to release these slices. *Makes 8 servings.*

BRAISED BONED LEG OF LAMB

Once learned, the braising technique works with almost any piece of meat. It is especially recommended for less tender cuts. Instead of a leg of lamb, braise a duck or a chicken, a piece of veal, a shoulder of lamb, or a cut of beef. But change the braising liquid. As a rule of thumb, you should use red wine and beef stock for the red meats and white wine and chicken stock for the white meats. You may always vary this, of course.

1 7-lb. leg of lamb, boned
2 tablespoons vegetable oil
6 tablespoons butter
3 cups chopped onions
1 cup chopped carrots
1 cup chopped celery
1½ cups dry white wine

1 cup chicken stock (see p. 241)
2 cloves finely chopped garlic
½ teaspoon thyme
1 bay leaf
1 tablespoon chopped pars-

ley, plus chopped parsley
for garnish
1 cup fresh tomatoes, peeled,
seeded, and chopped, or
canned Italian plum toma-
toes

1 teaspoon salt
½ teaspoon freshly cracked
black pepper
1 teaspoon meat glaze (see
p. 244), optional

1. Brown lamb on all sides—use wooden spatulas to turn it, for if it's pricked with a fork, the juices will escape—in oil and 2 tablespoons of the butter in a heavy casserole. The heat should be high.

2. When lamb is nicely browned, remove it from casserole and add the remaining ¼ cup of butter and the onions, carrots, and celery. Stir vegetables to coat them well with the butter.

3. Lay lamb on top of vegetables. Pour in wine and chicken stock and add garlic, thyme, bay leaf, 1 tablespoon of chopped parsley, and tomatoes (break up canned tomato pieces with a fork). Season with salt and pepper.

4. Cover casserole with foil to condense the steam, put on lid, and bring to a boil.

5. Place casserole on the middle shelf of a preheated 350° oven and cook for about 2 hours—18 minutes a pound, that is—or until lamb is very tender.

• For pink lamb, cook a shorter time, about 1½ hours.

6. When lamb is done, remove it to a warm serving platter and keep it warm. Discard bay leaf. Work the vegetables and liquid through a food mill or sieve or purée them in a blender (filled less than half full, so it won't overflow). Skim to remove all fat, and boil over high heat until mixture is reduced by one-fourth. This reduction intensifies the sauce's flavor. If further intensification is desired, stir in meat glaze.

7. Carve the lamb and arrange it on the platter in overlapping slices. Spoon sauce over meat and garnish with chopped parsley. Serve with Soissons (see p. 166). *Makes 8 servings.*

BRAISED LAMB SHANKS

When buying the lamb shanks for this recipe do not let the butcher crack the bones, use the shanks as they are.

8 lamb shanks
½ cup flour
¼ cup vegetable oil

1 teaspoon salt
½ teaspoon freshly cracked
black pepper

2 tablespoons butter
2 cloves finely chopped garlic
1 cup chopped onions
1 cup chopped carrots
1 cup chopped celery
1 cup dry red wine

1 cup chicken stock (see p. 241), about
½ teaspoon rosemary
1 tablespoon chopped parsley
1 bay leaf

1. Roll shanks in flour and shake off excess.

2. Heat oil in a large heavy casserole. When oil is hot, brown the shanks over high heat on all sides, doing just 2 or 3 at a time, turning them with tongs, and sprinkling them with salt and pepper as they're turned.

3. Set aside shanks, add butter to casserole and remove from heat, then stir in chopped garlic; the casserole heat is enough to cook it. Return to high heat, stir in onions, carrots, and celery, and cook 3 to 5 minutes—or until vegetables are well coated.

4. Remove casserole from heat and lay shanks on the bed of vegetables. Pour in wine and 1 cup of the chicken stock. Sprinkle with rosemary and parsley; lay bay leaf on top. Cover casserole with foil to condense the steam and put on lid. Bring to a boil, then put casserole in a pre-heated 325° oven and bake for 1½ hours.

5. Remove lamb shanks to a serving platter and keep warm. Discard bay leaf, then make a sauce by puréeing the vegetables and liquid in a blender (filled less than half full, so it won't overflow) or working them through a food mill or sieve. If sauce is too thick, thin it with a little chicken stock. Reheat and pour over shanks. ***Makes 8 servings.***

RAGOUT OF LAMB

The secret of a superb lamb stew is cooking all the vegetables separately, as in this recipe.

4 lbs. lamb, cut from the shoulder or leg into 2-inch cubes, plus a few cubes of lamb breast meat
½ cup flour, about
¼ cup butter
2 tablespoons vegetable oil
½ teaspoon freshly cracked black pepper
1 teaspoon salt

2 cloves finely chopped garlic
2½ cups chicken stock (see p. 241)
½ cup dry red wine
Bouquet garni (see p. 7)
1 cup shelled fresh peas
24 small carrots, peeled, or 6 medium carrots, peeled and sliced on the diagonal

12 *small turnips, peeled*
12 *small white onions*
 2 *whole tomatoes, peeled, seeded, and quartered*

8 *large sautéed mushroom caps (see p. 11)*
2 *tablespoons chopped parsley*

1. Trim excess fat from meat cubes, then toss them in flour and shake off excess.

2. Heat butter and oil in a large heavy casserole. When mixture is hot and no longer foaming, brown the lamb over high heat, a few cubes at a time, on all sides. Do not crowd the pan; do not let the cubes touch; use tongs to turn them.

3. When all the cubes are browned, return them to the casserole and sprinkle with salt and pepper. Add garlic, pour on chicken stock and wine, and lay the bouquet garni on top.

4. Cover casserole with foil and put on lid. Bring to a boil, reduce heat, and simmer for 45 minutes. Baste several times while cooking.

5. While the lamb cooks, prepare vegetables: put peas in a saucepan with a little cold salted water, bring to a boil, then simmer until almost tender when tasted. Drain and set aside.

6. Put carrots in another saucepan with cold salted water to cover, bring to a boil, then reduce heat and simmer carrots until they are almost tender. Drain and set aside.

7. Put turnips in another saucepan, cover with cold salted water, bring to a boil, and cook until almost tender. Drain and set aside.

8. Drop onions in boiling water for 30 seconds to loosen skins. Drain and peel them, then put them in a saucepan, cover with cold salted water, and cook over high heat until they are almost tender. Drain and set aside.

9. When lamb has cooked 45 minutes, remove bouquet garni, skim off excess fat, and add the prepared vegetables and the mushroom caps. Cover and cook over medium-high heat 15 to 20 minutes or until vegetables are tender. Taste for seasoning. Sprinkle with chopped parsley. Serve from the casserole with hot French bread and green salad. *Makes 6 to 8 servings.*

ROAST VEAL

Fat adds flavor as well as tenderness to meat, and since veal is not a fatty meat, this particular dish is better when it is larded—when it has strips of fat inserted into it, that is—and barded, or covered with a layer of fat.

1 5-lb. rump or leg of veal, boned and tied
½ lb. salt pork for larding
¼ cup cognac
1 tablespoon coarse salt
½ teaspoon freshly cracked white pepper
Pork fat for barding, if necessary

2 cups mixed chopped carrots, onions, and celery
1½ cups dry white wine
½ cup chicken stock (see p. 241) or veal stock (see p. 242)
½ cup heavy cream
Few drops lemon juice

1. Cut salt pork in thin 5- to 6-inch strips to fit larding needle. Soak strips in cognac for 1 hour, then put them in freezer to stiffen; they'll be easier to work with. Reserve 2 tablespoons cognac to add to sauce later.

2. Lay a strip of salt pork in the hollow of the larding needle and push the needle through the veal, keeping a thumb on the fat in the needle. Hold the strip inside the meat with your fingers while withdrawing the needle. Repeat with other strips, spacing them to make a mosaic design.

3. Rub veal with salt and pepper. If there is no fat on the outside of the veal, bard it with thin sheets of pork fat (available from most butchers). Lay the fat over the top of the meat and tie it every inch or so.

4. Place chopped vegetables in a roasting pan and lay veal on vegetables. Pour on 1 cup wine and roast in a preheated 350° oven for 20 minutes per pound.

• Test veal for doneness by pricking it with a small knife. If juices run pink, cook 20 minutes longer.

5. Remove veal to a serving platter and keep warm. The vegetables in the roasting pan will be brown and glazed. Pour in the remaining ½ cup of wine and bring it to a boil, scraping up the vegetables. Add chicken or veal stock and cook over medium-high heat to reduce. Strain into another pan, add heavy cream and cook until mixture thickens slightly. Taste for seasoning—salt and pepper may be needed—and add a little lemon juice and the reserved cognac.

6. Remove barding fat and strips, carve, and pour sauce over slices. *Makes 8 servings.*

ÉPAULE DE VEAU FARCIE

(Stuffed Shoulder of Veal)

4 lemons
1 cup raisins
½ teaspoon salt, about
½ teaspoon freshly cracked black pepper, about
2 tablespoons chopped shallots
1 tablespoon butter, plus butter to rub on veal
6 slices white bread, crusts removed and crumbed
¼ cup chopped parsley
5 tablespoons coarsely chopped walnuts or almonds

2 beaten eggs
1½ cups dry vermouth, about
1 5- to 6-lb. shoulder of veal, boned
1 2-oz. can anchovies, drained
2 large cloves garlic
4 bay leaves
1 cup chicken stock (see p. 241) or veal stock (see p. 242)
½ cup heavy cream
1 teaspoon potato starch, optional
1 bunch watercress

1. Make stuffing as follows. Juice 1 lemon and grate its peel. In a large bowl mix together lemon juice, grated peel, raisins, ½ teaspoon salt, ¼ teaspoon pepper, shallots sautéed in 1 tablespoon butter (to

soften them), the bread crumbs, parsley, walnuts or almonds, the beaten eggs, and enough vermouth (about ½ cup) to make a moist mixture.

2. Trim excess fat from veal. With a small sharp knife, make little slits all over the top of the veal. Stuff slits with anchovies and garlic chopped finely and mixed together. Rub veal with butter and ¼ teaspoon freshly cracked black pepper.

3. The boned veal will have a pocket for stuffing. Enlarge it if necessary, then sprinkle it lightly with salt and more freshly cracked black pepper and stuff it with the raisin-bread-crumb mixture. Sew with a trussing needle and string.

4. Place veal in a roasting pan. Cut 2 lemons into thin slices and cover surface of the veal with them.

5. Put bay leaves in pan and pour on ½ cup vermouth and ½ cup chicken or veal stock. Roast in a preheated 350° oven for 2 hours. Baste every ½ hour with a bulb baster. Take the pan from the oven and tilt it back and forth to lift the glaze. Keep 1 cup of liquid in the pan at all times, adding more stock or vermouth when needed.

6. At the end of 2 hours test veal by pricking it with a small sharp knife; if juices run pink, roast ½ hour longer.

7. Remove veal from roasting pan to carving board and keep warm. Strain juices into a saucepan. Deglaze roasting pan with vermouth or stock if needed; bring it to a boil, and loosen brown bits. Add to strained juices.

• Shoulder of veal is not fatty, but skim the mixture if necessary, leaving about 1 tablespoon of fat for flavor.

8. Stir heavy cream into mixture in saucepan and bring it to a boil. Boil until mixture thickens slightly. For a thicker sauce, mix potato starch in 1 tablespoon of cold water and add to sauce.

9. Before serving, remove trussing string and carve veal into neat slices with a portion of stuffing in each. Garnish with watercress and lemon slices cut from the remaining lemon. Pass the sauce separately.

• Potatoes Savoyard (see p. 184) and Whipped Carrots (see p. 170) are excellent as accompaniments for this roast. *Makes 8 servings.*

STUFFED VEAL

The veal used for this recipe should be about 3 inches thick. It may be prepared ahead if desired—simply stuffed, or stuffed and baked—and stored in refrigerator. Undercook it if it is to be reheated.

1 4- to 5-lb. leg of veal, boned
½ teaspoon salt
¾ teaspoon freshly cracked black pepper
¾ cup dry Marsala wine
6 thinly sliced mushrooms
1 large diced truffle
¼ lb. chopped prosciutto
¼ cup grated Gruyère cheese
2 tablespoons melted butter, plus melted butter to brush on veal
1 tablespoon coarse salt
¼ cup bread crumbs (see p. 7)
¼ cup grated Parmesan cheese
2 tablespoons chopped shallots
½ cup chicken stock (see p. 241) or veal stock (see p. 242)

1. Lay veal flat on a cutting board, and with a large knife, slit it, lengthwise, not quite all the way through. Open it, like a book, and sprinkle with salt, ¼ teaspoon pepper, and 2 tablespoons of the Marsala.

2. Make stuffing by combining mushrooms, truffle, prosciutto, and Gruyère cheese. Pat it over bottom half of the veal and cover with top half. Sew around the three open sides with a large trussing needle and string.

3. Place veal in a baking pan, fatty side up. Brush it with melted butter and sprinkle with coarse salt and ½ teaspoon pepper.

4. Place in a preheated 350° oven to roast for a total of about 2 hours —25 minutes per pound, that is. During roasting period, baste 3 times with Marsala, using 2 tablespoons each time.

• To do this, take meat pan out of oven, sprinkle wine over the meat, then tilt pan back and forth to lift the glaze. This helps to mix the nice brown bits with the sauce.

5. Twenty minutes before roasting time is up, remove pan from oven, brush veal with more melted butter, and pat on a coating of bread crumbs, grated Parmesan cheese, and 2 tablespoons melted butter.

• The coating can be omitted if desired.

6. Return pan to oven for 20 minutes to finish cooking veal and to set coating.

• Test for doneness by pricking it with a small knife. If juices run pink, cook 20 minutes longer.

7. Remove pan from oven and place meat on a serving platter to keep warm.

8. Make sauce in the roasting pan, as follows. Pour off any excess fat and deglaze pan with the remaining ¼ cup of Marsala. Add chopped shallots and chicken or veal stock. Boil until syrupy. Remove trussing string, carve meat, and pour on sauce.

• Serve the veal with Chestnut Croquettes (see p. 173) and Celery Sticks (see p. 172). *Makes 8 to 10 servings.*

VITELLO TONNATO

A marvelous cold dish—great for a summer buffet—from the north of Italy, Vitello Tonnato is even better when made ahead. Try to get a long cylindrical piece of veal for it, or have the meat rolled and tied to make this ideal shape. Ask for the bones too.

1 4-lb. piece of boned veal, shoulder, rack, leg, or rump, and bones from the veal
4 chopped anchovy fillets
1 clove chopped garlic
¾ cup chopped onion
½ cup chopped carrot
1 teaspoon salt
½ teaspoon freshly cracked white pepper
Bouquet garni (see p. 7)

1½ cups chicken stock (see p. 241)
1 cup dry white wine
1 13-oz. can white tuna
1 cup mayonnaise (see p. 251)
2 tablespoons chopped capers
1 lemon
2 tablespoons chopped parsley

1. With a small sharp knife, make little slits, about 1 inch deep, all over the veal. Using the knife blade as a slide, stuff bits of anchovy into the slits.

2. Put the veal and the bones into a large heavy casserole and add the garlic, onion, carrot, salt and pepper, and the bouquet garni.

3. Pour on chicken stock and wine, then add the tuna, with its oil. Bring to a boil, skim, cover casserole and reduce heat to simmer. Cook for 2 hours.

4. Remove bouquet garni and veal bones and let veal cool in the stock, which will jell as it cools.

5. Remove veal from casserole, scraping off any jelled stock, and carve the veal in very thin slices. Arrange them, overlapping, on a large oval platter.

6. Make sauce by putting the stock and vegetables through a blender or puréeing them through a food mill or sieve, chilling for 1 hour, then beating in the mayonnaise. Spoon the sauce over the sliced veal and sprinkle the slices with chopped capers.

7. Garnish the platter with chopped parsley and serrated slices of lemon made by using a lemon stripper to carve grooves at ¼-inch intervals from end to end of lemon, then cutting the lemon into thin slices.

• Serve with Rice Salad (see p. 197), either plain or stuffed into hollowed-out tomatoes. *Makes 8 servings.*

SALTIMBOCCA

I agree with the Romans who gave this dish its name—it means "jump into the mouth." To make the best possible saltimbocca, get the palest pink veal available. By European standards, most U.S. veal is too robust, the pink-to-red color indicating that the animal has already been weaned from milk to grain or grass and that the flesh is less tender than it would otherwise be. Ideally, the slices for saltimbocca should be cut from the leg right above the knee.

8 ¼-inch slices of veal, cut from leg	½ teaspoon salt
½ cup grated Parmesan cheese	¼ teaspoon freshly cracked black pepper
8 paper-thin slices prosciutto	1 teaspoon tomato paste
¾ cup dry Marsala wine, about	¾ cup beef stock (see p. 240), about
8 small sage leaves, or 1 teaspoon dried sage leaves	1 tablespoon lemon juice
3 tablespoons butter	1 teaspoon potato starch or arrowroot, optional
1 tablespoon olive oil	8 large fluted sautéed mushroom caps (see p. 11)
1 medium clove chopped garlic	2 tablespoons chopped parsley
¼ teaspoon thyme	

1. Lay veal slices on waxed paper and sprinkle with grated Parmesan cheese, then cover with another sheet of waxed paper and pound with the side of a cleaver to flatten the veal and work the cheese into it.

2. Remove waxed paper and lay a slice of prosciutto on each slice of veal.

• Prosciutto, an imported air-cured Italian ham, is available in most Italian markets. As a substitute, use Westphalian ham; have it sliced paper thin.

3. Brush ham slices with a little dry Marsala—use about 2 tablespoons in all.

• If dry Marsala is not available, substitute dry Madeira.

4. Lay a small leaf of fresh (⅛ teaspoon of dried) sage on each slice of ham.

5. Roll ham and veal carefully but loosely. Tie with string.

6. Heat butter and olive oil in a skillet, and when mixture is hot and no longer foaming, brown veal rolls over high heat on all sides. Brown a few at a time, and do not crowd the pan—in particular, do not let the rolls touch each other, for if they do touch, the result is braised, not browned, meat.

7. When all the rolls are browned, place them in the pan and flame with 2 tablespoons of dry Marsala—that is, warm the wine in a small, long-handled pan, then ignite it and while it is flaming, pour it over the veal rolls.

8. Remove rolls from pan and stir in garlic, thyme, salt, pepper, and tomato paste. Add beef stock and ½ cup dry Marsala. Stir to loosen brown bits. Return rolls to pan and cook over low heat, covered, for about 15 minutes.

9. When meat is done, remove to serving platter and keep warm. Add lemon juice to pan sauce, then taste for the seasoning.

10. Boil the sauce for a few minutes to reduce it slightly, or thicken it with potato starch smoothed into 1 tablespoon cold beef stock or Marsala.

11. Remove strings from rolls and place them in a serving dish (I like to use an oval one), then pour sauce over and place a mushroom cap on each roll. Sprinkle chopped parsley over all. *Makes 6 to 8 servings.*

VEAL DECAMERON

Boned chicken breasts can be substituted for the veal in this recipe. The only difference is that chicken breasts must cook in the sauce for 15 rather than 5 minutes.

8 *large fresh or canned arti-*
choke bottoms
3 *tablespoons butter, plus*
butter to brush on arti-
choke bottoms
8 *veal scallops, cut from leg,*
as round as possible and
about ¼ inch thick
2 *tablespoons Calvados or*
apple brandy
1 *tablespoon lemon juice*
1½ *cups sliced mushrooms*
1 *teaspoon salt*
½ *teaspoon freshly cracked*
white pepper
2 *tablespoons chopped shal-*
lots

½ *cup dry white wine*
2 *tablespoons fresh tarragon,*
or 2 teaspoons dried
1 *cup chicken stock (see*
p. 241)
½ *teaspoon tomato paste*
1 *teaspoon meat glaze (see*
p. 244)
1¼ *cups heavy cream*
2 *tablespoons grated Parme-*
san cheese
1 *teaspoon potato starch,*
optional
8 *slices of truffle*

1. If freshly cooked artichoke bottoms are used, arrange them, still warm, on a serving dish and brush them with melted butter; if canned artichoke bottoms are used, drain, wash in cold water, and pat dry, then

brush with melted butter and put in a low (250°) oven to warm before placing on serving dish. Keep them warm while proceeding with recipe.

2. Melt 2 tablespoons butter in a skillet, and when it is hot and no longer foaming, sauté the veal, a few pieces at a time, over high heat, until lightly browned. This will take about 2 minutes for each side. Do not crowd the pan; do not let pieces touch.

3. When all pieces are sautéed, return them to pan and flame with Calvados—that is, warm the Calvados in a small long-handled pan, then ignite it, and while it is flaming, pour it over the veal. Shake pan until flames die, then remove veal and keep it warm.

4. Add 1 tablespoon butter to the skillet, if needed, and heat until foaming. Add sliced mushrooms and sprinkle over them 2 teaspoons lemon juice, ½ teaspoon salt, and ¼ teaspoon pepper. Sauté by shaking them over high heat for 3 minutes. Remove mushrooms from pan and set aside.

5. Add shallots and wine to pan and cook, stirring, over high heat to lift the glaze, until wine is reduced by half.

6. Remove pan from heat and stir in tarragon, chicken stock, tomato paste, meat glaze, and heavy cream. Season with remaining ½ teaspoon of salt and ¼ teaspoon of pepper. Stir in grated Parmesan cheese and remaining 1 teaspoon of lemon juice. Return to high heat and cook, stirring, until mixture thickens slightly. Or thicken it, if desired, with 1 teaspoon potato starch mixed with 1 tablespoon cold water.

7. Return mushrooms and veal to pan and continue cooking gently for 5 more minutes.

8. Put 1 veal scallop on each artichoke bottom, pour pan sauce over veal, and garnish each piece with a slice of truffle. *Makes 8 servings.*

Veal Viennoise

The veal cooks in minutes, so have all the garnishes ready and at hand. They make a beautiful platter!

1 *lemon*	2 *eggs*
1 *2-oz. can flat anchovy fillets*	¾ *cup bread crumbs (see*
3 *hard-cooked eggs*	*p. 7)*
8 *veal scallops cut from leg,*	9 *tablespoons butter*
as round as possible, and	½ *cup dry white wine*
about ¼ inch thick	12 *olives, stuffed with pi-*
½ *teaspoon baking powder*	*mientos, sliced thin*
¾ *cup flour*	2 *tablespoons chopped pars-*
1 *tablespoon vegetable oil*	*ley*

1. Using a lemon stripper, carve grooves from end to end of lemon, making them about ¼ inch apart. Cut lemon into thin slices, making at least 8. The edges will be serrated.

2. Put anchovy fillets in a sieve and rinse them in cold water. Pat them dry on paper towels.

3. Peel hard-cooked eggs, chop the whites, and work the yolks through a sieve.

4. Place the veal scallops between 2 sheets of waxed paper and pound them paper thin with the side of a cleaver or the bottom of a heavy skillet.

5. Stir baking powder into the flour. Beat oil into the eggs. Dip veal pieces in the flour mixture, shake off excess, then dip into egg mixture and roll in bread crumbs.

• Breading is fast and neat done this way: line up 3 bowls, 1 for flour, 1 for egg, 1 for bread crumbs, and next to them place a baking tray; work from bowl to bowl, ending with breaded food on tray.

• Veal can be breaded in the morning, covered loosely with waxed paper, and refrigerated, but because the scallops are thin, they dry out too quickly to be reheated satisfactorily.

6. Melt ½ cup of the butter in a skillet. When it is hot and no longer foaming, sauté breaded veal over high heat 3 minutes on each side. Do a few pieces at a time; do not crowd them—in particular, do not let them touch each other. Remove sautéed veal to serving platter and keep warm.

• The sautéed scallops can be held in a low oven for 15 minutes. But remember, this is really a last-minute dish.

7. Deglaze the pan with wine by boiling it for a minute, then scraping up the brown bits. Swirl in the remaining 1 tablespoon of butter, then pour over veal.

8. Place a serrated lemon slice on each piece of veal, with anchovy fillets crisscrossing the lemon slices. Use the rest of the lemon slices and the egg whites and yolks, the olive slices, and the chopped parsley to fill in spaces between the veal so that the platter doesn't show through.

• The platter looks prettiest if colors are placed symmetrically—i.e., chopped egg whites on opposite sides of it. *Makes 6 to 8 servings.*

VEAL PICCATA

2 lbs. veal, cut from leg, ¼ inch thick	2 tablespoons butter
	2 tablespoons olive oil
½ cup flour, about	2 tablespoons lemon juice
1 teaspoon salt	¼ cup dry Marsala, optional
½ teaspoon freshly cracked white pepper	2 tablespoons chicken stock (see p. 241)

1. Cut veal in 2-inch squares. Place them between 2 sheets of waxed paper and pound paper thin with the side of a cleaver or the bottom of a heavy skillet.

2. Dip veal pieces in flour, shaking off excess, then season with salt and pepper.

3. Heat butter and oil in a skillet. When it is hot and no longer foaming, brown veal over high heat, a few pieces at a time, 2 minutes on each side.

4. Return all pieces to pan, add lemon juice, Marsala (if desired), and chicken stock. Cook 2 minutes over high heat. Remove veal to a warm serving platter and pour pan sauce over it. *Makes 4 to 6 servings.*

VEAL CASSEROLE

1 cup plump white raisins	2 teaspoons lemon juice
1 cup white wine	2 1-lb. cans (about 1½ cups)
4 lbs. veal, cut from the leg	small artichoke hearts
into 1-inch cubes	3 tablespoons flour
¾ cup butter	1½ cups chicken stock (see
¼ cup cognac	p. 241)
2 cups sliced mushrooms	Bouquet garni (see p. 7)
¾ teaspoon salt	1½ cups dairy sour cream
⅛ teaspoon freshly cracked	
white pepper	

1. Soak raisins in wine for 1 hour.

2. Dry veal with paper towels. Melt ¼ cup butter in a large heavy casserole, and when foaming subsides, brown veal over high heat, on all sides, a few cubes at a time. Use tongs to turn them. Do not crowd the pan or let the veal cubes touch each other.

3. When all the cubes are browned, place them in the casserole and flame them with cognac—that is, warm the cognac in a small long-handled pan, light it, and pour it, flaming, over the veal.

4. When flames die down, remove veal and set aside. Drain and dry raisins, saving the wine, then add 2 tablespoons butter to casserole and sauté raisins briskly for 2 to 3 minutes. Remove raisins and set aside.

5. Add 2 more tablespoons butter to casserole. When butter is hot and no longer foaming, sauté mushrooms for 3 minutes, first seasoning them with ¼ teaspoon salt, ⅛ teaspoon pepper, and 2 teaspoons lemon juice. Remove and set aside.

6. Add 2 more tablespoons butter to casserole; drain, rinse, and dry artichoke hearts and sauté them for 3 to 5 minutes. Remove and set aside.

7. Add 2 more tablespoons butter to casserole. When it melts, blend in flour smoothly to make a roux. Cook it, stirring, for 2 minutes, but do not let it brown.

8. Remove casserole from heat, add chicken stock and whisk vigorously. Return to heat and cook, stirring constantly, until mixture comes to a boil, then add wine drained from raisins, season with ½ teaspoon salt and ¼ teaspoon pepper, and add the bouquet garni.

9. Return veal to casserole and simmer for 30 to 40 minutes, or until meat is tender. During last 10 minutes of cooking, add mushrooms, raisins, and artichoke hearts.

10. Remove bouquet garni. Blend in sour cream and bring to a boil.

• When sauce is fortified with flour, as this one is, sour cream can be boiled without fear of curdling.

11. Serve with green noodles. Cook them according to package directions, drain, and dress with ½ cup of melted butter and chopped truffle. Season to taste with salt and freshly cracked pepper. *Makes 8 servings.*

BLANQUETTE DE VEAU WITH RICE TIMBALES

4 lbs. veal cut from the leg, shoulder, or rump into 2-inch cubes, plus a few cubes of lamb breast meat for added flavor	*1 bay leaf*
	1 cup sliced celery
	1 cup leeks, whites plus 1 inch of the green, sliced
	2 cups sliced carrots
3 teaspoons salt, about	*¾ cup sliced onion*
½ teaspoon freshly cracked white pepper, about	*6 peppercorns*
	18 tiny white onions
6 cups chicken stock (see p. 241), about	*Velouté Sauce (recipe follows)*
	2 tablespoons chopped parsley
2 tablespoons fresh lemon juice	*Rice Timbales (see p. 187)*

1. Sprinkle veal cubes with salt and pepper—use about 1 teaspoon of salt and ½ teaspoon of pepper—and let them stand for 1 hour to season well.

2. Put the cubes in a large flameproof casserole or saucepan and cover with 6 cups chicken stock. Bring slowly to a boil and skim the surface.

3. Add lemon juice, bay leaf, celery, leeks, carrots, sliced onion, peppercorns, and 2 teaspoons salt.

• Be sure to clean the leeks carefully: split them lengthwise and hold them under running water, separating the layers to rinse out all the sand.

4. When liquid returns to a boil, reduce heat, cover, and simmer 25 to 45 minutes or until meat is tender.

• Some veal will cook in 20 minutes; other veal will take 1 hour and 20 minutes. Take out a piece to test it.

5. Peel the tiny onions, then with a little pointed knife, cut an X in the root end of each onion (this will help keep the onion whole) and boil the onions in salted water to cover for 5 to 15 minutes, or until barely tender. Cooking time depends on the size of the onions; drain the onions and add them to the casserole when veal is almost done.

• A quick way to peel tiny onions is to put them into boiling water for 20 to 30 seconds, then to drain them, trim the root and stem ends, and rub the skins off under running water.

6. Before serving, drain veal and tiny onions. Add veal to the Velouté Sauce and arrange it on a large heated platter. Sprinkle chopped parsley over the top. Arrange the onions in mounds around the veal, and if it's possible, fish out the leeks and carrots and alternate them around the veal. Arrange Rice Timbales around the platter (tip out the molds onto it), 3 on each side, 1 at each end.

Velouté Sauce with Mushrooms

5 tablespoons butter	¼ to ½ cup heavy cream
¼ cup flour	2 egg yolks, optional
1 teaspoon salt	1½ cups mushrooms, sliced
⅛ teaspoon cayenne pepper	1 teaspoon lemon juice
½ teaspoon Dijon mustard	¼ teaspoon freshly cracked
1 cup stock, strained from veal pot	white pepper

1. Melt 3 tablespoons butter in a heavy saucepan, then add flour, ½ teaspoon salt, cayenne pepper, and mustard and work this with a wooden spatula, cooking over high heat for 3 minutes to cook the flour.

2. Remove pan from heat, pour in stock and whisk vigorously.

3. Return pan to heat and cook over high heat, whisking constantly, until mixture is thick.

4. Add ¼ cup heavy cream and simmer 10 minutes.

5. To enrich sauce, if desired, beat egg yolks in a small bowl with ¼ cup heavy cream; add a little bit of the hot mixture from the pan to the egg-cream mixture to warm it gradually; then add warmed egg mixture to pan and heat. Do not boil.

• If you are making the sauce ahead and planning to reheat it, do not enrich it, for when egg-enriched sauces are reheated there is a risk of curdling.

6. Heat remaining butter in skillet until foaming, add mushrooms, sprinkle with lemon juice, ½ teaspoon salt, and white pepper, and cook over high heat, shaking the skillet, for 3 minutes. Add mushrooms to sauce. *Makes 8 servings.*

VEAL KIDNEYS

8 veal kidneys
1½ cups mushrooms
2 teaspoons lemon juice, plus lemon juice to clean mushrooms
6 tablespoons butter
1 teaspoon salt
¼ teaspoon freshly cracked white pepper
¼ cup cognac
1 tablespoon Dijon mustard
1½ cups heavy cream
¼ teaspoon freshly cracked black pepper

1. Soak kidneys in cold water for 1 hour, then carefully remove membrane, core, and any fat. Cut into 1-inch slices.

2. Wipe mushrooms clean with a paper towel dipped in acidulated water (water with lemon juice) and wipe dry. Trim off ends of stems and slice mushrooms vertically, through cap and stem.

3. Heat 3 tablespoons of butter in a large skillet, and when foaming subsides, add mushrooms and toss them over high heat for 3 minutes, adding 2 teaspoons lemon juice, ½ teaspoon salt, and white pepper. Remove mushrooms and set aside.

4. In the same pan, heat the remaining 3 tablespoons of butter. When it is hot and no longer foaming, sauté sliced veal kidneys over high heat for 2 minutes on each side.

5. Flame kidneys with cognac—that is, warm the cognac in a small long-handled pan, ignite it, and pour it, flaming, over the kidneys. Shake pan until flames die.

6. Stir in mustard and heavy cream and cook over high heat for a few minutes to reduce the sauce. Return mushrooms to pan and heat through. Season with the remaining ½ teaspoon of salt and the black pepper. Serve with rice. *Makes 8 servings.*

RIS DE VEAU WITH MADEIRA SAUCE

(Calves' Sweetbreads with Madeira Sauce)

2 large pairs calves' sweetbreads
¼ cup flour
¼ cup butter
2 tablespoons cognac
Madeira Sauce (see p. 250)

1. Put sweetbreads in a pan and cover them with cold water. Slowly bring them to a boil and cook them slowly, uncovered, for 5 to 7 minutes, depending on their size. Turn them over once during cooking.

2. Drain sweetbreads and plunge them immediately into iced water. This helps to keep them firm. Carefully remove all the skin, sinews, and tubes. Sweetbreads are very delicate.

3. Cut them in half lengthwise and lay them on a plate. Put another plate on top, weight it with something heavy, and place in a refrigerator for at least 1 hour.

4. When ready to cook, dry sweetbreads with paper towels and dust them lightly with flour.

5. Heat butter in a large skillet. When butter is foaming, add sweetbreads—do not let them touch each other—and cover them with a flat lid and weight, to keep them flat. Brown sweetbreads 1 minute on each side.

6. Flame sweetbreads with cognac—that is, warm the cognac in a small long-handled pan, light it, and pour it, flaming, into the skillet. Shake the pan until flames die, and scrape up the brown bits.

7. Arrange sweetbreads on a warm serving platter and spoon Madeira Sauce over them.

• Sweetbreads are good served with Pea Purée (see p. 182). *Makes 4 to 6 servings.*

POULTRY

From Henri IV to Herbert Hoover, chicken has figured in political life. "A chicken in every pot"—remember the slogan?

Poultry is without doubt the cook's best friend. The number of recipes is almost endless. And most of the dishes in these pages aren't as extravagant as they sound. They may take a little time to make, but it is time well spent.

It helps to know the chicken family. Broilers weigh up to 2½ lbs., fryers are between 2 and 3½ lbs.; roasters start at 3½ lbs. and go to 5 or 6. Then there are stewing hens and capons, which reach the larger weights.

Mass production and artificial feeding make it increasingly difficult to find poultry of real flavor. If possible, poultry should be bought from a farmer or poulterer who specializes in freshly killed birds; next best is frozen.

Some of the recipes that follow involve boning and skinning chicken breasts (butchers and poulterers will bone them, but it's good to know how it should be done), boning a whole chicken or turkey, trussing, and carving. Here are the directions.

How to Bone and Skin a Chicken Breast

1. Place the whole chicken breast (whole chicken breasts are easier to bone than are split ones) on a cutting board, breastbone up, and, if

you're right-handed, wishbone to the left. Then, with a short sharp boning knife or a 3-inch utility knife, make a slit the full length of the breast-bone.

2. Working first on the side away from you—it's easier to see what you're doing that way—use the knife with a cutting-scraping motion against the breastbone and rib bones, peeling back the flesh with your free hand as you cut.

3. Turn the breast around so that the wishbone is at the right; then free the other side in the same way.

4. Pull off the skin.

• Chicken breasts can be boned the day before they're to be used if, after boning, they're covered with plastic wrap and refrigerated. Bring breasts to room temperature before using.

How to Bone a Chicken or Turkey

Before trying to bone a chicken or turkey, visualize what it is you're about to do. In boning a bird you work from the top of the bird down —that is from the neck to the vent—completely boning one side before beginning the other. Essentially, you'll open the skin at the back (along the backbone) and then cut and scrape against the rib cage and breastbone to free the flesh all in one piece—hopefully without cutting through the skin except for the original cut. There are a few roadblocks along the way: cutting through the leg and wing joints and freeing the wishbone (the tendons in these areas make them harder to cut through) and, at the very last, scraping flesh free from the ridge of the breastbone which is very close to the skin. But once tried, you'll find the job not at all difficult.

1. Place the bird on a cutting board, breast down, and if you're right-handed, neck to the left. Use a small, very sharp knife to make a slit along the backbone from neck to tail, then cut and scrape against the bones (the cutting edge of the knife should free the flesh by scraping the bones). With the hand that's not holding the knife (the thumb, mostly) push aside the flesh that's scraped loose.

2. The first obstacle to be faced is the bird's equivalent of a shoulder blade—a long, thin, flat bone on the back, floating loose. Scrape it free of flesh and continue on to the wing joint. Cut through it.

3. Now do the lower back. There's a nugget of flesh in a hollow on each side of the backbone, just above the ball joint of thigh. Scrape it out and cut through the thigh joint.

4. Continue down the side of the bird, scraping against the rib bones.

5. You'll come next to the breastbone, which is shaped like the keel of a boat. Scrape against it, but just to the ridge. Do the other side of the bird, again scraping just to the ridge.

6. Getting out the wishbone requires a bit of painstaking work, for this bone is buried in the flesh of the breast, between the "keel" and the neck. Scrape carefully all around this V-shaped bone to free it. Keep your goal in mind: to end with all the bones in one hand, all the flesh in the other.

7. Finally, very carefully, so as not to pierce the skin, scrape right along the ridge of the breastbone. This will free the carcass from the flesh.

• I usually leave the leg and wing bones in, to give the bird more shape, but take out the thigh bones if you wish. They're partly exposed and rather easy to do: scrape the flesh from around each until you can cut through the leg joint and remove the thigh bone.

• Taking out wing bones is harder, for there are several tendons in each wing, and you must virtually turn the flesh inside out until you expose the next joint. Do not remove the second bone of the wing.

• Do not remove the leg bones (drumsticks).

How to Carve a Duck

INFORMAL METHOD: Place bird on its back and cut from neck to vent right next to breast. You may use poultry shears. Open wide. Turn over and cut back from neck to vent. Cut each half into 2 pieces making 4 pieces of duck in all.

FORMAL METHOD: Lay bird on its back on a carving board. Remove leg from carcass by cutting through skin close to carcass. Bend leg and thigh back to remove. Separate leg from thigh at the joint. Remove other leg in the same way. Carve off breast on one side all the way down to frame of the bird, taking wing off with breast. All breasts and wings should come off together. Lay breast on board and cut across on a diagonal giving 2 pieces of breast, one with wing attached. Repeat on other side.

How to Truss a Bird (see illustrations, p. 128)

1. Cut a length—about 1 yard—of butcher's cord. Lay the bird on its back, tail toward you. Bring the cord under the tail and legs and loop it, making a half knot, then draw legs close to tail.

2. The string now has two equal ends. Pass each end of the cord between a leg and the body of the bird.

3. Flip the bird over, breast down, then go under the wings with the cord ends and bring the neck flap down over the bird's back.

4. Loop the cord over the flap, making a half knot to hold the flap in place.

5. Turn the bird onto its back again, then bring the cord ends over the wings and tie a knot on the breast.

CHICKEN BREASTS DUXELLES WITH WHITE WINE SAUCE

Here is the recipe that made my cooking school famous. It's an original with me, and it's the first entrée that I teach beginning students. When they show off what they learned at Saturday dinner parties, my phone starts ringing early Monday morning.

4 whole chicken breasts
2 tablespoons cognac, plus cognac to brush on breasts
Salt
Freshly cracked white pepper
1 cup Duxelles (recipe follows
¼ cup butter, plus butter to brush on artichoke bottoms
1 medium clove finely chopped garlic
2 tablespoons finely chopped shallots
1 tablespoon chopped truffle

1 tablespoon chopped fresh tarragon, or 1 teaspoon dried
1 teaspoon meat glaze (see p. 244)
1¼ cups chicken stock (see p. 241)
¼ cup dry vermouth or other dry white wine
2 tablespoons chopped parsley
8 fluted and sautéed mushrooms (see p. 11)
8 canned artichoke bottoms

1. Bone and skin chicken breasts (see directions, p. 125) and trim them into neat ovals. These are called *suprêmes;* there will be 8 of them, 2 from each breast.

• Reserve the bones and skin cut from the breast and use them in making chicken stock.

2. Cut pockets in the 8 suprêmes by laying each one flat on a cutting board, placing a hand on top to hold it, and cutting, not all the way through, from the thicker side.

3. Brush the insides of the pockets with a little cognac and sprinkle with salt and a few grains of pepper. Fill pockets with duxelles, but *don't stuff them too full.* Close pockets by pulling the top over the bottom and pressing it with your thumb.

• There's enough gelatin in chicken to hold the edges together, providing the pockets haven't been stuffed too full. Browning the chicken breasts under a weighted lid will also help to keep the pockets closed. It isn't necessary to sew them or to hold them together with toothpicks.

4. Heat butter in a large heavy skillet until it is foaming. Brown chicken quickly over high heat—just enough to be a little crusty (remember, this is not fried chicken)—on both sides, under a flat lid (or flat pan) pressed down with a 2- to 3-lb. weight. Brown what was the skin side first. Don't let suprêmes touch in the pan.

5. Remove the chicken from the pan, pour off all but 1 tablespoon of fat, take the pan off heat, and lift the glaze with 2 tablespoons of cognac heated in a small long-handled pan until it is warm to the touch, then lighted and poured into the chicken pan. When flames die down, scrape up the brown bits that have been loosened by the cognac.

6. Make sauce as follows. Add garlic and shallots to pan and cook for 1 minute over high heat. Stir in truffle and tarragon, then add meat glaze, chicken stock, and wine. Bring to a boil while stirring and boil to reduce the sauce by one third. It will thicken by itself.

• When using dried herbs it's a good idea to rub them between the palms of your hands, over the pan, and drop them in. Rubbing releases their flavor.
• Dried herbs can be substituted for fresh herbs (vice versa) but not in the same amounts. Since dried herbs have more intense flavor than do fresh ones, use one third as much of the dried herbs as you would of the fresh.

7. Return chicken breasts to pan and baste them once with the sauce.

• The recipe can be prepared in advance to this point, with final cooking of chicken breasts done just before serving. Cover the pan and store it in a refrigerator for no longer than 24 hours. Let the chicken breasts and sauce come to room temperature before continuing.

8. Turn heat to simmer and cook chicken breasts, covered, until tender, about 15 to 18 minutes. Don't overcook them.

• The only place you might run into trouble with this recipe is here. Boned chicken breasts don't take long to cook, and once overcooked, they're as hard as rocks. To test for doneness, press them with a fork: if the flesh is still soft, the breasts are not done; if the flesh springs back when touched, they are.

9. Before serving, arrange suprêmes in a large au gratin dish and coat with sauce. Sprinkle with chopped parsley, and in addition, garnish with fluted mushrooms and with artichoke bottoms that have been rinsed and dried, then brushed with butter and heated through in a 325° oven. *Makes 8 servings.*

Duxelles

Duxelles, which *Larousse Gastronomique* defines as "a kind of mushroom hash," is one of the most useful basics in cooking, worth keeping on hand at all times. Frozen, it can be stored almost indefinitely, and it will keep in a refrigerator for up to 10 days. There are literally dozens of uses for duxelles. Here are a few: when baking a fish, fill it with duxelles; combine duxelles with bread crumbs and use to stuff chicken; hollow out whole tomatoes or (for a sensational hot hors d'oeuvre) little cherry tomatoes, spoon duxelles in the shells, and bake; combine duxelles with mashed hard-cooked egg yolks and pack them back into the whites; or spread duxelles on Melba toast, sprinkle with grated Parmesan cheese and melted butter, and heat under a broiler.

¼ lb. very finely chopped mushrooms	½ teaspoon salt
¼ cup butter	¼ teaspoon freshly cracked black pepper
¼ cup finely chopped shallots	

1. Put the chopped mushrooms in the corner of a tea towel and wring them out to get rid of excess liquid.
2. Melt butter in a skillet, and when it is foaming, add the chopped shallots. Cook over high heat for a few minutes, stirring with a wooden spatula, until shallots are transparent. Don't let them brown.
3. Add mushrooms and cook 15 to 20 minutes, stirring constantly with wooden spatula, until the mushrooms look dry. Season with salt and pepper and cool. *Makes about 1 cup.*

Petti di Pollo

4 whole chicken breasts
1 teaspoon salt
½ teaspoon freshly cracked
white pepper
¾ cup flour, about
¼ cup butter
2 tablespoons vegetable oil

¾ cup grated Swiss cheese
¾ cup chopped prosciutto
¼ cup dry Marsala wine
1 cup Basic Brown Sauce (see
p. 248)
2 tablespoons tomato paste

1. Bone and skin chicken breasts (see directions, p. 125).
2. Lay the 8 pieces of chicken on waxed paper, with what was the skin side facing down. Cover them with another sheet of waxed paper and pound them thin with the flat side of a cleaver.
3. Season with salt and pepper and dip in flour, shaking off the excess.
4. Heat 2 tablespoons butter and the oil in a heavy skillet. When hot and no longer foaming, sauté chicken quickly over high heat for 1 minute on each side.
5. Melt the remaining butter and brush a baking dish with it. Transfer chicken pieces to baking dish, leaving a little space between them if possible. Mound ham and then cheese on top of each piece. Set aside.
6. Deglaze the skillet by pouring in wine and cooking over high heat for 1 minute, scraping up the brown bits.
7. Make sauce by stirring in Brown Sauce and tomato paste and bringing to a boil.
8. Pour sauce around chicken in baking dish. Place in a preheated 325° oven to bake until chicken is tender, about 10 to 15 minutes.

• To test for doneness, press chicken breasts with a fork: if the flesh is still soft, the breasts are not done; if the flesh springs back when touched, they are.
• Serve with Sautéed Mushroom Caps and Pine Nuts (see p. 176). **Makes 8 servings.**

Chicken Pajorsky

3 whole chicken breasts
1 cup unsalted butter
2 egg whites
2 slices bread
½ cup heavy cream
1½ teaspoons salt

½ teaspoon freshly cracked
white pepper
¼ teaspoon freshly grated
nutmeg
¾ cup flour
2 beaten eggs

1 tablespoon vegetable oil,
optional
¾ cup fine dry bread crumbs
(see p.7)

¼ cup cognac
1 bunch watercress

1. Bone and skin chicken breasts (see directions, p. 125). Work the flesh through a meat grinder, using the finest blade, or chop it finely with a knife.

2. Put ground chicken into mixer bowl and (with the flat whip if the mixer is a heavy-duty one) beat in ¾ cup of softened butter. Add egg whites and beat until mixture is well blended, about 5 to 10 minutes.

3. Trim crusts from bread, then cut in cubes, and soak in heavy cream until soft.

4. Mash cubes with a fork to make a paste, add to chicken mixture, and beat well. Season with salt, pepper, and nutmeg. If mixture is too soft to shape, refrigerate until it stiffens, or about ½ hour.

5. Sprinkle board with flour. Drop 2 heaping tablespoonfuls of the chicken mixture on the board and with your hands form it into a kidney-shaped cutlet. Coat the cutlet completely with flour, shaking off excess.

6. Shape and flour the remaining mixture—mixture should yield 6 to 8 cutlets—then dip the floured cutlets first in beaten egg (add 1 tablespoon oil to the beaten eggs if you wish; it will help to make the coating adhere), then in bread crumbs.

7. Melt the remaining ¼ cup of butter in a skillet, and when foaming subsides, add cutlets (do not let them touch). Sauté over high heat for 3 minutes on each side. Then warm cognac in a small long-handled pan, ignite it, and pour it, flaming, over the cutlets.

8. Arrange cutlets on a round serving platter with watercress in the center. Pour pan juices over.

• If you want a sauce with these cutlets, Hollandaise Sauce (see p. 246) and Béarnaise Sauce (see p. 248) are excellent. Or make a Velouté Sauce (see p. 246) with chicken stock and fold in 2 tablespoons Duxelles (see p. 130). *Makes 6 servings.*

CHICKEN À LA KIEV WITH PAPRIKA SAUCE

4 whole chicken breasts
2 tablespoons cognac
¾ cup frozen unsalted butter
4 teaspoons fresh chopped
chives
2 teaspoons dried tarragon
1 teaspoon salt
½ teaspoon freshly cracked
white pepper

¾ cup flour, about
2 beaten eggs
¾ cup bread crumbs (see
p. 7)
2 cups vegetable shortening
1 bunch watercress
Paprika Sauce (recipe follows), optional

1. Bone and skin the chicken breasts (see directions, p. 125).

2. Lay the 8 pieces of chicken on waxed paper, with what was the skin side facing down. Cover them with another sheet of waxed paper and pound them thin with the flat side of a cleaver. Remove top piece of waxed paper.

3. Brush each piece of chicken with cognac.

4. Cut frozen butter into fingers and lay a finger of butter on each piece of chicken, along one side.

• When butter is frozen, it's much easier to handle and roll up in the chicken.

5. Sprinkle each piece of chicken with ½ teaspoon chopped chives, ¼ teaspoon tarragon, and salt and pepper.

• Classic Chicken Kiev has no herbs, only butter. But I think it's rather too bland. Instead of tarragon, you can use an equal amount of thyme or any other herb you prefer.

6. Roll edge of each piece of chicken over butter, tuck ends in to encase butter, and continue to roll like a jelly roll.

• The rolls don't have to be tied up or fastened with toothpicks; chicken is gelatinous and will adhere to itself.

7. One by one, dip chicken rolls in flour, shake off excess, dip in beaten egg, and roll in bread crumbs. Be sure to flour, egg, and crumb the ends.

8. Place rolls on a baking sheet or on a flat dish or pan, seam side down, and put them in a freezer for at least ½ hour or in a refrigerator for at least 1 hour.

• The rolls can be made ahead to this point and frozen for future use. Wrap them in plastic wrap or foil for storage.

9. Heat vegetable shortening to 375° in a deep-fat fryer or heavy saucepan.

• Use a fat thermometer to check temperature. Or test with a bread cube: if it browns nicely in 1 minute, the fat is about the right temperature. A thermometer is surer.

10. Fry rolls 2 at a time (if too many are put into fat at once, the temperature of the fat drops too low to cook the rolls properly), turning to brown both sides. It will take a total of about 5 minutes to cook 2 rolls. When they are deep golden brown, remove them from fat with a slotted spoon and drain on paper towels. Be sure fat is back to 375° before frying more rolls.

11. Arrange rolls on a serving platter, garnish with a bunch of watercress, and either serve as is or with Paprika Sauce, strained and poured over the rolls.

Paprika Sauce

½ cup finely chopped onion
2 tablespoons butter
½ cup dry white wine
2 tablespoons sweet Hungarian paprika
2 cups Velouté Sauce made with chicken stock (see p. 246)

Bouquet garni (see p. 7)
½ teaspoon salt
¼ teaspoon freshly cracked white pepper

1. Cook onion in butter over high heat until transparent. Stir with a wooden spatula, and don't let the onion brown.
2. Add wine and cook over medium heat until wine is reduced by half.
3. Remove from heat. Stir in paprika and Velouté Sauce. Add bouquet garni, salt and pepper, and simmer for at least ½ hour. **Makes 8 servings.**

COLD CHICKEN MOUSSE

3 whole chicken breasts
2 cups chicken stock (see p. 241)
½ cup chopped carrot
¾ cup chopped onion
½ cup chopped celery
1 cup butter
¼ cup flour
1½ cups milk
1 teaspoon salt
½ teaspoon freshly cracked white pepper

2 tablespoons chopped parsley
2 teaspoons dried tarragon
3 tablespoons dairy sour cream
Vegetable oil to grease mold
1 bunch watercress
1 cup cherry tomatoes and/ or black olives

1. Put chicken breasts in a saucepan and cover with chicken stock. Add carrot, onion, and celery and bring to a boil. Reduce heat to simmer, cover, and cook for 20 minutes. Cool breasts in the stock.
2. Meanwhile, make a *panade*, or thickening agent, by melting ¼ cup of butter in a small saucepan, stirring in flour with a wooden spatula, and cooking over high heat, stirring, for 2 minutes (do not let the mixture brown), then removing from heat and adding milk, whisking vigorously, returning to high heat and cooking 3 minutes, stirring, until very thick. Pour the panade into a baking dish and chill in a refrigerator about ½ hour or until set.
3. When chicken is cool enough to handle, remove skin and bones and

work the meat through a meat grinder, using the finest blade, or chop finely with a knife.

4. Put the ground chicken into a bowl and beat in ¾ cup of softened butter either with a mixer (use the flat whip, if it's a heavy-duty mixer) or, over ice, with a wooden spatula.

• If you are beating the mixture by hand, chilling it causes the natural gelatin in the chicken to react to thicken it and thus helps compensate for the lack of the forcefulness of the mixer beating.

5. Beat in the chilled panade and add salt, pepper, parsley, tarragon, and sour cream. Mix thoroughly.

6. Pour the mixture into an oiled 1-quart mold or soufflé dish, cover with waxed paper, and put it in refrigerator to chill at least 3 hours.

• This can be done the day before the mousse is to be served.
• To unmold, run a little knife around the edge of the mold, using an up-and-down motion, put a serving plate over the mold, invert, give a shake, and lift off mold.

7. Garnish with watercress and with cherry tomatoes and/or black olives.

• If a ring mold was used, fill center with cherry tomatoes, or if you like with Cucumber Salad with Yoghurt (see p. 193). **Makes 6 servings.**

POACHED CHICKEN CUTLETS

This is an exquisite dish, made by packing a chicken mousse mixture into cutlet molds and poaching in chicken stock. As the mousse cooks, it floats out of the molds in light and lovely cutlet shapes. The molds, which are about 4 inches long and ½ inch deep, are available in most gourmet shops. For this recipe, 8 to 10 are needed.

2 *whole chicken breasts*
3 *egg whites*
1 *cup light cream*
1 *tablespoon chopped shallot*
1 *medium clove chopped garlic*
3 *tablespoons butter, plus butter to grease molds*
1½ *teaspoons salt*
½ *teaspoon freshly cracked white pepper*
2 *teaspoons dried tarragon*
½ *cup flour*
1 *egg*
2 *tablespoons dairy sour cream*
2 *tablespoons cognac*
2 *quarts chicken stock (see p. 241)*
1½ *cups Velouté Sauce made with chicken stock (see p. 246)*
⅓ *cup heavy cream*
8 *to 10 slices truffle*
1 *bunch watercress*

1. Bone and skin chicken breasts (see directions, p. 125), then work the flesh through a meat grinder, using the finest blade, or chop finely with a knife.

• The discarded bones and skin can be used in making the chicken stock.

2. Put ground chicken into a bowl, add 2 egg whites, and beat—either with a mixer (use the flat whip if it's a heavy-duty mixer) or, over ice, with a wooden spatula—until smooth and fluffy.

3. Add light cream, 1 tablespoonful at a time, and beat it in.

4. Cook shallot and garlic at high heat in 2 tablespoons of butter until transparent. Do not let it brown. Beat it into chicken mixture along with 1 teaspoon salt, pepper, and tarragon.

5. Make the panade, or thickening agent, by putting ½ cup of water, ½ teaspoon of salt, and 1 tablespoon of butter into a small saucepan, bringing to a rolling boil, and immediately, all at once, dumping in ½ cup of flour, then beating over high heat with a wooden spatula until the mixture is smooth and leaves the side of the pan, then removing from heat and thoroughly beating in the whole egg and the 1 remaining egg white.

6. Add panade, a spoonful at a time, to chicken mixture, beating it in. Beat in sour cream and cognac.

7. Butter 8 to 10 cutlet molds and fill them with the chicken mixture, smoothing off tops with a wet spatula. Bang the molds on a table to settle the mixture.

• The cutlets can be made ahead to this point and poached at the last minute. Cover the filled molds with waxed paper and store in a refrigerator. Let the molds come to room temperature before poaching.

8. Fill a 4-quart saucepan half full of chicken stock and bring to a boil. Then reduce heat to simmer, drop in the molds, bottoms down (stock should cover the molds), and poach gently for about 15 minutes, or until the mousse floats out of the molds and to the surface of the stock.

9. Gently lift the mousse cutlets out of the stock with a slotted spoon and arrange them in a circle on a warm round platter.

10. Pour a ribbon of Velouté Sauce over each cutlet, first thinning the Velouté with a little heavy cream. Garnish each cutlet with a slice of truffle. Place a bunch of watercress in the center of the platter.

• If dinner is delayed, the cutlets will hold for a short while, about 15 minutes, in a warm oven. *Makes 4 to 5 servings of 2 cutlets each.*

Hungarian Chicken Paprika

1 3½-lb. chicken
1½ teaspoons salt
¾ teaspoon freshly cracked
  white pepper
6 tablespoons butter
½ cup sliced carrot
1 cup sliced celery
1 cup chopped yellow onion
¼ cup medium sweet Hun-
  garian paprika

¼ cup flour
2 tablespoons tomato paste
2 cups strong chicken stock
  (see p. 241)
1 cup dairy sour cream
2 green and/or red peppers
  cut into rings

1. Wash and dry chicken and cut into 6 serving pieces, leaving wings attached to breast meat. Season with 1 teaspoon salt and ½ teaspoon pepper.

2. Melt ¼ cup of butter in a heavy casserole. When foaming subsides, add chicken pieces and brown all over, over high heat, turning with wooden spatulas. Don't let pieces touch. Remove chicken from casserole and set aside.

3. Add the remaining 2 tablespoons of butter to casserole. When hot, stir in carrot, celery, and onion and cook over high heat 5 to 7 minutes, or until onion is transparent but not brown.

4. Add paprika, blending it in with a spatula. Stir in flour and cook at high heat for a couple of minutes until completely blended, stirring constantly. Add tomato paste, remaining ½ teaspoon of salt, remaining ¼ teaspoon of pepper and pour in chicken stock, stirring vigorously. Bring to a boil, reduce to a simmer, and cook, covered, about 20 minutes, or until vegetables are tender but not mushy.

5. Pour into a blender jar (to avoid overflows, never fill a blender more than half full of a hot mixture) and purée.

6. Return mixture to casserole, add browned chicken pieces—slit the legs to the bone so they'll cook in the same length of time as the breast meat—cover, and simmer until chicken is tender, about 20 minutes (to test for tenderness, prick flesh with fork; juice should run clear).

7. Arrange chicken pieces on a platter and keep warm. Whisk sour cream, 1 tablespoon at a time, into sauce in the casserole and heat through.

• You can even boil this sauce; it won't curdle—the flour in it does the trick.

8. Pour sauce over chicken. Garnish with blanched pepper rings over-lapped on top of chicken.

• Serve with rice, Italian Gnocchi (see p. 180), noodles, or Spaetzle (see p. 181). *Makes 4 to 6 servings.*

CHICKEN DAUPHINOISE

I adapted this from a recipe made popular by Jean Noel Escudier, an authority on Provençale cooking, better known as Monsieur Provence. The original recipe calls for 40 to 50 cloves of garlic! But garlic in Provence is not as strong as that in the United States. Blanching the garlic first removes some of the pungency.

30 medium cloves garlic	*1 teaspoon salt*
3 to 4 lbs. chicken pieces, breasts, thighs, legs, or a combination	*½ teaspoon freshly cracked white pepper*
2 tablespoons olive oil	*½ cup chicken stock (see p. 241)*
3 tablespoons butter	*2 tablespoons chopped parsley*
1 small bay leaf	
½ teaspoon thyme	*¼ cup dry white wine*

1. Peel the garlic cloves (30 cloves is correct) and put them into a saucepan. Blanch them by covering with cold water, bringing to a boil, and cooking 2 minutes at a rapid boil. Drain the cloves in a sieve and pat them dry with paper towels.

2. Wash and dry the chicken pieces. Then heat oil and 2 tablespoons of butter in a heavy skillet (or a casserole) and sauté the pieces over high heat for about 15 minutes, or until brown. Do not let chicken pieces touch: do only as many at one time as the pan (or casserole) will accommodate. Turn them with wooden spatulas to brown evenly.

3. When chicken is golden brown, remove from skillet and set aside.

4. Add the remaining 1 tablespoon of butter to the skillet. Add blanched garlic and sauté, over medium heat, stirring the cloves around until they're well coated with butter; do not let them brown.

5. Return the chicken pieces to the skillet. (If you have included legs, slit them to the bone so they'll cook in the same length of time as the breasts.) Add bay leaf and thyme, sprinkle with salt and pepper, and add chicken stock. Bring to a boil, reduce heat to simmer, then cover the skillet and cook very gently for about ½ hour, or until chicken is tender.

6. Remove the chicken to a platter. Scoop up the garlic cloves with a slotted spoon and scatter them over the chicken. Sprinkle with chopped parsley.

7. Deglaze the skillet by adding wine and bringing it to a boil. Scrape up the brown bits and boil to reduce the mixture a little. Check seasoning, and pour over chicken. **Makes 6 servings.**

POULET EN VESSIE

(Chicken in a Sealed Pot)

3 to 4 lbs. chicken pieces, breasts, thighs, legs, or a combination
6 tablespoons butter
¼ cup cognac
18 small white onions
2 large fluted sautéed mushroom caps (see p. 11)
1 medium clove finely chopped garlic
2 teaspoons potato starch
½ teaspoon meat glaze (see p. 244)

1 bay leaf
¼ teaspoon thyme
¾ cup chicken stock (see p. 241)
½ teaspoon salt
½ teaspoon freshly cracked white pepper
1 cup dry red Burgundy
2 cups flour
1 egg yolk
2 tablespoons chopped parsley

1. Wash and dry the chicken pieces. Then melt ¼ cup of butter in a heavy 3- to 4-quart casserole, and when foaming subsides, brown chicken, over high heat, a few pieces at a time. Do not let the pieces touch. Turn them with wooden spatulas to brown evenly, and don't prick them with a fork. It takes about 15 minutes to brown chicken nicely.

2. Put all the browned pieces in the casserole and flame with 2 tablespoons cognac—that is, warm the cognac in a small long-handled pan, ignite it, and pour it, flaming, over the chicken.

3. Peel the onions (the smaller they are, the better), then, in a frying pan, melt 2 tablespoons butter and brown them, over high heat, shaking the pan so they roll around and brown evenly. Add to chicken in casserole.

• If you can't get small onions, cut larger ones in half or boil them 15 minutes before browning.
• To peel onions the easy way, drop them into boiling water for 30 seconds before removing the skins.

4. Add sautéed mushroom caps to chicken in casserole.

5. Make sauce by stirring the potato starch and meat glaze into the butter and juices remaining in the pan, then adding garlic, bay leaf, thyme, chicken stock, salt, pepper, and wine and bringing to a boil, stirring constantly.

6. Pour sauce over chicken in casserole, add the remaining 2 tablespoons of cognac, and seal the casserole with a lute (sealing paste) made by mixing flour with 1 cup of water to form a paste, laying it on a board and rolling it into a long rope. Place the rope around the rim of the casserole and press the lid on top, tightly. Press the lute with fork tines, and brush it with egg yolk mixed with 1 tablespoon water so it will shine.

7. Put the sealed casserole into a preheated 350° oven and bake for 45 minutes.

8. Bring the sealed casserole to the table and break the seal (you may need a chisel and a small hammer) there—the fragrance is glorious! Sprinkle with chopped parsley before serving. *Makes 6 servings.*

ROAST CHICKEN BALLOTTINE

A ballottine is a fowl or piece of meat that is boned, stuffed, and pressed back into shape, usually served hot. This one is stuffed—ever so deliciously—with chicken mousse, tongue (or ham), and pistachio nuts, and it's excellent served hot or cold.

1 3½-lb. chicken	*1 tablespoon chopped truffle*
2 whole chicken breasts	*8 slices bacon*
2 egg whites	*¼ cup melted butter, plus*
1½ cups light cream	*butter to brush on arti-*
6 tablespoons cognac	*choke bottoms*
1 teaspoon salt	*8 fluted and sautéed mush-*
½ teaspoon freshly cracked	*room caps (see p. 11)*
white pepper	*1 bunch watercress*
½ cup natural pistachio nuts	*8 canned artichoke bottoms*
¼ lb. tongue or ham	

1. Wash and dry chicken and bone it (see directions, p. 126). Cut off the wing tips and the knobby ends of the leg bones. This is done so the bird will look more shapely when it's re-formed.

• The carcass can be used to make chicken stock.

2. Prepare chicken mousse as follows. Bone and skin chicken breasts (see directions, p. 125) and work the flesh through a meat grinder, using the finest blade, or chop finely with a knife. Put the flesh in a bowl and beat in egg whites either with a mixer (use the flat whip if it's a heavy-

duty mixer) or, over ice, with a wooden spatula. Then beat in cream gradually, 1 tablespoonful at a time.

• If you are beating the mixture by hand, chilling it causes the natural gelatin in the chicken to react to thicken it and thus helps compensate for the lack of the forcefulness of the mixer beating.

3. Lay the boned chicken, with what was the skin side facing down, on a cutting board and spread it open. Brush the flesh with cognac—use 2 tablespoons of it—and sprinkle with salt and pepper.

4. Spread chicken mousse over boned chicken, leaving a ½-inch margin all around. Sprinkle with pistachio nuts. Then cut pieces of tongue or ham the shape and size of your index finger, lay them on top of the nuts, and scatter chopped truffle over all.

5. Form the chicken into a compact roll and sew it up with needle and thread.

6. Cover the rolled chicken with overlapping slices of blanched bacon —that is, bacon that has been put in a saucepan, covered with cold water, brought to a boil, and boiled 1 minute. Drain the bacon in a sieve before using it.

7. Tie the bacon on with string every inch or so, but don't tie it too tightly, for if there's no give, the expansion of the mousse inside the chicken will cause string marks on the roasted bird.

8. Place chicken on a rack in a roasting pan and put it into a pre-heated 375° oven to roast for 1 hour. Every 15 minutes baste it, twice with 2 tablespoons melted butter and 2 tablespoons of cognac; the third time use a bulb baster to draw up the liquid in the pan and squirt it over chicken.

9. Before serving, remove strings, bacon, and threads holding roast together; cut into neat slices and overlap them on a platter. Garnish platter with mushroom caps, watercress, and artichoke bottoms that have been rinsed and dried, brushed with butter, and heated through in a 325° oven.

• Pass Basic Brown Sauce (see p. 248) if you wish, but this chicken is good plain. *Makes 8 servings.*

Truffled Chicken or Turkey Flambé

This is a fast method for roasting a bird. The skin gets beautifully crisp, and the meat is unbelievably moist. I've tried roasting birds both slowly and quickly. This is the method I prefer. Note that to allow time for the perfume of the truffle to permeate the bird, truffle slices should be placed under the skin and the bird should be trussed (steps 1 to 5, below) 24 hours before it is to be roasted.

8 ⅛-inch slices truffle	2 tablespoons lemon juice
7 tablespoons armagnac, or more	2 tablespoons finely chopped shallots
1 4-lb. roasting chicken or 1 5-lb. turkey	½ cup dry red wine
1 tablespoon salt	½ teaspoon meat glaze (see p. 244)
1 teaspoon freshly cracked white pepper	½ teaspoon tomato paste
10 tablespoons unsalted butter	¾ cup chicken stock (see p. 241)
	1 bunch watercress

1. Marinate truffle slices in ¼ cup of armagnac for 1 hour. When finished, reserve the armagnac to use for basting the bird.

• Armagnac is a brandy made southeast of Bordeaux, in what was ancient Gascony. It has a drier taste than most brandies.

2. Remove giblets and neck from the bird's cavity, trim wing tips, and wash the bird, drying it thoroughly. Season the cavity with 1 teaspoon of salt and ½ teaspoon pepper and put a lump of unsalted butter—¼ cup —in it.

3. Loosen the skin on breast and legs: start at the neck, lifting the skin over the breast—don't use a knife, just push the skin away from the flesh with thumb and fingers, taking care not to tear the skin; when the breast skin is loosened, go to work on the skin over the thighs.

4. Insert 1 truffle slice under the skin on each thigh. Place the remaining 6 slices under the breast skin, 3 on each side, making a design.

5. Rub the outside of the bird with lemon juice, 2 tablespoons softened butter, remaining 2 teaspoons salt, and remaining ½ teaspoon pepper. Truss the bird (see directions, p. 127), wrap it in foil and refrigerate it for 24 hours.

6. The next day take the bird from the refrigerator, bring it to room temperature, and place it on its side, on a rack in a shallow roasting pan. Roast in a preheated 475° oven for 15 minutes; meanwhile make a basting mixture of ¼ cup of melted butter and ¼ cup of reserved armagnac,

baste the bird, turn it onto its other side, baste it, and roast it for another 15 minutes.

7. Turn the bird breast side up. Reduce oven to 425°, baste again and every 15 minutes until roast is done.

• Use a bulb baster to draw up the liquid in the pan and squirt it over the bird.
• A 4-lb. chicken takes about 45 minutes, a 5-lb. turkey takes about 1½ hours.

8. Remove bird to an ovenproof platter and keep warm.

9. Pour out all but 2 tablespoons of fat from the roasting pan. Place pan over high heat, add shallots and cook for 1 to 2 minutes, without browning them.

10. Add red wine, meat glaze, tomato paste, and chicken stock. Bring to a boil over moderate heat and boil 15 minutes to reduce mixture until it is syrupy. Taste for and, if desired, adjust seasoning, then pour into a bowl to serve as sauce.

11. Garnish bird with watercress. Heat remaining 3 tablespoons of armagnac in a small long-handled pan until just warm to the touch. Ignite the armagnac, pour it over the bird, and take the bird, flaming, to the table.

12. When carving bird, take off first one side of the breast (including wing), then the other; cut the 2 breast sections across into 3 pieces each —this way there will be 6 servings of breast meat with skin and truffle, then remove legs and thighs. *Makes 6 servings.*

ROAST GOOSE

To many people, Christmas wouldn't be Christmas without a succulent goose. For any occasion, try to get a fresh goose; a nice, plump one.

1 10-to-12-lb. goose	*1 teaspoon freshly cracked*
1 tablespoon coarse salt	*black pepper*

1. Wash the goose inside and out and dry it carefully with paper towels. Remove as much fat as possible (you'll find large chunks of fat under the neck skin and in the cavity).

• Stuff the goose if you wish, with 2½ lbs. of sauerkraut, or with 2½ lbs. of sausage meat, or with 4 cups of chopped onions sautéed in goose fat until they're lightly browned.

2. Rub the goose all over with coarse salt and pepper. Truss it (see directions, p. 127), and put it on a rack in a roasting pan, breast up, and

place in a preheated 375° oven. Roast for a total of 20 minutes per pound but before the last ½ hour remove goose, prick it all over with a fork (this will release a lot of the fat), and before returning goose to finish roasting, reduce oven heat to 325°.

• To test for doneness, prick a leg with a fork; if the juices run clear, the goose is done.

3. Serve goose with all the traditional holiday vegetables: glazed turnips, onions, mashed parsnips, glazed carrots, sweet potatoes, chestnuts, Brussels sprouts. *Makes 8 to 10 servings.*

Canard à la Normande

Heavy cream, apples, and Calvados are all products of Normandy. Hence the name for this delicious duck.

2 *4- to 5-lb. Long Island ducklings*	4 *beaten eggs*
8 *slices firm home-style white bread, plus heels of the loaf*	¾ *cup Calvados, or apple brandy, about*
6 *cups roughly chopped peeled-and-cored apples*	½ *cup chicken stock (see p. 241), about*
2 *teaspoons cinnamon*	1 *cup melted apple jelly*
1 *tablespoon salt*	1 *cup heavy cream*
1 *teaspoon freshly cracked black pepper*	

1. Wash and dry ducks; stuff paper towels into the cavities to dry them thoroughly.

2. Cut the bread slices into cubes (trim off crusts or not, as you prefer), put the cubes in a large bowl and make stuffing by tossing them with apples, cinnamon, 2 teaspoons salt, and ½ teaspoon pepper, then adding eggs and enough Calvados—about 3 to 4 tablespoonfuls—to moisten the mixture.

3. Stuff ducks *loosely*. (Stuffing expands as ducks roast.) Close the cavity of each duck with heel of a loaf of bread, then truss ducks (see directions, p. 127), rub them all over with the remaining salt and pepper, place them on a rack in roasting pan, and put them in a preheated 325° oven to roast for a total of 20 minutes per pound. During all but the last 20 minutes of roasting, baste ducks every ¼ hour with Calvados mixed with chicken stock, using about ¼ cup of each in all. (Use a bulb baster to draw up the liquid in the pan and squirt it over the ducks.)

4. About 20 minutes before ducks are done, take them out of the oven and glaze them with apple jelly. Apply it with a pastry brush.

5. Return the ducks to oven, and when they are done, remove them to a carving board and keep warm.

• To test for doneness, prick a thigh with a fork; when juices are no longer pink, the duck is done.

6. Pour off all but 1 tablespoon of fat from the roasting pan and de-glaze the pan with the remaining ¼ cup Calvados, like this: pour the Calvados into the pan, give it a few seconds to warm, then ignite it.

7. Scrape up the brown bits, add the remaining ¼ cup chicken stock and the heavy cream, and make sauce by bringing to a boil, then cooking to reduce sauce and thicken slightly. Strain sauce and serve it separately, in a bowl. **Makes 4 to 6 servings.**

Canard aux Pêches

1 4- to 5-lb. Long Island duckling
1 tablespoon coarse salt
1 teaspoon freshly cracked black pepper
2 1-lb. cans white peach halves, or 6 peeled, pitted, and halved fresh white peaches
8 to 10 tablespoons dry white wine

¼ to ½ cup sugar
¼ cup wine (or cider) vinegar
2 cups Basic Brown Sauce (see p. 248)
1 tablespoon dry Madeira
1 tablespoon cognac
⅓ cup melted apricot jam
2 teaspoons potato starch, optional
1 bunch watercress

1. Wash duck and dry thoroughly. Remove giblets, neck, and wing tips, then truss the duck (see directions, p. 127), rub it all over with salt and pepper, and place it, breast up, on a rack in a roasting pan along with giblets and trimmings. Roast in a preheated 350° oven for 1 hour.

2. Put canned peach halves, with their juice, into a saucepan, add ¼ cup wine, and simmer slowly for 3 to 5 minutes until heated through. Or bring a mixture of ¼ cup wine, ¼ cup sugar, and ¾ cup water to a boil, add fresh peach halves, and simmer for 10 minutes. Drain and set aside the peaches—and save the liquid in which they cooked for possible addition to sauce (see step 9, below).

3. Make caramel by dissolving ¼ cup of sugar in vinegar over low heat in a heavy pan. After sugar dissolves, do not stir, just tip the pan back and forth over the heat until the contents turn a clear caramel color.

4. Add Brown Sauce very slowly to caramel. Stir over low heat adding Madeira and cognac. Taste for seasoning and add salt and pepper if desired. Set aside.

5. After duck has roasted 1 hour, remove it from the oven and brush it with apricot jam, using a pastry brush. Return duck to oven for another 15 minutes, or until done.

• To test for doneness, tip the duck so juice runs out of its cavity; when juices run yellow, duck is done. Or prick a thigh with a fork; when juices are no longer pink, duck is done.

• The duck and the sauce (see steps 7 to 9, below) can be made several hours ahead of when the duck is to be served if the duck is under-cooked—that is, cooked 15 minutes less than called for—refrigerated, then brought to room temperature and reheated for 10 minutes in a 350° oven.

6. When duck is done, remove it to a carving board or a serving platter and keep warm.

7. Pour off all but 1 tablespoon fat from the roasting pan and deglaze the pan by pouring in ¼ cup wine, and bringing the wine to a boil.

8. Scrape up the brown bits and strain contents of pan into the caramel mixture to make sauce.

9. Thicken the sauce, if necessary, by adding potato starch that has been stirred into 2 tablespoons of dry white wine and cooking over high heat, stirring constantly, for 1 or 2 minutes. If sauce is too thick, thin it with some of the liquid in which the peaches cooked.

10. Place peach halves around the duck, spoon a little sauce on each half and serve the remaining sauce in a bowl. Garnish the carving board or serving platter with watercress and carve duck (see directions, p. 127) at table. *Makes 2 to 3 servings.*

SQUABS WITH CUMBERLAND SAUCE

Squabs are in season in the wintertime. They are domestically raised little birds, with all dark meat, and they tend to be dry if not faithfully basted. Plan on 1 whole squab per person. And serve squabs with finger bowls: it's not only proper but quite necessary to nibble on the little bones.

1 cup wild rice	¾ cup butter, plus butter to
¾ cup very finely chopped	brush on squabs
onion	4 teaspoons salt
1 medium clove finely	1 teaspoon freshly cracked
chopped garlic	black pepper

2 tablespoons chopped parsley

2 cups seedless white grapes,
washed and stemmed

8 1¼- to 1½-lb. squabs

Cumberland Sauce (recipe
follows)

1 teaspoon potato starch, optional

1 tablespoon port wine, optional

1 bunch watercress, optional

Frosted White Grapes (see
p. 95), optional

1. Soak rice in 1½ cups of cold water for 1 hour. Drain, then put in a saucepan with 2 cups cold water and bring to a boil, lower heat, and simmer, covered, for 30 minutes, or until done.

• To test for doneness, pinch a grain between your fingers: it should have a little hardness but not be mushy.

2. When rice is done, drain it and put it in a bowl.

3. Sauté onion and garlic over high heat, in 1 tablespoon of butter, stirring with a wooden spatula until transparent.

4. Add onion-garlic mixture, 1 teaspoon salt, ½ teaspoon pepper, 3 tablespoons melted butter, and the chopped parsley to rice. Mix together with fork, adding 1 cup of grapes. Set aside.

5. Wash the squabs and dry them thoroughly. Trim off wing tips and cut off necks. Stuff squabs with rice-grape mixture.

6. Truss squabs (see directions, p. 127), then brush them with melted butter—use 2 tablespoonfuls—and sprinkle with the remaining salt and pepper.

7. Put squabs in a roasting pan and roast them, uncovered, in a preheated 375° oven for 45 minutes. Baste them often—at least 3 times while roasting—with melted butter, using about ½ cup.

• If tender squab is preferred, roast an extra 10 to 15 minutes, but keep in mind that squab tends to become dry as it's cooked.

8. When squabs are done, remove them to a warm platter and keep warm.

9. Make sauce by pouring off all but about 2 tablespoons of fat from the roasting pan, then pouring in Cumberland Sauce and bringing to a boil, scraping up brown bits. Thicken the sauce, if you wish, by adding potato starch that has been stirred into port wine and boiling 1 minute, stirring constantly.

10. Add the remaining cup of grapes to sauce and heat through. Remove trussing cords from squabs and arrange them on the platter. If desired, decorate the platter either with a watercress garnish or with Frosted White Grapes. Serve sauce separately, in a sauce boat.

Cumberland Sauce

Cumberland Sauce can be served hot or cold. It is excellent with poultry, ham, or tongue. Try it with Pâté Maison (see p. 28), too.

1 cup red currant jelly	*Grated peel of 1 orange*
½ cup fresh orange juice	*Grated peel of 1 lemon*
½ teaspoon dry mustard	*1 cup port wine*
¼ teaspoon powdered ginger	

Put all ingredients in a saucepan and cook over low heat, stirring constantly, until jelly melts. ***Makes 8 servings.***

SQUABS WITH PINEAPPLE

1 large ripe pineapple	*1 cup unsweetened canned*
8 1¼- to 1½-lb. squabs	*pineapple juice*
½ cup pâté de fois gras	*1 cup Basic Brown Sauce*
1 tablespoon salt	*(see p. 248)*
1 teaspoon freshly cracked	*1 teaspoon potato starch,*
black pepper	*optional*
1 cup butter	*1 recipe Chestnut Purée (see*
2 tablespoons cognac	*p. 173)*
1½ cups port wine	

1. Remove plumage from pineapple and save for garnish. Peel the pineapple (the easiest way is by standing it on a cutting board and slicing down, all around, with a large sharp knife), dig out the eyes, and cut the pineapple in half, then cut the halves into slices ½ inch thick. Cut out and discard the core, and after reserving 8 of the most attractive slices as garnishes for the squabs, cut the remaining pineapple slices in half.

2. Wash and dry the squabs. Trim off wing tips and cut off necks. Reserve giblets and trimmings.

3. Into the cavity of each squab put 1 tablespoon of pâté and a piece of pineapple. Truss squabs (see directions, p. 127), then rub them with salt and pepper.

4. Melt ¼ cup of butter in a large heavy casserole and when no longer foaming, brown squabs, giblets, and trimmings thoroughly, over high heat, turning them with wooden spatulas. Don't prick the skins with a fork; don't let the pieces touch each other—that is, brown at once only as many as can fit into the casserole without crowding, and allow plenty of time—about 15 minutes for each batch.

• If the birds touch, they will braise instead of browning.

5. Put all the squabs, giblets, and trimmings into the casserole and flame them with cognac—that is, warm the cognac in a small long-handled pan, ignite it, and pour it, flaming, into the casserole.

6. Scrape up the brown bits in the casserole. Then pour in ¾ cup of melted butter and roast, uncovered, in a preheated 375° oven for 45 minutes. Baste often—at least 3 times during roasting—with pan juices, using a bulb baster to take them up and squirt them over squabs.

7. While squabs roast, poach reserved pineapple slices in wine and pineapple juice for 10 minutes. Remove slices and keep them warm. Boil liquid to reduce it by half, then add Basic Brown Sauce, bring to a boil again, and remove from heat. Taste for seasoning and add salt and pepper if desired. Thicken slightly, if desired, by adding potato starch that has been mixed with 1 tablespoon of cold water and cooking over high heat, stirring constantly.

8. When birds are done, arrange them on a platter and keep warm.

• If you want crisp brown skin on them, put squabs under a broiler for about 5 minutes before arranging them on the platter.

9. Pour off all but 2 tablespoons of the fat in the casserole, add the wine-brown-sauce mixture and the giblets—chop them first—and bring to a boil, scraping up the brown bits. Strain into a serving bowl.

10. Arrange a pineapple slice over each squab and garnish with a rosette of Chestnut Purée made by putting the purée into a pastry bag fitted with a star tube and piping the rosette on each pineapple slice. Decorate the platter with reserved pineapple plumage. *Makes 8 servings.*

EGGS AND CRÊPES

Eggs

Eggs are one of the best buys on the food market today. They are high in protein yet low in price. And eggs will keep well in a refrigerator for up to two weeks.

I always prefer to use large eggs; this is especially important if you plan to serve eggs whole—they just look so much better when they're large. But please note that there is no difference in the nutritional value or taste of brown eggs compared with white ones, and brown eggs are often less expensive.

Eggs are the most versatile food imaginable. They can be served for breakfast, lunch, or supper, and they can be baked, boiled, fried, or poached, or turned into omelettes and soufflés. Eggs can also be combined with almost any ingredient you have on hand to provide an endless variety of new dishes.

You'll find that it's a good idea always to have some eggs on hand; with just a few eggs, and only a few minutes' time in the kitchen, you can create a quick yet elegant brunch, luncheon, or light supper.

FRENCH OMELETTES

A French omelette should be a perfect oval, pointed at both ends and plump in the center; the outside should be pale yellow (if it's brown, the pan was too hot); and inside, the omelette should be mellow and creamy (what the French call *baveuse*).

Learn to make a perfect French omelette and you'll have one of the most useful skills in a cook's repertoire. With 3 eggs in the house, you can always offer an unexpected guest a plain omelette, a flaming jam omelette, or an omelette filled with vegetables, ham, herbs, cheese—whatever happens to be handy. And giving an omelette party for large groups—I've had as many as sixty people at once—can be great fun. In my family room is an antique stove I've had electrified; I use it to make omelettes to order. First I serve a good hearty potage, then the omelettes with green salad and French bread; the dessert is fruit and cheese.

For making omelettes it's wise although not absolutely necessary to have a pan with some weight, and one that's not too large, since individual omelettes are easier to make than are large ones. The pan I like best is of cast aluminum, with a comfortable wooden handle; the pan measures 10 inches across the top and 8 inches across the bottom and is the perfect size for a 3-egg omelette—for 1 serving, that is.

To season an omelette pan, fill it ¾ full of vegetable oil (don't use olive oil), set it over low heat, and when the oil reaches the point of smoking—this takes about 20 minutes—turn off heat and let the pan stand at room temperature overnight. In the morning pour off the oil and discard it. Wipe out the pan with paper towels, and from this point on, *never, never* wash it—just wipe it out with paper towels. If the pan should inadvertently be washed, season it again before using. Use this pan only for omelettes. And if you've never made omelettes before, use it first for practice—making omelettes requires it. Buy yourself a couple of dozen eggs and make one omelette right after the other; feed them to the dog, or throw them away if you have to—it's worth the slight investment in eggs and time.

But if an omelette made for a guest isn't quite perfect, don't panic—just cover the top more generously than usual with chopped parsley. No one will know.

3 *eggs, at room temperature*
Scant ½ *teaspoon salt*
¼ *teaspoon freshly cracked*
  white pepper

Generous 1 *tablespoon butter,*
  plus butter to brush on top
  of omelette
1 *tablespoon chopped parsley*

1. Break eggs into a bowl, add salt and pepper, and beat with a fork just enough to mix—about 30 strokes.

2. Put a seasoned omelette pan on low heat and heat slowly—the slower, the better—until a tiny bit of butter if put in the pan sizzles briskly without browning.

• If the butter browns, swing the pan through the air a couple of times to cool it; then try again.

3. When the pan is the right temperature, put 1 generous tablespoon butter into it. The butter will sizzle and foam as it melts. Be ready to add the eggs the instant the butter stops foaming (before it browns, that is).

• At the moment the eggs go into the pan, increase heat to medium high.

4. As soon as the eggs hit the pan, stir them quickly with a fork held in one hand while shaking the pan back and forth over the heat with the other. Keep the tines of the fork flat on the pan and stir vigorously, first clockwise, then counterclockwise. Stir and shake with enthusiasm. It takes only 30 seconds to cook the omelette, so really bend over the pan and move.

• The shaking and stirring motion takes practice and coordination. It's rather like patting your head and rubbing your stomach at the same time. But once you get the hang of it, it's easy.

5. The omelette is now ready to fold and turn out. As soon as the egg mixture *starts* to set but while it is still quite moist and creamy-looking, pat it out evenly over the bottom of the pan with the fork.

•If the omelette is to be filled, the filling goes in now.

6. Rotate the pan about ¼ turn (to the left if you're right-handed so you can change the position of your hand on the handle and grip it with palm underneath). Tip up the pan, and keeping it tipped with one hand, use the fork with the other to loosen the omelette around the edge near the handle, then to fold it over and roll it—guiding it with the fork and tucking in the edges as you go—until it is in the curve of the pan opposite the handle.

7. Bring the edge of a warm plate to the edge of the pan and, literally turning the pan upside down over the plate, tip the omelette out onto the plate.

• The omelette won't stick if the pan was well seasoned, if it was the right temperature, and if a generous tablespoon of butter was used. If it does stick, put butter at the sticking points and let the melting butter help your fork loosen the omelette.

• Sometimes fillings get under the eggs and into the pan and cause sticking. Loosen the omelette with butter, and before making another omelette, rub the pan out with paper toweling, and if necessary, a little coarse salt.

8. Before serving the omelette, brush the top with melted butter and sprinkle with chopped parsley. *Makes 1 serving.*

Cheese Omelette

Proceed as above, but before folding the omelette, drop about 2 table-spoons of grated cheese—use Cheddar, Swiss, Gruyère, or any other well-flavored kind—in the center of the egg mixture.

Mincemeat Omelette Flambé

Put 2 tablespoons of hot mincemeat in the omelette before folding it. Tip the omelette out onto a stainless steel or other flameproof serving dish, sift confectioners' sugar over it, and flame it by warming 2 tablespoons of rum in a small long-handled pan, igniting the rum, then pouring it, flaming, over the omelette.

Jam Omelette Flambé

Before folding the omelette, fill it with 2 tablespoons of raspberry, strawberry, or apricot jam, or 2 tablespoons of orange marmalade. Tip the omelette out onto a stainless steel or other flameproof serving dish. Sift confectioners' sugar over it. Decorate the top with crisscross lines burned into the sugar with a red-hot skewer. Flame the omelette by pouring over it 2 tablespoons of rum, cognac, framboise, or kirsch that has been warmed in a small long-handled pan, then ignited.

Truffle Omelette Flambé

When the egg mixture goes into the pan add to it as many truffle slices as the budget allows. Tip the omelette out onto a stainless steel or other flameproof serving dish, decorate with a slice of truffle, and flame by warming 2 tablespoons of cognac in a small long-handled pan, igniting the cognac, and pouring it, flaming, over the omelette.

Ham or Bacon Omelette

When the egg mixture goes into the pan add to it, stirring, ½ cup of diced cooked ham or ½ cup of bacon that has been cut in tiny pieces, fried until crisp, and drained on paper towels.

Mushroom Omelette

Before cooking omelette, slice 4 or 5 mushrooms, sprinkle them with 2 teaspoons of lemon juice, ½ teaspoon of salt, and ¼ teaspoon of freshly cracked white pepper, and sauté them (in another pan) in 2 tablespoons of foaming butter, tossing them over high heat for 3 minutes only. Add mushrooms to the omelette just before folding it. Decorate omelette with a fluted sautéed mushroom cap (see p. 11) and chopped parsley.

Caviar Omelette

After omelette has been tipped from the pan to a plate, slit it from end to end and fill it with red or black caviar. Put a big spoonful of sour cream on the side and garnish with chopped fresh dill.

Watercress Omelette

Before cooking omelette, trim stems off and wash and dry enough watercress (or baby spinach, or sorrel leaves) to have a handful (about ½ cup) of the leaves. Add them, stirring, to the egg mixture at the time it goes into the pan and cook the omelette just a bit longer than usual. Because of water in the leaves, it needs a few extra seconds over heat. Spoon a little sour cream over the omelette.

Herb Omelette

Before cooking omelette, chop 2 tablespoons of any fresh herb or combination of herbs, and when the egg mixture goes into the pan, add them to it, stirring; or stir 1 teaspoon of dry herbs into 2 tablespoons of sour cream and add to omelette just before folding it. Garnish omelette with 1 tablespoon of the fresh herbs or with chopped parsley.

COLD POACHED EGGS

This is an inexpensive, handsome-looking luncheon dish.

6 *eggs*
¾ *cup red wine vinegar*
3 *peeled, stemmed tomatoes*
2 *tablespoons tarragon or red wine vinegar*
5 *tablespoons olive oil*
½ *teaspoon salt*
¼ *teaspoon freshly cracked black pepper*

1 *recipe Seven-Minute Green Beans (see p. 164)*
6 *large lettuce leaves*
1 *cup mayonnaise (see p. 251)*
2 *tablespoons chopped parsley*

1. Poach eggs as follows. Fill 8-inch skillet ¾ full of water, add ¾ cup wine vinegar, and heat to simmering. Break 3 eggs close to the surface of the water and drop them in one after the other. With a skimmer in one hand gently smooth the top of the water just enough to keep it moving on the surface, and at the same time, use the other hand to tip the pan just a bit, also to keep the water moving. Smoothing the water and keeping the pan tipped, poach eggs for 2 to 2½ minutes. Remove eggs from water with a slotted spoon and plunge immediately into cold water to stop the cooking. Set aside, and follow the above procedure for the 3 remaining eggs.

2. Place eggs in refrigerator, still in the cold water, to chill about ½ hour.

3. Cut the tomatoes in half. Hollow out the halves just enough to make beds for the eggs.

4. In a mixture of the remaining 2 tablespoons of vinegar, oil, salt, and pepper marinate the cooked green beans in a refrigerator ½ hour.

5. Before serving, arrange a lettuce leaf on each of 6 plates, put a tomato half in the lettuce, an egg in the tomato half, mask with mayonnaise, and sprinkle with parsley. Arrange the marinated beans alongside. **Makes 6 servings.**

EGGS IN GELATIN

6 *eggs*
2 *tablespoons (2 envelopes)*
unflavored gelatin
1 *quart chicken stock (see*
p. 241)

6 *small slices truffle*
12 *leaves fresh tarragon*
6 *small pieces of thin-sliced*
ham (about 1 inch square)
6 *large lettuce leaves*

1. Poach the eggs, following directions in step 1 of the recipe for Cold Poached Eggs (see p. 155). Place eggs in refrigerator to chill.

2. Soften gelatin by sprinkling it in ½ cup of cold chicken stock. Set the container of gelatin and stock in a pan of hot water, and stirring occasionally, heat until gelatin is dissolved.

3. Heat the remaining chicken stock in a saucepan, then stir the dissolved gelatin into it and remove from heat.

4. Stir mixture over ice until it reaches the syrupy stage and is about ready to set, then put a spoonful of it—reserve the rest—in the bottom of each of 6 oval dariole molds—oval molds 3 inches wide and 1½ inches deep—and refrigerate for about 15 minutes or until set.

5. Dip slices of truffle into the reserved gelatin mixture, then put the slices in the middle of the molds on top of the gelatin. Return to refrigerator for about 5 minutes to set.

6. Cover the truffle layers with a bit more of the gelatin mixture and crisscross two tarragon leaves over the top. Refrigerate again for about 15 minutes or until set.

• If you don't have fresh tarragon, cut long thin leaf shapes from scallion tops or sprinkle the molds with chopped parsley to get the green color.

7. When the tarragon layers have set, coat the pieces of ham with gelatin mixture and lay them on top.

• The ham should be a little bigger than the truffle, so the pink will later (after unmolding) show around the black.

8. Coat the ham layers with more gelatin and put the molds back in refrigerator to set.

9. Carefully lay a chilled poached egg in each mold, and cover with remaining gelatin mixture, this time to the top of each mold. Return to refrigerator and chill thoroughly, about 1 hour.

• The molds in this recipe can be prepared and refrigerated the day before they are to be served.

10. To unmold, run the tip of a small knife around each mold with an up-and-down motion. Place lettuce on a serving plate, invert mold over serving plate with a bang, then lift off mold.

• If a mold sticks set the bottom of it in warm water for 1 or 2 seconds, then try again.

11. Serve with cold cooked vegetables or Rice Salad (see p. 197). Pass mayonnaise (see p. 251) if you wish. *Makes 6 servings.*

EGG MOUSSE WITH CUCUMBER

This is good for luncheon, as an hors d'oeuvre, or as a first course.

1 tablespoon (1 envelope) unflavored gelatin
⅓ cup dry white wine
¾ cup mayonnaise (see p. 251)
1 tablespoon anchovy paste
½ cup grated onion
3 tablespoons chopped parsley
12 coarsely chopped hard-cooked eggs

1 cup medium Béchamel Sauce (see p. 245) at room temperature
1 cup heavy cream
3 to 4 drops Tabasco sauce
Vegetable oil to grease soufflé dish
1 cucumber

1. Soften gelatin by sprinkling it in wine. Set the container of gelatin and wine in a pan of hot water, and heat, stirring occasionally, over high heat, until gelatin is dissolved.

2. In a large bowl, mix together mayonnaise, anchovy paste, onion, and 2 tablespoons of the parsley. Add chopped eggs and fold together.

3. Mix dissolved gelatin into Béchamel Sauce and fold sauce into egg mixture.

4. Whip cream lightly, season it with Tabasco, then fold it into egg-sauce mixture. Taste for seasoning and add salt, if desired.

5. Pour mixture into a lightly oiled 6-cup soufflé dish and chill in refrigerator at least 2 hours.

• I usually do this much the day before I want to serve the mousse so that flavors have a chance to blend.

6. When set, unmold on a serving plate.

• To unmold, run a little knife around the edge of the mold with an up-and-down motion. Place serving dish over mold, invert, give a shake, and lift off mold.

7. Garnish the edge of the mold with cucumber ruffles made by slicing the cucumbers (with the skins on) into thin rounds, slitting each round from an outside edge to just beyond the center, then grasping the cut ends and twisting in opposite direction. Garnish the center of the mold with the remaining chopped parsley. *Makes 12 to 16 servings.*

Crêpes

No matter what goes inside of a crêpe, the result is an elegant one. The simplest dishes become party fare when they are wrapped in a crêpe and covered with a sauce. Crêpes can be made ahead and kept in a refrigerator or freezer, and with prepared crêpes on hand you are always ready for last-minute entertaining or for a lovely treat for the family.

Crêpes can be served at almost any time of the day and can be an appetizer, a main dish, or a dessert (for dessert crêpes, see pp. 204–207). And crêpes can be served flaming for an extra festive touch.

Try some of your favorite dishes wrapped in crêpes for new and exciting variations.

CRÊPES

This is the recipe to use when plain unsweetened crêpes are needed.

½ cup flour
¼ teaspoon salt
2 eggs
2 egg yolks

¼ cup vegetable oil, plus oil
to grease crêpe pan
½ cup milk

1. Make batter by putting all ingredients (except the oil to grease pan) into a blender jar or a bowl and either blending at top speed or whisking until smooth.

• If lumps or flour specks remain in the batter, strain it.

2. Put the batter into a refrigerator for at least 1 hour to give the flour granules time to swell and thus to make the resulting crêpes tenderer than they would otherwise be.

• When it is removed from the refrigerator the batter should be the consistency of heavy cream. If it is too thick, thin it with a little milk or water.

3. Fry crêpes 1 at a time in a seasoned 5- or 7-inch iron crêpe pan. Brush the pan lightly with a little oil (or film the pan with oil by wiping it with a folded paper towel dipped in oil), and place pan over high heat. When the oil is very hot (at the point of smoking), pour in a scant ¼ cup of batter, then quickly tilt the pan in all directions to coat the bottom with it. (The crêpe should be very thin. If there's too much batter —more than enough to coat the bottom of the pan—pour the excess back into the jar or bowl. The first crêpe will help you judge the amount of batter to use for subsequent ones.) Fry the crêpe about 1 minute, or until the edges brown and pull away from the sides of the pan, then turn the crêpe (use a spatula for the whole turn, or lift a corner of the crêpe with a spatula and use your fingers to flip over the rest) and fry the other side, which will not brown evenly (so this is the side to always roll or fold inward), for about 30 seconds. Brush the pan lightly with oil (or film it) again before frying the next crêpe.

• Crêpes can be frozen if they're stacked with plastic wrap or waxed paper between them, then either overwrapped tightly with plastic wrap or foil or sealed in a plastic bag. Defrost in a refrigerator, or in a 250° oven.

• To season a crêpe pan, fill it ¾ full of vegetable oil, heat the oil to the point of smoking, let it stand overnight in the pan, and in the morning, discard the oil and wipe out the pan with paper towels. Never wash the pan—just wipe it out with paper towels after each use. *Makes 8 7-inch or 12 5-inch crêpes.*

CRÊPES STUFFED WITH CHEESE SOUFFLÉ

6 tablespoons butter, plus
    butter to grease pan
3 tablespoons flour
¾ cup milk
3 to 4 drops Tabasco sauce
1½ cups grated Parmesan,
    Swiss, or Cheddar cheese

5 egg yolks
7 egg whites
¼ teaspoon cream of tartar
8 7-inch crêpes (see p. 158)

1. Make a roux by melting 3 tablespoons butter in saucepan, stirring in flour with a wooden spatula, and cooking over high heat, stirring, for about 2 minutes. Do not let it brown.

2. Remove pan from heat and add milk, whisking vigorously. Return pan to heat and bring to a boil, whisking constantly. Mixture will be very thick.

3. Remove from heat and stir in Tabasco sauce and 1 cup of the cheese.

• Any well-flavored cheese may be used. I prefer freshly grated imported Parmesan.

4. Beat in egg yolks. Mixture will be fairly stiff.

5. Beat egg whites until very stiff, adding the cream of tartar just after egg whites begin to foam.

• Egg whites are stiff if most of the mixture can be scooped onto the whisk or beater at one time or if, when the bowl is turned over, the mixture doesn't fall out.

6. Make soufflé mixture by stirring a spoonful of the beaten whites into the cheese mixture to lighten it, then, with a rubber spatula, lightly folding in the remaining whites.

7. Lay the 8 crêpes out on 2 generously buttered baking sheets or in buttered ramekins. Put a big spoonful of soufflé mixture on one half of each crêpe, then fold the other half over, but do not line up the edges— leave about ½ inch margin.

8. Sprinkle the top of each crêpe with 1 teaspoon of melted butter and 1 tablespoon of grated cheese.

9. Put baking sheets or ramekins into a preheated 375° oven and bake for 8 to 10 minutes, or until soufflés puff. Serve immediately, plain or with Hollandaise Sauce (see p. 246) or Mornay Sauce (see p. 245). **Makes 8 servings.**

SPINACH CRÊPES

2 *(10 oz.) packages frozen chopped spinach*
1 *recipe basic crêpe batter (see p. 158)*
1 *cup dairy sour cream*
¼ *teaspoon freshly grated nutmeg*
½ *teaspoon salt*
¼ *teaspoon freshly cracked black pepper*

1½ *cups finely diced prosciutto*
2 *tablespoons melted butter*
2 *cups Mornay Sauce (see p. 245)*
3 *beaten egg yolks, optional*
¼ *cup freshly grated Parmesan cheese*

1. Cook spinach in a covered pan over high heat just until thawed; do not add water. Drain and squeeze dry—press it in a sieve to release all moisture.

2. Add 2 tablespoons of the spinach to crêpe batter and fry crêpes as recipe directs, using a 7-inch pan. Stack crêpes on a plate until ready to fill.

3. To make filling: return remaining spinach to saucepan; add sour cream, nutmeg, salt, pepper, and prosciutto. Combine and cook over high heat 5 to 7 minutes or until heated through.

4. Butter an ovenproof serving dish. Put 2 tablespoons of spinach-prosciutto filling on the edge of each crêpe (on the undercooked, or second side), roll up and place seam side down in serving dish.

5. Make Mornay Sauce, enriching it if desired with 3 egg yolks. Spoon the sauce over the crêpes, sprinkle with cheese, and bake in a preheated 375° oven for 15 minutes or until bubbly. **Makes 8 servings.**

VEGETABLES
AND OTHER
ACCOMPANIMENTS

It's much easier to cook vegetables right than to ruin them. The key word is *simplicity*, for vegetables are at a peak of deliciousness when simply steamed or cooked in very little liquid, seasoned with salt and pepper, and dressed with melted butter. And there are other easy ways with vegetables. Try, for example, Sautéed Cherry Tomatoes (see p. 189), Minted Cucumbers (see p. 174), Seven-Minute Green Beans (see p. 164), Whipped Carrots (see p. 170), or Pea Purée (see p. 182). All are perfect!

While admittedly a convenience, frozen vegetables never have the exquisite flavor of those just gathered from the earth. Americans are fortunate to be living in a land that supplies such a bountiful variety the whole year around. But few Americans seem to know that for the best flavor, vegetables should be picked just after ripening when they are as small as possible. Prizes are often awarded gardeners for gargantuan green beans or peas the size of cannonballs; my prizes go to the growers of matchstick green beans and minuscule peas.

A well-balanced meal should include at least one vegetable or a green leafy salad. Certain vegetables—artichokes and asparagus, for example, and all vegetable soufflés—deserve to be served as a separate course. Individual serving plates designed for these elite vegetables are very nice to own.

Many other vegetables go hand in hand with some particular main dish: imagine poached fish without its parslied potato or a fine steak or roast without a perfectly baked potato. Vegetables can be wonderful!

ARTICHOKES WITH VINAIGRETTE SAUCE

6 large artichokes   *Vinaigrette Sauce (see p. 252)*
2 tablespoons salt

1. Break off stems and trim bases—remove the few short outer leaves around them—so that artichokes stand evenly. With scissors, cut the tips off the leaves, and with a knife, cut ½ inch off the very top of each artichoke.

2. Put the artichokes in a large kettle and cover them with water— enough so they swim around. Add salt, bring to a boil, uncovered, and boil 25 to 35 minutes, or until done.

• The time will depend on the size of the artichokes. To test, pull out a leaf: if it comes easily, the artichoke is done.

3. Turn artichokes upside down to drain. When they are cool enough to handle, spread the leaves apart so that the little center cone of leaves can be pulled out with your fingers. Below this cone is the fuzzy choke. Use a spoon to scrape out all the fuzz, exposing the meaty artichoke bottom.

4. If desired, Vinaigrette Sauce can be poured into the hollowed-out centers, or the sauce can be served in little cups alongside the artichokes.

• Instead of Vinaigrette, Hollandaise Sauce (see p. 246) can be served. **Makes 6 servings.**

ASPARAGUS HOLLANDAISE

For this recipe, try to choose a bunch of asparagus with all spears about the same thickness.

1 2- to 2½-lb. bunch asparagus   *Hollandaise Sauce (see p. 246)*
1 teaspoon salt

1. Cut off ½ inch from the hard white end of each asparagus spear. Peel the spears with a vegetable peeler, ¾ of the way up to the tip.

• This helps the spears to cook in about the same time as the tender tips; it also removes any dirt hiding under the scales.

2. Lay the spears in a skillet and add cold water to ⅔ its depth. Add salt. Do not cover. Bring to a boil and boil 10 to 20 minutes until bases of stalks are tender when tested with a fork. (The time will depend on the thickness of the spears.) Drain well.

3. Serve asparagus as a separate course, putting 4 to 5 spears on each plate. Sprinkle with salt and pepper to taste and serve with Hollandaise Sauce.

• Or serve asparagus spears cool, but not cold, with Vinaigrette Sauce (see p. 252). ***Makes 4 to 6 servings.***

SEVEN-MINUTE GREEN BEANS

1½ lbs. green beans	½ teaspoon freshly cracked
4 teaspoons salt	black pepper
2 tablespoons lemon juice	¼ cup melted butter

1. Top and tail the beans, wash them, and put them into a large saucepan with 2 quarts of water and 1 tablespoon of salt.

2. Bring to a rolling boil, reduce heat to simmer, and cook for 7 minutes only, uncovered. (The beans lose their bright color when covered during cooking.)

3. Drain beans and plunge them immediately into cold water to refresh and set their color.

• This can be done in the morning and the beans refrigerated until dinner.

4. Return beans to the saucepan, add lemon juice, the remaining 1 teaspoon of salt, pepper, and melted butter, and shake over high heat until the beans are warmed—about 5 minutes. ***Makes 6 servings.***

GÂTEAU DE HARICOTS VERTS

1 lb. very finely minced mushrooms	2 lbs. whole green beans or 3 10-oz. pkgs. frozen whole
1 cup minced yellow onion	green beans
¼ cup butter	4 beaten eggs

1 cup grated Gruyère cheese
¼ cup bread crumbs (see p. 7)
1 teaspoon salt
½ teaspoon freshly cracked
   black pepper

¼ teaspoon freshly grated
   nutmeg
1 cup Lemon Butter (see
   p. 253)

1. Sauté mushrooms and onion in foaming butter over high heat until mushrooms are dry. Set aside.

• Before sautéing the mushrooms, put them, a handful at a time, in the corner of a tea towel and wring them out. Not absolutely necessary, but it helps get rid of excess moisture.

2. Cook fresh beans in a small amount of boiling water for 7 minutes, or cook frozen beans according to the package directions, but for just half the recommended time.

3. Drain beans and mix with onion and mushrooms in a big bowl.

4. Add beaten eggs, cheese, bread crumbs, salt, pepper, and nutmeg, then pack the mixture into an oiled 10-inch ring mold or a kugelhof mold.

5. Stand the mold in a pan of boiling water, put it in a preheated 350° oven, and bake for ½ hour.

• If dinner is delayed, the mold can remain in the water bath, in a 200° oven, for about ½ hour longer.
• The mold can be baked ahead, refrigerated overnight, then brought to room temperature and reheated in the water bath in a preheated 350° oven. Reheating will take 10 minutes.

6. Remove mold from water bath, let it stand 5 minutes, then run a knife around the edge to loosen it, invert it on a platter, and shake to unmold.

7. Serve with hot Lemon Butter. **Makes 12 to 16 servings.**

FLAGEOLETS

Flageolets are green kidney beans from France. Since they are quite bland, the little beans, which are especially good with Rack of Lamb (see p. 104), need the chopped garlic for flavor.

1 box (about 2 cups) dried or
   1 large can flageolets
1 quart chicken stock (see
   p. 241)
2 tablespoons lamb drippings
   or melted butter

1 medium clove chopped
   garlic
½ teaspoon salt
¼ teaspoon freshly cracked
   black or white pepper
1 tablespoon chopped parsley

1. Soak dried beans overnight in enough cold water to cover.
2. Drain beans and put them in a saucepan with chicken stock.
3. Bring to a boil, cover pan, reduce heat to simmer, and cook until beans are tender, about 1 hour.
4. Drain beans and toss them in lamb drippings, or butter, flavored with the chopped garlic. Season with salt and pepper and garnish with chopped parsley.

• If canned beans are used, drain and rinse them, place in saucepan with drippings or butter and garlic and cook over medium heat 5 to 10 minutes or until heated through. *Makes 6 servings.*

SOISSONS

Almost any kind of dried bean can be used in this recipe, but I prefer the small dried pea bean. I like to serve this with Braised Boned Leg of Lamb (see p. 107).

1 lb. dried pea beans
1 to 1½ quarts light chicken stock (p. 241)
1 teaspoon salt
½ teaspoon freshly cracked black pepper

¼ cup braising liquid from lamb or other meat, optional
2 tablespoons chopped parsley

1. Put beans in enough cold water to cover and either soak them overnight or bring the water to a boil, boil 2 minutes, cover the pan, and let the beans soak 1 hour; but, first, read the package directions, since these days some dried beans are presoaked, hence quicker to prepare.
2. Drain beans, cover with chicken stock, and bring to a boil. Cover the pan and turn heat down to simmer. Cook until the beans are tender and all the stock is absorbed. This should take about 1 hour, but it's difficult to give an exact cooking time for beans: sometimes they'll take only 20 minutes, but in hard water, they may never get tender—unless a pinch of baking soda is added. Start testing the beans, by pressing one between your thumb and forefinger, after 20 minutes of cooking, and watch them closely if soda has been added.
3. Before serving, season the beans with salt and pepper and moisten them with a little braising liquid if available. Garnish with chopped parsley.

• Soissons may be cooked the day before or in the morning. Undercook them if they're to be reheated.
• To keep beans warm without additional cooking, stand them in a pan of warm water. *Makes 8 servings.*

Braised Brussels Sprouts

1 quart Brussels sprouts, the   *½ cup butter*
   smallest available   *½ teaspoon freshly cracked*
1 teaspoon salt, plus salt to   *black pepper*
   clean sprouts   *¼ cup lemon juice*

1. Trim wilted leaves from the Brussels sprouts and trim around the bases—but not too deeply, or the sprouts will fall apart.
2. Let the sprouts soak for a few minutes in a bowl of salted water.

• Sometimes there are tiny bugs in Brussels sprouts. Salted water draws them out.

3. Drain the sprouts and put them in a heavy casserole—one with a tight-fitting lid. Lay butter on the sprouts, sprinkle with 1 teaspoon salt, pepper, and lemon juice, cover, and place in a preheated 350° oven to braise for 25 to 35 minutes, or until barely tender. Every 10 minutes remove cover and stir the sprouts to be sure they don't stick.

• They will cook in the butter juice, and the small amount of moisture clinging to them. Neither water nor broth is needed. But do keep an eye on them, lest they scorch.
• Baby onions and turnips can be cooked the same way; sprinkle them with 1 teaspoon of sugar when adding the salt, pepper, and lemon juice. **Makes 6 servings.**

Broccoli Soufflé

2 10-oz. pkgs. frozen broccoli   *¼ teaspoon cayenne pepper*
¼ cup butter   *¼ teaspoon freshly grated*
¼ cup flour   *nutmeg*
2 cups milk   *6 beaten egg yolks*
½ cup grated Parmesan cheese   *8 egg whites*
½ teaspoon salt   *¼ teaspoon cream of tartar*

1. Cook broccoli according to package directions. Drain and purée in a blender or through a food mill, using the medium disk.
2. Melt butter in a saucepan, stir in flour, and cook over high heat, stirring with a wooden spatula, for 2 minutes.
3. Remove from heat, add milk and whisk vigorously.
4. Return to high heat and cook until thick and smooth, stirring with a whisk.

5. Stir in cheese, salt, cayenne pepper, and nutmeg; then remove from heat.

6. Stir a little of the hot mixture into the egg yolks to warm them, then stir the warmed yolks into the saucepan, return pan to heat, and cook 1 minute more, but do not boil (or mixture will curdle).

7. Stir in broccoli purée and set aside.

• The soufflé may be made ahead up to this point and stored in a refrigerator several hours.

8. Beat egg whites and cream of tartar until very stiff.

• Egg whites are stiff when most of them can be scooped onto the beater at one time.

9. Put the broccoli mixture in a large bowl, add about ⅓ of the egg whites and fold in well to lighten the mixture, then lightly and quickly fold in the rest of the egg whites.

• Don't overmix when folding in egg whites. It's better to leave little fluffs of white showing than to risk the soufflé's not rising properly.

10. Pour the mixture into an unbuttered 8-cup soufflé dish and bake 45 minutes in a preheated 350° oven. Serve at once—soufflés wait for no one. *Makes 6 to 8 servings.*

CABBAGE STUFFED WITH CABBAGE

Green, white, or red cabbage can be used. The red is especially good with game or pork. As a change, add meat—about ¾ cup of chopped ham or sausage meat, or ground beef—to the stuffing. Little new potatoes boiled in the water with the cabbage are delicious.

1 medium-size (1½- to 2-lb.) cabbage
¾ cup butter
½ cup finely chopped onion
¼ cup fine bread crumbs (see p. 7)
4 teaspoons salt
½ teaspoon freshly cracked white pepper
¼ teaspoon freshly grated nutmeg
3 tablespoons chopped parsley
2 lightly beaten eggs
2 tablespoons lemon juice

1. Remove and discard damaged leaves from cabbage, then peel off 5 or 6 leaves, keeping them as perfect as possible.

• The trick here is to cut the leaves loose at the base to release them. If the cabbage head is firm, run it under warm water to loosen the leaves.

2. Line a 2-quart bowl with a cloth at least 12 inches square and place the 5 or 6 leaves, stem ends up, in it, overlapping them to form a cup or nest.

3. Remove the core from the remaining cabbage and chop the cabbage very fine.

4. Melt ¼ cup of butter in a large skillet and sauté cabbage with chopped onion over high heat for about 15 minutes, or until cabbage is limp. Do not let it brown.

5. Put the sautéed cabbage and onion into a bowl and add bread crumbs, 1 teaspoon salt, pepper, nutmeg, 2 tablespoons of parsley, and the beaten eggs.

• The cabbage will be hot, so stir the eggs in quickly to avoid curdling.

6. Stuff the mixture into the cloth lined with cabbage leaves and twist the cloth very tight. Tie with a string, leaving a long end with which to pull the cabbage out of the water.

7. Drop the tied cloth into a large kettle of boiling salted—about 1 tablespoon of salt—water, reduce heat, and simmer, uncovered, for 1 hour. Turn once during cooking.

• The cabbage can be prepared ahead by tying it and cooking it for 45 minutes, then setting it aside, for up to 3 hours, then reheating it by simmering for the remaining 15 minutes in water that has been first brought to a boil.

8. Drain the cloth in a large strainer. Untie it and turn the cabbage out on a serving dish.

9. Make sauce by melting the remaining ½ cup of butter and adding the remaining 1 tablespoon of parsley and the lemon juice.

10. Pour sauce over cabbage. Cut in pie-shaped wedges to serve. *Makes 6 servings.*

CARROTS VICHY

10 *peeled carrots*
½ *cup melted butter*
2 *teaspoons sugar*
1 *teaspoon salt*
½ *teaspoon freshly cracked*
  white pepper

2 *tablespoons finely chopped*
  parsley
1 *tablespoon finely chopped*
  mint, optional

1. Cut carrots into very thin slices, using a vegetable cutter or *mandoline*.

2. Put the slices into a pan with ¼ cup of the butter, 2 tablespoons of cold water, sugar, salt, and pepper. Cover with foil, pressing it right down on the carrots, and put the lid on the pan.

3. Place the pan over moderately high heat, and shaking it occasionally, cook about 20 minutes, or until carrots (which will cook in their own juices) are tender.

4. Place carrots in a serving bowl, add the remaining ¼ cup of butter, and sprinkle with parsley, and if desired, with mint. *Makes 6 to 8 servings.*

WHIPPED CARROTS

12 *peeled carrots*
1 *teaspoon salt*
3 *tablespoons butter*
1 *teaspoon lemon juice*
¼ *teaspoon freshly grated*
  nutmeg

¼ *teaspoon freshly cracked*
  white pepper
2 *tablespoons chopped parsley*

1. Cut carrots in half crosswise and put them in a saucepan with enough water to cover generously.

2. Add salt, bring to a boil, cover, reduce heat, and simmer about 10 minutes, or until carrots are tender.

3. Drain carrots and purée them through a ricer or food mill or beat them in an electric mixer.

4. Beat in butter, lemon juice, nutmeg, and pepper.

5. Taste for seasoning and add more salt if desired. Garnish with chopped parsley. *Makes 8 servings.*

CARROT RING

This carrot custard can be prepared ahead of time to the point of baking. Or it can be underbaked prior to dinner, left to stand in warm water for 1 hour and then reheated. Or it can be baked, unmolded, and reheated in a 250° oven—if you do this, I'd recommend serving the ring with piping hot Lemon Butter (see p. 253).

5 *cups peeled and grated raw carrots*
2 *teaspoons salt*
4 *well-beaten eggs*
1½ *cups light cream*
½ *teaspoon freshly cracked white pepper*
1 *teaspoon sugar*

1 *tablespoon lemon juice*
½ *cup blanched shredded almonds*
¼ *cup bread crumbs (see p. 7)*
Vegetable oil to grease mold
1 *lb. fluted and sautéed mushrooms (see p. 11)*

1. Boil carrots in water with 1 teaspoon of salt added for 5 minutes. Drain and put in a bowl.
2. Add the remaining ingredients, except mushrooms (and oil), and mix together.
3. Pour mixture into an oiled 9-inch ring mold, set in a pan of hot water and bake in a preheated 350° oven for 1 hour, or until mixture starts to shrink from the sides of the mold.
4. Let stand for 5 minutes. Turn out on a serving platter. Fill the center of the ring with mushrooms. *Makes 8 to 10 servings.*

CAULIFLOWER MOUSSE

This is good to serve with any kind of roast.

2 *lbs. (2 average-size heads) cauliflower*
1 *tablespoon salt*
⅛ *teaspoon cayenne pepper*
¼ *teaspoon freshly grated nutmeg*
1 *cup medium Béchamel Sauce (see p. 245)*

6 *eggs*
Butter to grease soufflé dish
2 *tablespoons bread crumbs (see p. 7)*
2 *tablespoons chopped parsley*

1. Trim leafy stalks from cauliflower and cut heads into large pieces.
2. Put cauliflower in a saucepan with 1 tablespoon of salt and enough water to cover, and cook over high heat until tender. Drain.

3. Add cayenne pepper and nutmeg to cauliflower and purée through a food mill, using the finest disk. Do not put it in a blender.

• Catch the purée in a large bowl. By the time sauce and egg are mixed in, you will see why.

4. Mix the sauce into the cauliflower purée.

5. Beat eggs just enough to mix them (they should not be frothy), then fold them into the cauliflower mixture.

6. Taste for salt, and if desired, add some.

• For a flavor change, add ½ cup of grated Parmesan cheese or 2 tablespoons of chopped chives.

7. Pour mixture into a buttered 6- to 8-cup soufflé dish that has been dusted with bread crumbs.

8. Set the dish in a pan of hot water and bake it in a preheated 350° oven for 45 to 55 minutes, or until the mousse begins to pull away from the edge of the dish (or until a knife inserted in the mousse comes out clean).

• The water bath keeps the mousse creamy and smooth in texture. It is the equivalent of a double boiler that is used to cook a sauce over hot water.
• The mousse will continue to cook after it's taken out of the oven. If overcooked, it will tend to separate and become watery.

9. Bring the soufflé dish to the table to serve or unmold the mousse onto a platter. Garnish with parsley sprinkled around the edge and in the center.

• Serve plain or with Mornay Sauce (see p. 245) or Beurre Noir (see p. 253). *Makes 8 to 10 servings.*

CELERY STICKS

1 large bunch celery	*½ teaspoon salt*
2 cups chicken stock (see p. 241)	*¼ teaspoon freshly cracked white pepper*
1 medium cored green pepper	*1 tablespoon chopped parsley*
½ cup butter	

1. Remove leaves from celery and cut the ribs into sticks 2½ inches long and ¼ inch wide. Tie the sticks into bundles—about 10 to a bundle —with string.

2. Put bundles into a saucepan, add stock, and bring to a boil, then cover, reduce heat, and simmer 12 to 15 minutes, or until celery is tender-crisp.

3. Remove from heat and drain.

4. Circle the bundles with ¼-inch-thick pepper rings—or top the bundles with half circles of pepper—that have been put in a saucepan of cold water, brought to a boil, boiled 1 minute, then drained and plunged immediately into cold water to set their color. Then arrange the bundles in a serving dish and remove the strings.

5. Heat butter in a small skillet until brown but not burned.

6. Season celery with salt and pepper, pour the Beurre Noir on top, and sprinkle with chopped parsley.

• If the celery sticks are prepared in advance, arrange them in an oven-proof serving dish, and before serving, pour the hot butter over them and put them in a preheated 350° oven for 5 minutes to heat through. *Makes 8 servings.*

CHESTNUT PURÉE

2 lbs. fresh chestnuts	½ teaspoon freshly cracked
2½ cups beef stock (see p. 240)	black pepper
1 teaspoon salt	3 tablespoons butter

1. Put the chestnuts in a saucepan, cover them with water, and bring to a boil. Remove the chestnuts from the pan 2 or 3 at a time, peel with a small sharp knife, and remove the inner brown skins.

• If the peel on any nut is especially stubborn, return the nut to boiling water for a few seconds—no chestnut is easy to peel, but warm ones seem a bit easier. A special chestnut knife helps cut through the shell.

2. Simmer nuts in beef stock about ½ hour, or until tender. When nuts are tender a knife blade should go in easily.

3. Purée the nuts through a ricer or through a food mill, using the medium disk.

4. Add salt, pepper, and butter and beat until smooth. The consistency should be suitable for piping through a pastry bag, to make rosettes.

• Use purée to garnish ducks or squabs. *Makes 6 to 8 servings.*

CHESTNUT CROQUETTES

1 16-oz. can unsweetened chestnut purée or 1 recipe chestnut purée (see above)	½ teaspoon salt
	¼ teaspoon freshly cracked black pepper
2 tablespoons chopped shal-lots	1 tablespoon dry Madeira or dry sherry
2 tablespoons butter	3 beaten eggs

¾ *cup ground almonds, about*   ¾ *cup bread crumbs (see*
½ *cup flour*   *p. 7)*
1 *tablespoon vegetable oil*   2 *cups vegetable shortening*

1. Put chestnut purée in a mixer bowl and beat until creamy.

2. Sauté shallots in butter until transparent; do not let them take on color.

3. Add sautéed shallots, salt, pepper, Madeira, and 1 beaten egg to the chestnut purée.

4. Taste and add more salt if desired.

5. Beat in ¾ cup of ground almonds and chill for ½ hour. If mixture seems too thin to shape, add more ground almonds.

6. Form mixture into cork-shaped croquettes about 2 inches long and roll in flour, shaking off the excess.

7. Dip the croquettes into a mixture of 2 beaten eggs and oil, then roll them in bread crumbs. Chill ½ hour.

8. Heat vegetable shortening to 375° in a heavy saucepan or an electric skillet and fry croquettes, 2 at a time, until brown and crisp. Drain on paper towels.

• Chestnut Croquettes may be fried in the morning, refrigerated and reheated. To reheat: set cake racks on a baking sheet, cover with two layers of brown paper, and lay the croquettes on the paper, and place in a preheated 350° oven for a few minutes. *Makes 8 servings.*

Minted Cucumbers

6 *large peeled cucumbers*   1 *tablespoon chopped fresh*
¼ *cup butter*   *mint, or 1 teaspoon dried*
1 *teaspoon salt*   *mint*
½ *teaspoon freshly cracked*
   white pepper

1. Cut ends off cucumbers, cut them in half lengthwise, and scoop out the seeds with the tip of a spoon. Cut the halves crosswise into pieces 1 inch long.

2. Put the pieces in a pan, cover with water, bring to a rolling boil, and boil for 1 minute. (This parboiling takes away any bitterness.)

3. Drain the cucumber pieces, run cold water on them, and return them to the pan. Add butter, salt, pepper, and mint.

4. Cover with foil, pressing it down on the cucumber pieces, then put the lid on the pan and cook the cucumber pieces in their own juice over moderately high heat for 8 minutes. Shake the pan frequently.

• Instead of mint, 1 tablespoon of chopped parsley or chopped fresh dill can be used. The dill is especially good when cucumbers are served with fish. ***Makes 6 to 8 servings.***

BRAISED BELGIAN ENDIVE

12 *heads Belgian endive*	1 *teaspoon sugar*
1 *tablespoon salt*	½ *teaspoon freshly cracked*
1 *slice bread*	*white pepper*
½ *cup butter*	

1. Wash endive. Trim around the root of each head, but do not detach the leaves. Remove any brown or wilted leaves.

2. Put the endive in a saucepan and add 3 to 4 cups of water. Add 2 teaspoons of salt, bring to a boil, and lay the slice of bread, crust and all, in the water. (The bread will take away some of the bitter flavor of the endive.) Boil for 7 minutes.

3. Melt ¼ cup of butter in a sauté pan—one with a tight-fitting lid.

4. Drain the heads of endive and put them into the butter with the water that clings to them.

5. Top with the remaining ¼ cup of butter and sprinkle with sugar, pepper, and the remaining 1 teaspoon of salt.

6. Cover the pan and shake it back and forth over high heat until the endive is golden on all sides. This will take about 20 minutes. Endive should be barely tender. ***Makes 6 servings.***

BRAISED BOSTON LETTUCE

5 *heads Boston lettuce*	1 *teaspoon salt*
2 *tablespoons butter, about*	½ *teaspoon freshly cracked*
¼ *lb. thickly sliced bacon*	*white pepper*
¾ *cup finely chopped onion*	2 *tablespoons chopped pars-*
½ *cup chicken stock (see*	*ley*
p. 241)	

1. Remove any damaged or loose outer leaves from the lettuce, then cut the heads in half, wash them, and shake off excess moisture.

2. Butter a large oval ovenproof dish—use about 2 tablespoons of butter—and arrange the lettuce in the dish, cut sides down.

3. Dice the bacon and sprinkle it over the dish, pushing some pieces underneath the lettuce halves.

4. Sprinkle with onion, pour on chicken stock, and season with salt and

pepper, then cover the dish with a piece of foil and set it in a preheated 350° oven for 1 hour.

5. Remove the dish from the oven and if there is too much liquid in the dish, pour it into a saucepan and boil rapidly to reduce it, then pour it back over the lettuce.

6. Before serving, sprinkle with chopped parsley. **Makes 10 servings.**

Sautéed Mushroom Caps and Pine Nuts

1½ lbs. mushrooms	½ cup pine nuts
2 teaspoons lemon juice, plus lemon juice to clean mushrooms	½ teaspoon salt
	¼ teaspoon freshly cracked white pepper
¼ cup butter	

1. Wipe mushrooms with a paper towel dipped in acidulated water (1 quart of water with 1 tablespoon lemon juice) to clean them. Wipe them dry and trim off stems.

2. Heat butter in a large skillet, and when foaming subsides, add pine nuts and sauté them over high heat until lightly browned.

3. Add mushrooms, salt, pepper, and 2 teaspoons lemon juice. Shake the pan, tossing the mushrooms over high heat, for 3 minutes. Serve immediately. **Makes 8 servings.**

Mushroom Roll

Serve this hot, with Hollandaise Sauce (see p. 246) or hot melted butter; or serve it cold, without a sauce.

Vegetable oil to grease pan and baking paper	¼ teaspoon freshly cracked white pepper
1½ lbs. very finely chopped mushrooms	2 tablespoons lemon juice
6 separated eggs	4 or 5 fluted and sautéed mushrooms (see p. 11)
½ cup melted butter	2 tablespoons chopped parsley
½ teaspoon salt	

1. Brush a jelly-roll pan with vegetable oil, then line it with waxed paper, letting the paper extend 4 inches on each end. Brush the paper with vegetable oil and set aside.

2. Put the chopped mushrooms in the corner of a tea towel, a handful at a time, wring them out to remove excess moisture, and put them in a bowl.

3. Beat egg yolks until fluffy. Add them, the melted butter, salt, pepper, and lemon juice to the mushrooms.

• Good flavor change: add 1 tablespoon chopped fresh tarragon, rosemary, or parsley to the mushroom mixture.

4. Beat egg whites until they form soft peaks and fold them into the mushroom mixture.

5. Pour the mixture into the prepared pan, spread it evenly, and bake in a preheated 350° oven for 15 minutes, or until the mixture starts to pull away from the sides of the pan.

6. Turn the mixture out of the pan onto 2 overlapping sheets of waxed paper, and with the paper to help, roll it up like a jelly roll.

• For a cool summer luncheon, roll it up with a crab-meat-and-sour-cream mixture inside (1 lb. crab meat mixed with 1 cup sour cream).

• The roll can be made in advance, then reheated, but it's better when it's fresh. If it's made ahead, place it in a preheated 300° oven for 10 minutes to warm it, and before serving, pour ½ cup of sizzling hot melted butter over the top.

7. Place the roll on a long narrow platter or board, garnish it with mushroom caps placed down the center, and sprinkle it with parsley. *Makes 8 to 10 servings.*

Mushroom Soufflé

Should you butter a soufflé dish or not? We have found in our Creative Cooking classes that the soufflé climbs higher when the dish is not buttered. If you like a soufflé that's a bit crusty around the edges, bake this one as directed. If you prefer one that's tender, set the soufflé dish—use a 6-cup one or a 4-cup one with a paper collar tied around it—in a pan of hot water during baking.

1 lb. finely chopped mush-   ½ teaspoon salt
  rooms   ¼ teaspoon freshly cracked
6 tablespoons butter   black pepper
1 cup finely chopped onion   ¼ teaspoon freshly grated
2 tablespoons flour   nutmeg
½ cup chicken stock (see   4 beaten egg yolks
  p. 241)   6 egg whites
½ cup light cream

1. When mushrooms are chopped as finely as possible, squeeze out the excess juice by wringing them, a handful at a time, in the corner of a tea towel.

• There's a lot of moisture in mushrooms, and for this recipe it should be removed so the soufflé doesn't take too long to bake.

2. Melt ¼ cup of butter in a skillet, and when it is hot and foaming, add mushrooms and onion. Cook over high heat, stirring constantly with a wooden spatula, for about 15 minutes, or until mixture looks dry. Set aside.

3. Melt the remaining 2 tablespoons of butter in a small saucepan, stir in flour with a wooden spatula, and after it is blended in, continue stirring over high heat for 2 minutes.

4. Remove pan from heat and whisk in chicken stock and cream.

5. Return to high heat and cook, whisking constantly, until mixture begins to thicken.

6. Season with salt, pepper, and nutmeg.

7. Stir some of the hot mixture into the beaten egg yolks to warm them gradually, then stir the warmed yolks into the pan, cook over medium heat 1 minute more—but do not boil, or egg yolks will curdle—and set aside to cool slightly.

8. Beat egg whites until very stiff.

• Egg whites are stiff when most of them can be scooped onto the beater or whisk at one time.

9. Combine mushroom-onion mixture and contents of the saucepan in a large bowl and add about ⅓ of the egg whites. Fold whites in well to lighten the mixture, then lightly and quickly fold in the rest of the egg whites.

• It's better to leave little fluffs of egg white showing than to overmix and risk the soufflé not rising properly. It is the air bubbles beaten into the egg whites that make the soufflé rise.

10. Pour mixture into a soufflé dish (6-cup size or 4-cup size with a paper collar attached), put in a preheated 375° oven and bake 25 minutes

for a moist soufflé, 30 to 35 minutes for a drier one. As soon as the soufflé is taken from the oven, serve it—soufflés won't wait. *Makes 4 to 6 servings.*

Stuffed Mushrooms

Serve these as appetizers or as an accompaniment to meat. Either way, they're very good.

1 lb. large white mushrooms	*½ teaspoon salt*
Lemon juice to clean mushrooms	*¼ teaspoon freshly cracked black pepper*
¼ cup bread crumbs (see p. 7)	*1 to 2 tablespoons cognac*
	¼ lb. sliced bacon
1 tablespoon chopped shallots	*1 tablespoon melted butter*

1. Wipe mushrooms with a damp cloth or paper towel wrung out in acidulated water (water with a little lemon juice in it), then remove and chop the stems and set the caps aside.

2. Put the chopped stems in a bowl with an equal amount of freshly made bread crumbs, then add shallots, salt, pepper, and enough cognac to moisten.

3. Partly cook the bacon, drain it on paper towels, chop it into little pieces. Combine bacon with the crumb mixture, and pack this stuffing into the cavities of the mushroom caps.

4. Sprinkle the caps with melted butter, place them on a baking sheet, and put in a preheated 350° oven to bake for about 15 minutes, or until stuffing is nicely browned. *Makes 6 servings.*

Noodle Nests

To make noodle nests, which can be filled with peas (or any other vegetable) and served as the accompaniment for a roast, a wire "bird's nest" basket is necessary. It's a French utensil (imported by gourmet shops and mail order houses) that consists of two bowllike baskets, one larger than the other, with long handles. The baskets clamp together, and the noodles are held between them for deep frying.

1 8-oz. pkg. very fine noodles	*4 cups vegetable shortening*

1. Cook the noodles in 3 quarts of boiling water for 3 minutes only (they should be undercooked for frying), then drain them in a colander, rinse them with cold water, and spread them on paper towels to dry thoroughly.

2. In a deep saucepan, heat shortening to 375°.

• Check the temperature either with a fat thermometer or by dropping a bread cube into the fat: if the cube browns nicely in 1 minute, the fat is the right temperature.

3. Heat a "bird's nest" basket in the fat. Put about ⅙ of the noodles into the bottom part—be careful, for the basket will be very hot when removed from the fat—clamp on the top to shape the nest, and put the basket back into hot fat for 5 minutes, or until the noodles turn brown; then unclamp the top part of the basket, let the noodle nest cool for a few seconds, and turn it out.

4. Proceed as above with the remaining noodles. *Makes 6 servings.*

ITALIAN GNOCCHI

2 *cups milk*	2 *teaspoons Dijon mustard*
2 *teaspoons salt*	¾ *cup grated Parmesan cheese*
¾ *cup semolina*	6 *tablespoons butter*
½ *teaspoon freshly cracked white pepper*	

1. Put milk, salt, and 2 cups of water into a saucepan and bring to a boil. Slowly add semolina, stirring all the while with a wooden spatula (to prevent lumping). Continue stirring and cooking over high heat until the mixture pulls away from the sides of the pan.

2. Stir in pepper, mustard, ½ cup of grated cheese, and ¼ cup of butter.

3. Rinse a baking sheet with water and spread the mixture—it should form a layer about ½ inch thick—on the wet sheet. Chill it in a refrigerator ½ hour.

4. With a knife or a cookie cutter, cut the chilled mixture into diamonds, crescents—whatever shape or shapes you wish.

5. Overlap the cut pieces in an au gratin dish or an ovenproof baking dish, drizzle them with 2 tablespoons of melted butter and sprinkle with the remaining ¼ cup of cheese.

• This much can be done ahead, and the mixture stored in a refrigerator, ready for heating.

6. Before serving, put the dish under a broiler until the pieces are brown and bubbly—5 to 10 minutes—or set it in a preheated 250° oven for 10 to 15 minutes (the gnocchi can be held in a low oven for a little while longer if dinner is delayed), then brown the pieces under a broiler. *Makes 6 servings.*

SPAETZLE

Spaetzle are little dumplings that go perfectly with Hungarian Chicken Paprika (see p. 137) and Hungarian Goulash (see p. 91). They can be shaped in a spaetzle machine which looks like a food mill with holes the size of half a dime, or the dough can be pressed through a colander or cut into tiny pieces with a knife.

2 eggs	*½ cup melted butter*
4 teaspoons salt	*¼ teaspoon freshly cracked*
2¼ cups flour	*black pepper*
⅔ cup milk	

1. Beat eggs in a bowl with a fork. Add ½ teaspoon salt, flour, a little at a time, and mix together.
2. Add milk, beating it in with a wooden spatula or an electric mixer.
3. The dough will be soft. Let it rest for about ½ hour.
4. Bring 2 quarts of water and 1 tablespoon of salt to a boil in a saucepan.
5. Put the dough into a spaetzle machine or press it through a colander with large holes, hold it over the boiling water, and tipping or shaking the pan just enough to keep the water moving (this helps to keep the spaetzle from sticking together), drop little bits of dough into the water by turning the handle of the machine or by pressing the dough through the colander with a wooden spatula, or cut the dough in tiny pieces with a knife and drop the pieces into the boiling water.
6. Boil spaetzle until they rise to the surface. This will take 3 to 4 minutes.
7. Before serving, drain spaetzle in a colander, put them in a warm serving dish, and toss with melted butter, pepper, and ½ teaspoon salt.

• Another serving idea: sauté the cooked spaetzle in butter and sprinkle with bread crumbs (see p. 7) before serving. **Makes 6 servings.**

ONIONS À LA GRECQUE

These can be served as a relish with ham or tongue. Or they are delicious as appetizers, served either hot or at room temperature. Don't serve them cold.

36 small white onions
¼ cup olive oil
⅔ cup dry white wine
1 teaspoon sugar
1 teaspoon salt
1 sprig fennel, if available

½ teaspoon dried thyme
1 bay leaf
½ teaspoon saffron
1 cup white raisins or currants

1. Peel the onions, then with the point of a knife, cut a little cross in the root end of each (this will help keep the onion in shape).

• The easiest way to peel small onions is by dropping them into boiling water for 30 seconds, draining them, then slipping off the skins.

2. Put the onions into a sauté pan along with the olive oil and wine, ½ cup of water, and the sugar, salt, fennel, thyme, and bay leaf. Bring to a boil, cover, then reduce heat and simmer until the onions are barely tender—the time, depending on the size of the onions, can be as little as 10 minutes or up to ½ hour.

3. Remove lid and discard bay leaf and fennel, add saffron and white raisins or currants, and toss onions around in the pan. If there is a surfeit of pan sauce, remove the onions, boil the sauce to reduce it, then return the onions. *Makes 6 servings.*

PEA PURÉE

Most lovely light, delicate pea purées one gets in fine restaurants are made in commercial blenders. This recipe comes as close as is possible.

2 10-oz. pkgs. frozen peas
1 teaspoon salt
1 teaspoon sugar

1 tablespoon melted butter
2 tablespoons heavy cream or
 dairy sour cream, optional

1. Put peas in a saucepan with ¼ cup of water, salt, and sugar. Cover and bring to a boil. Boil for 3 to 4 minutes.

2. Drain peas well, and either purée them through a food mill, using the medium disk, then whip in melted butter, or for additional flavor, put them in a blender with the melted butter and heavy or sour cream and blend until smooth.

• Another way to give the peas more flavor is by puréeing them, then adding, instead of the melted butter, ½ teaspoon of salt, 1 tablespoon of sour or whipped cream, and a brown roux made by melting 3 tablespoons of butter in a small saucepan, stirring in 3 tablespoons of flour, and cooking over high heat, stirring constantly with a wooden spatula, until the mixture is brown (this takes at least 5 minutes).

• Still another way: purée peas, then, instead of adding melted butter, beat in ½ teaspoon of salt, ¼ teaspoon of freshly cracked black pepper, 2 tablespoons of heavy cream, and 1 tablespoon of bacon fat. *Makes 4 servings.*

POTATOES ANNA

6 *large baking potatoes*   ½ *teaspoon freshly cracked*
¾ *cup butter, about*   *white pepper*
2 *teaspoons salt*

1. Peel the potatoes, wash and dry them well, then slice them ⅛ inch thick with a cutter or *mandoline*.
2. Butter a shallow ovenproof baking dish (or a 9- to 10-inch pie plate) generously—use about 2 tablespoons of butter.
3. Lay the potato slices, overlapping them, in concentric circles on the bottom of the dish (or pie plate). Build up layers of slices, sprinkling each layer with salt and pepper and dotting generously with butter. Potatoes should fill the container.
4. Lay a flat lid on the potatoes and weight it down with a 3-lb. weight. Bake in a preheated 375° oven for 1 hour.
5. Remove weight and lid from potatoes. Turn oven heat to 450° and bake potatoes about 15 minutes or until they brown on top. Turn out on a warm platter before serving. *Makes 6 to 8 servings.*

POTATOES DAUPHINOISE

Serve this potato casserole with Truffled Chicken (see p. 142), Rack of Lamb (see p. 104) or Rib Roast (see p. 81).

6 *large baking potatoes*   1 *teaspoon freshly cracked*
2 *cups milk*   *white pepper*
6 *tablespoons butter*   1¼ *cups grated Swiss cheese*
1 *clove chopped garlic*   1 *egg*
¼ *teaspoon freshly grated*
   nutmeg

1. Peel the potatoes, wash and dry them well, and slice them ⅛ inch thick with a cutter or *mandoline*.
2. Put the slices into a saucepan, cover with milk, bring to a boil, and simmer, uncovered, for 10 minutes.
3. Drain the potatoes—reserve the milk—and dry them on paper towels.

4. Cream ¼ cup of butter, beat in the chopped garlic, and set aside.

5. Melt the remaining 2 tablespoons of butter and brush a large au gratin dish or an ovenproof baking dish with it.

6. Arrange ½ the potato slices in the dish and sprinkle with nutmeg, pepper, and ¾ cup of the cheese (no need for salt, since the cheese is salty). Put the remaining potato slices on top.

7. Beat egg with a fork and mix it into the reserved milk. Pour over the potatoes, dot the tops with the garlic-butter mixture, and sprinkle with the remaining ½ cup of cheese.

8. Set the dish in a pan of boiling water and bake in a preheated 375° oven for 45 to 60 minutes, or until potatoes are tender.

• This casserole can be made ahead if it's reheated (in the water bath) in a 375° oven.
• If dinner is delayed, an extra 30 minutes in a 250° oven won't hurt the potatoes a bit. *Makes 6 to 8 servings.*

POTATOES SAVOYARD

6 *large baking potatoes*	6 *tablespoons butter*
2 *cups chicken stock (see*	1 *teaspoon freshly cracked*
p. 241) or beef stock (see	*white pepper*
p. 240)	1¼ *cups grated Swiss cheese*

1. Peel potatoes and slice them ⅛ inch thick with a vegetable cutter or *mandoline.*

2. Put the slices into a saucepan with the stock, bring to a boil, and simmer, uncovered, for 10 minutes.

3. Drain the potatoes—reserve the stock—and dry them on paper towels.

4. Melt 2 tablespoons of butter and brush an au gratin dish or an ovenproof baking dish with it.

5. Arrange ½ the potato slices in the dish and sprinkle with pepper and ¾ cup of the cheese (no salt is needed, because cheese is salty). Put the remaining potato slices on top.

6. Pour enough of the reserved stock over potatoes to come ¾ of the way up the dish. Dot the top of the potatoes with the remaining butter and sprinkle with the remaining ½ cup of cheese.

7. Put the dish in a preheated 375° oven to bake 45 to 60 minutes, or until the potatoes are tender. *Makes 6 to 8 servings.*

POTATOES SARLANDAISE

These are truffled potatoes served in one large cake, crisp and brown on the outside, moist and tender inside.

6 *large baking potatoes*   1½ *cups vegetable shortening*
1 *large truffle*
4 *large canned artichoke*
bottoms

1. Peel the potatoes and slice them ⅛ inch thick with a vegetable cutter or *mandoline*.
2. Cut the slices into sticks the size of thin French fries. (Stack two or three slices together and cut them with a large knife—it's easy this way), and as the sticks are cut, put them in a bowl of cold water.
3. Soak the sticks for about ½ hour.
4. Cut the truffle into slivers and cut the artichoke bottoms into sticks the size of kitchen matches.
5. Drain the potato sticks, dry them thoroughly with paper towels, then combine them with the truffle slivers and cut artichoke bottoms.
6. Heat shortening in a heavy 8- to 10-inch iron skillet, and when the shortening is very hot—almost smoking—drop in the potato mixture and pat it into a flat cake with a spatula.
7. Cover the skillet and cook over high heat for about ½ hour, or until the potato cake is brown and crisp on the bottom. Then turn the potato cake over and cook until the other side is brown and crisp.

• A good way to turn the cake is by lifting it out onto a flat lid with a broad spatula, then turning the lid and the cake over together.

8. Drain the cake and cut it in wedges to serve. **Makes 8 to 10 servings.**

Pommes Pailles

Follow the recipe for Potatoes Sarlandaise (see above), but omit the truffle and artichoke bottoms and cut the potatoes like straws. (*Paille* means straw.)

German Potatoes

Follow the recipe for Potatoes Sarlandaise (see above) but do not cut the ⅛-inch potato slices into sticks, omit the truffle and artichoke bottoms, and put ½ the potatoes into the hot shortening, then sprinkle them with ½ a grated onion before adding the remaining potatoes and forming into a cake.

WAFFLED POTATOES

4 large baking potatoes   *2 teaspoons salt*
2 cups vegetable shortening

1. Peel the potatoes, wash and dry them, and using the serrated cutting edge of a *mandoline* or a vegetable slicer, cut them as thin as possible, in a waffle pattern.

2. Soak the slices in iced water for 1 hour.

• A lot of the starch is removed from potatoes when they're soaked. The potatoes can be sliced in the morning and kept in water, in a refrigerator, until cooking time. Don't add salt to the water, for potatoes that stand in salted water turn dark.

3. When ready to fry the potatoes, drain the slices and dry them on paper towels, then heat shortening to 375° in an electric skillet, a deep fat fryer, or a heavy saucepan and fry a few slices at a time, until golden brown. Remove with a slotted spoon and drain on paper towels.

• Waffled potatoes can be fried ahead of time and reheated. To reheat: set cake racks on a baking sheet, cover with brown paper, lay the potatoes on the paper, and place in a preheated 350° oven for a few minutes.

4. Sprinkle with salt just before serving. *Makes 8 servings.*

RICE PILAF

Rice Pilaf, which can be made with any stock or with water, can be served in the casserole in which it cooked, or it can be turned out onto an au gratin dish, the top first smoothed with a spatula, then indented to make a design. However you present it, give the rice a border of chopped parsley.

½ cup butter
1 finely chopped medium-size yellow onion
1 cup long-grain rice
2 cups chicken stock (see p. 241) or beef stock (see p. 240)

1 teaspoon salt
½ teaspoon freshly cracked black pepper
2 tablespoons chopped parsley

1. Melt ¼ cup of butter in a heavy casserole—one with a tight-fitting lid—and sauté the onion over high heat until it is translucent, about 2 minutes. Do not brown it.

2. Add the rice, stirring it around to coat the grains with butter.

3. Pour in the stock, add salt and pepper, bring to a full boil over high heat, then immediately put the lid on the casserole and turn the heat down to simmer.

4. Cook for 23 minutes (use a timer if you have one), without lifting the lid, then remove the lid, fluff the rice with 2 forks, sprinkle it with the remaining ¼ cup melted butter, and add a border of chopped parsley.

• Rice Pilaf can be cooked a day in advance, refrigerated, and reheated. To reheat: place the casserole, uncovered, over low heat and stir in ½ cup of melted butter. ***Makes 6 to 8 servings.***

Rice Timbales

1 recipe of Rice Pilaf (see p. 186)
2 tablespoons finely chopped celery

1 clove chopped garlic
¼ teaspoon freshly grated nutmeg
Oil to grease molds

1. Follow recipe for Rice Pilaf adding celery, garlic, and nutmeg to cooking liquid. Bring liquid to boil and proceed with recipe as directed.

2. When rice is cooked, pack it, hot, into 8 small oval molds greased with oil. Pack firmly, then let molds set for 1 minute before tipping them out. ***Makes 8 servings.***

SAFFRON RICE

Saffron Rice is made like Rice Pilaf (see p. 186). The only difference is in the flavorings.

2 tablespoons butter
2 tablespoons olive oil
1 finely chopped medium-
size onion
½ teaspoon chopped garlic
1½ cups long-grain rice
1 teaspoon saffron filaments

3 cups shrimp stock, if available (see p. 72, step 2) or
3 cups chicken stock (see
p. 241)
1 teaspoon salt
½ teaspoon freshly cracked
white pepper

1. Heat butter and oil in a heavy casserole—one with a tight-fitting lid—and sauté onion and garlic in the mixture for about 3 minutes. Do not let it brown.

2. Add the rice, stirring it around to coat the grains with butter and oil.

3. Dissolve saffron in 1 tablespoon of stock, pour the remaining stock into the casserole, add the dissolved saffron, season with salt and pepper, and bring to a full boil over high heat, then immediately cover tightly and reduce heat to simmer.

4. Cook for 23 minutes, without lifting the lid, then remove the lid and fluff the rice with 2 forks.

• If dinner is delayed, keep the casserole warm in a 250° oven, without the lid (if it's left on, the rice will continue to steam), but covered with cheesecloth or a tea towel. To hold the rice even longer, pour ½ cup melted butter over it, stand the casserole in a pan of warm water, and half cover the pan with a lid. *Makes 6 to 8 servings.*

RICE RING

2 cups long-grain rice
14 tablespoons butter
1 teaspoon salt
½ teaspoon freshly cracked
black pepper

1 cup finely chopped parsley,
optional

1. Put rice and 1 quart of water into a heavy saucepan or a casserole with a tight-fitting lid. Bring the water to a boil, put on the lid, reduce heat to simmer, and cook for 20 minutes, after which the water should be absorbed. If some is left, drain it off.

2. Stir in ¾ cup of melted butter, salt, and pepper. If you want a green rice ring, add the parsley.

3. Use 2 tablespoons of butter to grease a 9-inch ring mold. Pack the rice into the mold, place the mold on a baking sheet, and put into a preheated 350° oven to bake for 10 minutes.

4. Let stand at room temperature for 5 minutes before unmolding onto a serving plate. *Makes 8 servings.*

Sautéed Cherry Tomatoes

Here's a quick vegetable garnish that looks beautiful on a meat platter.

2 boxes (1 quart) cherry tomatoes
¼ cup butter
½ teaspoon sugar
½ teaspoon salt

¼ teaspoon freshly cracked
black pepper
1 heaping tablespoon
chopped parsley

1. Remove stems, then wash and dry the cherry tomatoes.
2. Heat butter in a large sauté pan. When it is foaming, add the tomatoes. Toss them over high heat, shaking the pan back and forth and sprinkling the tomatoes with sugar (this gives them a shiny glaze), for about 3 minutes. Don't overcook, or the skins will split, and the tomatoes will be too soft.
3. Season with salt and pepper and garnish with chopped parsley. *Makes 6 to 8 servings.*

Stuffed Tomatoes Ménagère

4 large tomatoes
6 tablespoons butter
¾ cup finely chopped onion
1 clove finely chopped garlic
½ cup soft bread crumbs (see
p. 7)

2 tablespoons chopped parsley
½ teaspoon salt
¼ teaspoon freshly cracked
black pepper
½ cup grated Parmesan cheese

1. Cut tomatoes in half, crosswise, and cut off stem ends. Trim enough off the bottom of each half so that the tomatoes will stand without tipping.
2. Scoop out the tomatoes and reserve the pulp. Place the shells in a baking dish and set aside.
3. Melt 2 tablespoons of butter in a small pan, stir in onion and garlic, and cook over high heat, stirring, until transparent. Do not let the onions and garlic brown.
4. Stir in tomato pulp and cook over high heat 10 minutes.
5. Add bread crumbs, parsley, salt, and pepper, mix, then fill the set-aside tomato shells with the mixture. Dot the tomato halves generously with the remaining butter, sprinkle with grated cheese, and bake in a preheated 350° oven for 25 minutes. *Makes 8 servings.*

ROMAN TOMATOES

Tomato cups filled with Rice Salad—the perfect chilled vegetable to serve with Vitello Tonnato (see p. 115).

8 large tomatoes   *8 sprigs parsley*
1 recipe Rice Salad (see
    p. 197)

1. Cut slices off the stem ends of tomatoes thick enough to serve as lids; reserve them. Then hollow out the tomatoes and turn them upside down on paper towels to drain.
2. Fill tomato shells with Rice Salad, mounding it slightly, and use the remaining Rice Salad to make a bed on a long narrow platter.
3. Stand the stuffed tomatoes on the rice bed, slit the reserved lids to the center, thread a sprig of parsley through each slit, and put the lids with their parsley plumes on top of the stuffed tomatoes. ***Makes 8 servings.***

ZUCCHINI PROVENÇAL

This zucchini can be made in advance and reheated. In fact, it's even better the next day.

6 zucchini   *¼ teaspoon freshly cracked*
½ cup olive oil   *black pepper*
2 large or 3 small cloves   *2 tablespoons chopped pars-*
    minced garlic   *ley*
½ teaspoon salt

1. Scrub the zucchini, cut them in half lengthwise, then cut the halves in very thin slices.

• Use a vegetable cutter or a *mandoline* to get even slices.

2. Heat olive oil in a large skillet and cook garlic over high heat in the oil until transparent. Do not let it brown.
3. Add zucchini slices and toss over high heat for about 3 minutes. Season with salt and pepper, and just before serving, sprinkle with chopped parsley. ***Makes 6 to 8 servings***.

SALADS

Mutiny threatens in my kitchen whenever I make a salad, for I refuse to honor all the rules set down by the classicists. In particular, I use glass, pottery, stainless steel, aluminum, or plastic salad bowls—any kind but wooden, for the very idea of a wooden bowl that has been rubbed with oil and garlic time and time again is repugnant to me. (If, however, you are loyal to a wooden bowl, scrub it with warm soapy water and rinse and dry it well after every use.) And though classicists may consider it heresy, I cut greens with a knife or scissors, for I find that less damage is done to greens by cutting than by tearing. And, also, cutting is faster.

For formal dinners, I serve salad as a separate course after the main course. For informal meals, I like the idea of serving salad as a first course. Some salads, such as Salade Niçoise (see p. 196), *are* the main course for luncheon or supper.

Any of the salad greens—romaine, Bibb, or Boston, for example—may be used alone as the basis of a salad or mixed with other greens, such as watercress, endive, chicory, celery, dandelion leaves, or young spinach leaves. However they're used, greens should first be washed thoroughly in cold water, then shaken to remove excess water, and placed on paper towels, rolled up loosely in the paper towels, wrapped in a tea towel, and placed in a refrigerator for at least ½ hour to crisp and become completely dry.

The simplest and best dressing for most salads is made with oil (4 parts) and vinegar (1 part) and seasoned with salt and pepper. This is a true French dressing. To vary the flavor, try different vinegars—tarragon, cider, red- or white-wine vinegar—or substitute fresh lemon juice for the vinegar. The best oil is olive oil, but it's interesting to experiment with vegetable oils and peanut oils. Use coarse salt (kosher salt or sea salt) and freshly cracked pepper from a mill. A little crushed garlic can be added, as can mustard or herbs.

Salads should be served immediately after they're dressed; otherwise the greens wilt and become sodden. When sturdy greens, such as romaine, spinach, or Belgian endive are used, the dressing can be made in advance in the salad bowl and the greens placed on top; then the bowl can be covered with plastic wrap and refrigerated until serving time, when the salad can be tossed and served on chilled plates.

CELERIAC RÉMOULADE

The common name for celeriac is celery root, but do not confuse it with ordinary celery. Celeriac looks like a knobby turnip. It is a winter vegetable, and in the winter, when beautiful lettuce isn't around, it makes an excellent salad. Celeriac Rémoulade can also be served as a first course.

4 celeriac	*½ teaspoon freshly cracked*
⅔ cup mayonnaise (see p. 251)	*white pepper*
1 tablespoon Dijon mustard	*2 tablespoons chopped pars-*
1 teaspoon coarse salt	*ley*

1. Peel the celeriac and cut into matchstick-size pieces.

• The easy way to do this is to cut the celeriac in half, place the halves, cut sides down, on a chopping board, and slice, then to stack 3 or 4 slices and cut them into matchsticks.

2. Put the matchstick slices into a saucepan, add 2 cups of cold water, and bring to a rolling boil. Boil for 5 minutes.

• Not everyone parboils celeriac, but I prefer to do so. Parboiling seems to remove the bitter taste, and it makes celeriac more tender than it would otherwise be.

3. Drain the slices in a colander, rinse them with cold water, and dry them on paper towels or tea towels, then put them into a salad bowl, and add a mixture of mayonnaise, mustard, salt, pepper, and parsley, and toss with forks to mix.

4. Chill for at least 15 to 20 minutes in a refrigerator before serving.

• Celeriac Rémoulade can be made 2 to 3 hours in advance and kept in a refrigerator until ready to serve. **Makes 6 servings.**

CUCUMBER SALAD WITH YOGHURT

6 *cucumbers*	1 *tablespoon freshly chopped*
2 *teaspoons coarse salt*	*dill*
1 *clove minced garlic*	2 *tablespoons freshly chopped*
2 *tablespoons vinegar*	*mint leaves*
1 *cup yoghurt*	

1. Peel cucumbers, cut off the ends, and cut them in half lengthwise. Scoop out the seeds with the tip of a spoon, then cut the cucumber pieces in half crosswise and cut the resulting quarters into very thin julienne slices.

2. Put the slices in a salad bowl and sprinkle with salt and garlic.

3. Mix vinegar, yoghurt, and dill together, fold into cucumbers, and marinate them in a refrigerator.

4. Before serving, sprinkle with chopped mint leaves. Serve *very* cold.

• This salad is especially good with lamb. **Makes 6 to 8 servings.**

BELGIAN ENDIVE SALAD

This is a good buffet salad because Belgian endive holds up well after tossing. The dressing, a mustardy vinaigrette, can be mixed in the bottom of the salad bowl, the endive placed on top, and the bowl covered with plastic wrap and refrigerated until serving time, when the salad can then be tossed.

12 *heads Belgian endive*	½ *cup tarragon vinegar*
1 *teaspoon coarse salt*	½ *cup French olive oil*
½ *teaspoon freshly cracked*	2 *tablespoons chopped pars-*
white pepper	*ley*
1 *tablespoon Dijon mustard*	

1. Trim root ends of endive and wash and dry the heads well. Cut them into long thin strips with a chef's knife.

2. To make dressing, mix salt, pepper, mustard, vinegar, and oil together with a fork.

• Taste the dressing for seasoning and add more salt if desired.

3. Put the strips of endive into a salad bowl with the chopped parsley and toss the endive, parsley, and dressing together before serving. *Makes 12 servings.*

BELGIAN ENDIVE AND CITRUS SALAD

12 *heads Belgian endive*	½ *cup olive oil*
8 *scallions*	1 *teaspoon coarse salt*
2 *large navel oranges*	½ *teaspoon dried rosemary*
1 *medium grapefruit*	2 *tablespoons chopped pars-*
½ *cup lemon juice*	*ley*

1. Trim root ends of endive, wash and dry the heads thoroughly, then slice them crosswise, into rings, and put the rings into a salad bowl.

2. Trim roots and green tops from scallions, then cut the scallions into thin rings and scatter the rings over the endive rings.

3. Peel oranges and grapefruit, trim off all the bitter white inner covering, and section by cutting as close to membrane of each section as possible. Add to salad bowl.

• If desired, all oranges, or all grapefruit, can be used.

4. Make dressing by shaking lemon juice, oil, salt, and rosemary in a small jar or by stirring them together in a small bowl.

• The salad can be made to this point the day before it is to be served. Store the dressing and the salad bowl separately in a refrigerator, and toss contents together at the last minute.

5. Sprinkle chopped parsley over salad, pour on dressing, and toss. Serve on chilled plates. *Makes 6 to 8 servings.*

FRENCH GREEN SALAD

2 *or 3 heads of tender lettuce*	2 *tablespoons tarragon vine-*
2 *tablespoons chopped pars-*	*gar*
ley	½ *cup French olive oil*
1 *teaspoon coarse salt*	
½ *teaspoon freshly cracked black pepper*	

1. Separate the lettuce leaves, discarding any damaged ones, and wash in cold water. Dry the leaves in single layers on a double thickness of paper towels, roll the leaves loosely in the paper towels, then wrap in a tea towel, and put in a refrigerator to crisp.

• This can be done the day before the salad is to be served.

2. Cut the leaves into pieces with a large chef's knife or with kitchen shears, then put the pieces into a chilled salad bowl and sprinkle with chopped parsley.

• Instead of, or in addition to, chopped parsley, other chopped fresh herbs—1 tablespoon of chopped chives, for instance, or of tarragon, or basil—can be used.

3. To make dressing, combine salt, pepper, vinegar, and oil in a small bowl (or a small jar) and stir or shake until mixed.

• The dressing can be varied to taste by using 5 parts rather than 4 parts oil to 1 part of vinegar; by using red- or white-wine or cider vinegar instead of tarragon vinegar, or vegetable oil or imported French peanut oil instead of olive oil; or by adding 1 clove of crushed garlic to it or if you want it to coat the lettuce more heavily, 1 beaten egg.

4. Pour dressing on lettuce, toss lightly, and serve at once, on chilled plates.

• Overdressing the salad causes the lettuce to wilt. It is proper to use just enough dressing to coat the greens. *Makes 4 to 6 servings.*

RAW MUSHROOM SALAD

1 lb. fresh large white mushrooms
½ cup lemon juice, plus lemon
juice to clean mushrooms
½ cup French olive oil
1 teaspoon coarse salt
½ teaspoon freshly cracked
white pepper
¼ teaspoon oregano
2 tablespoons chopped parsley

1. Clean mushrooms either by dipping them in acidulated water—water with a little lemon juice (about 1 tablespoon to 1 quart of water) in it—or by wiping them with towels that have been dipped in acidulated water.

2. Dry the mushrooms with paper towels, then trim the stems even with the base of the caps and slice the caps paper thin.

3. Put the slices in a bowl, add lemon juice, olive oil, salt, pepper, and oregano, mix together, and marinate for 1 hour at room temperature.

4. Sprinkle with parsley and serve on chilled plates. *Makes 4 servings.*

SALADE NIÇOISE

This is my own variation on the classic recipe.

1 medium clove garlic

1 head romaine or other sturdy green

1 cooked chicken breast, cut in julienne strips

¼ lb. baked ham, or smoked tongue, cut in julienne strips

3 peeled and quartered hard-cooked eggs

2 peeled, seeded, and quartered tomatoes

1 can flat anchovy fillets

6 canned beets, cut in julienne strips

6 small boiled and sliced potatoes

2 sliced ribs celery

1 green or red pepper, sliced in rings

1 medium peeled red onion, sliced in rings

1 7-oz. can tuna

24 black olives

1 teaspoon coarse salt

1 teaspoon freshly cracked black pepper

1 teaspoon Dijon mustard

½ cup French olive oil

2 tablespoons red-wine vinegar

2 tablespoons chopped parsley

6 lemon slices

1. Cut garlic clove in half and use the halves to rub the inside of a large salad bowl.

2. Wash romaine, roll up in paper towels and then in a tea towel, and put in a refrigerator for ½ hour to crisp.

3. Cut the leaves into shreds with a large chef's knife, line the salad bowl with them, then arrange the chicken, ham or tongue, eggs, tomatoes, anchovies, beets, potatoes, celery, pepper, onion, tuna, and olives in layers on top.

4. Cover bowl with plastic wrap and place it in a refrigerator until serving time.

• This can be done in the morning.

5. Make dressing by shaking salt, pepper, mustard, olive oil, and vinegar in a small jar or stirring them in a small bowl.

6. When ready to serve, pour dressing over salad and toss. Sprinkle with chopped parsley and garnish with thin slices of lemon. *Makes 4 servings.*

FRENCH POTATO SALAD

8 *to 10 medium-size potatoes*
1 *teaspoon salt*
¼ *cup tarragon vinegar*
½ *cup French olive oil*
2 *tablespoons chopped fresh chives*
1 *teaspoon Dijon mustard*

½ *teaspoon freshly cracked black pepper*
1 *teaspoon coarse salt*
2 *tablespoons mayonnaise (see p. 251)*
2 *tablespoons freshly chopped parsley*

1. Put unpeeled potatoes into a saucepan of boiling water with 1 teaspoon salt added, and cook over medium high heat 15 to 25 minutes or until tender. Drain and cool slightly.

2. When the potatoes are comfortable to handle, peel them and slice them—¼ inch thick—into a bowl.

3. Mix together the vinegar, olive oil, chives, mustard, pepper, and 1 teaspoon coarse salt; while the potato slices are still warm, pour the mixture over them and toss with a fork.

4. Let the potato slices marinate at room temperature until cool, about 1 hour, turning them over in the bowl occasionally, then put them in a refrigerator to chill.

5. Serve cold, garnished with mayonnaise and chopped parsley. **Makes 6 servings.**

RICE SALAD

1 *cup long-grain rice*
1 *teaspoon salt*
½ *teaspoon freshly cracked black pepper*
¼ *cup olive oil*
2 *tablespoons wine vinegar*
2 *teaspoons Dijon mustard*

2 *cups mixed cooked vegetables—carrots, green beans, peas, corn kernels, or other vegetables*
½ *finely diced green pepper*
½ *peeled and diced cucumber*

1. Put rice, salt, pepper, and 2 cups of water in a small heavy pan or a casserole—one with a tight-fitting lid. Bring to a boil, cover, then reduce heat and simmer, covered, for 20 minutes.

2. Put cooked rice in a bowl, add oil, vinegar, and mustard, and toss with a fork to mix.

3. Gently mix in cooked vegetables (these can be leftovers, and in any combination you wish), green pepper, and cucumber.

4. Taste for, and if necessary, adjust seasoning. Serve cold.

• Foods to be served cold usually require more seasoning than do other foods.

• If desired, Rice Salad can be packed into an oiled ring or melon mold, an oiled loaf pan—even a mixing bowl—chilled, then unmolded (by inverting the container) on a serving platter. *Makes 8 servings.*

ROMAINE SALAD

2 *heads romaine*	2 *tablespoons red-wine vinegar*
½ *lb. sliced bacon*	*gar*
1½ *cups bread cubes*	½ *cup vegetable oil*
2 *teaspoons coarse salt*	2 *tablespoons French olive oil*
1 *teaspoon freshly cracked black pepper*	1 *egg*
1 *teaspoon Dijon mustard*	2 *tablespoons chopped parsley*
1 *teaspoon finely chopped garlic*	2 *hard-cooked eggs*
2 *tablespoons lemon juice*	8 *flat anchovy fillets*

1. Wash the romaine in cold water, then cut the leaves crosswise. Shake off all water, and wrap the cut leaves in paper towels and then, together, in a tea towel, and put them in a refrigerator to crisp for at least ½ hour.

2. Cut the bacon into small bits, fry slowly until crisp, then remove the bacon bits with a slotted spoon and pour off all but 2 tablespoons of the fat in the frying pan. Dry the bacon bits and set them aside.

3. Fry bread cubes in the bacon fat until brown and crisp. Set aside.

4. In the bottom of a big salad bowl, mix together salt, pepper, mustard, garlic, lemon juice, vinegar, vegetable oil, olive oil, and egg. Stir with a fork to mix thoroughly, then pile the romaine on top and sprinkle with bacon bits and bread cubes.

5. Sprinkle chopped parsley over all and either toss and serve immediately, or cover the bowl with plastic wrap, and refrigerate until time to serve, and toss then.

6. After tossing salad, shell, then quarter hard-cooked eggs. Arrange the quarters around the edge of the salad and lay an anchovy fillet on each quarter. *Makes 8 servings.*

RAW SPINACH SALAD

1½ *lbs. fresh young spinach*	2 *tablespoons white-wine vinegar*
1 *tablespoon grated onion*	*vinegar*
2 *teaspoons Dijon mustard*	½ *cup walnut oil (available in gourmet shops)*
⅛ *teaspoon freshly cracked black pepper*	4½ *teaspoons lemon juice*
½ *teaspoon coarse salt*	

1. Pick over spinach, eliminating damaged leaves, remove stems, and wash thoroughly, first in warm water, then in cold. Dry the leaves thoroughly by rolling them up in paper towels, wrapping them all in a tea towel, and putting in a refrigerator to crisp for at least ½ hour.

2. Mix remaining ingredients together in a small bowl. Pour over spinach, and toss.

• Taste the salad for seasoning before serving it. More salt may be necessary; nine times out of ten, it is. *Makes 6 servings.*

BEEFSTEAK TOMATO AND RED ONION SALAD

6 *beefsteak tomatoes*
2 *red onions*
1 *teaspoon coarse salt*
½ *teaspoon freshly cracked black pepper*

¼ *cup red-wine vinegar*
¾ *cup oil*
2 *tablespoons fresh chopped chives*
2 *cloves finely chopped garlic*

1. Do not peel tomatoes. Cut off tops and bottoms, then cut the tomatoes into ½-inch-thick slices.

2. Peel the onions and cut them into thin (⅛-inch) slices.

3. Arrange the tomato slices alternately with the onion slices, overlapping them, on a long narrow platter.

4. To make dressing, put salt, pepper, vinegar, and oil in a small bowl (or a small jar) and stir (or shake) until mixed.

5. Pour dressing over tomato and onion slices, sprinkle with chives and garlic, and let marinate for ½ hour at room temperature before serving. *Makes 6 to 8 servings.*

ENSALADA VALENCIANA

2 *large navel oranges*
1 *small red onion*
2 *heads romaine*
½ *cup Spanish olive oil (available in gourmet shops)*
2 *tablespoons red-wine vinegar*

2 *tablespoons dry sherry*
1 *teaspoon coarse salt*
½ *teaspoon freshly cracked black pepper*
½ *cup chopped black olives*
1 *4-oz. jar drained and slivered pimientos*

1. Peel oranges, trim off all the bitter white inner covering, and section by cutting as close to the membrane of each section as possible.

2. Peel the onion, cut it into thin slices, and press the slices to make onion rings.

3. Wash the romaine, cut the leaves crosswise. Shake off all water, dry

the cut leaves by rolling in paper towels, then wrapping in a tea towel, and put them in a refrigerator to crisp.

4. Make dressing by shaking olive oil, vinegar, sherry, salt, and pepper in a small jar or by stirring them together in a small bowl.

5. When ready to serve, put orange sections, onion rings, and romaine in a salad bowl, sprinkle with chopped olives and pimiento slivers, pour on dressing, and toss. Serve on chilled plates. *Makes 8 servings.*

COLD VEGETABLE SALAD VINAIGRETTE

2 cups cooked peas
2 cups diced cooked green beans
1 cup diced cooked potato
½ cup diced cooked carrot
1 cup diced canned beets
1 cup diced cooked ham
1½ teaspoons coarse salt

½ teaspoon freshly cracked white pepper
¾ cup oil
¼ cup red-wine vinegar
½ teaspoon freshly cracked black pepper
1 cup mayonnaise (see p. 251)
Lettuce, optional

1. Put peas, beans, potato, carrot, beets, ham, 1 teaspoon salt, and white pepper into a salad bowl.

2. Make a vinaigrette dressing by beating oil, vinegar, black pepper, and the remaining ½ teaspoon of salt together with a fork.

3. Pour dressing over vegetables, toss to coat, and let marinate in refrigerator for 2 hours.

4. Drain off the dressing, add mayonnaise, and toss to mix.

5. Spoon the salad onto individual beds of lettuce, or pack it into a mold and turn it out on a chilled serving platter. *Makes 6 servings.*

WATERCRESS AND MUSHROOM SALAD

3 bunches watercress
½ lb. fresh large white mushrooms
¼ cup walnut or other oil (walnut oil is available in gourmet shops)

4½ teaspoons lemon juice, plus lemon juice to clean mushrooms
1 teaspoon coarse salt
½ teaspoon freshly cracked black pepper

1. Wash watercress. Shake off excess water and trim heavy stems, then roll the watercress in paper towels and place it in a plastic bag. Put in refrigerator at least ½ hour.

• Instead of watercress, 3 heads of Bibb lettuce can be used. Wash the lettuce—separate the leaves to do this—and dry carefully. Wrap leaves in paper towels, then in a tea towel, and put in a refrigerator to crisp.

2. Clean mushrooms either by dipping them in acidulated water—water with a little lemon juice (about 1 tablespoon to 1 quart) in it—or by wiping them clean with towels dipped in acidulated water.

3. Wipe the mushrooms dry with paper towels, then trim the stems even with the base of the caps and slice the caps paper thin.

4. Mix dressing in a salad bowl by beating oil, lemon juice, salt, and pepper together with a fork.

5. Add mushrooms and watercress. Toss and serve immediately. *Makes 4 to 6 servings.*

ZUCCHINI SALAD

6 small- to medium-size zucchini	*2 tablespoons chopped fresh chives*
1 cup dairy sour cream	*1 tablespoon chopped fresh*
1 teaspoon coarse salt	*tarragon or 1 teaspoon dried*
½ teaspoon freshly cracked white pepper	*2 tablespoons chopped parsley*

1. Scrub, but do not peel, the zucchini, then slice them paper thin, using a vegetable cutter or *mandoline.*

2. Put the slices in a salad bowl and fold in sour cream, salt, pepper, chives, and tarragon. Chill thoroughly.

3. Before serving, toss, then sprinkle with chopped parsley. Serve icy-cold on chilled plates. *Makes 6 servings.*

DESSERTS

To many people, dessert is the most important part of the meal. These are the people you see in restaurants reading the menu from bottom to top, choosing an entrée to go with the sweet. If they're to be your guests, why not indulge them? After a rich dinner a light dessert is generally called for, but after a simple one, why not pull out all the stops and serve an extravagant, absolutely luscious concoction?

Both kinds of dessert—simple and extravagant—are in this chapter, in generous variety. Here, too, a reminder: fruit and cheese are still the perfect ending to many a meal, and with an abundance of fresh fruit the year around, and America's growing interest in cheese, dessert need never be a problem.

Many desserts—cold soufflés, mousses, and tarts, to name a few—can or must be prepared in advance. Meringue Shells (see p. 232), made days or even weeks ahead, then filled with ice cream, and covered with Chocolate Fudge Sauce (see p. 233) or fruit can make any dinner seem like a party.

A Sponge Cake (see p. 215) that has been baked and frozen is quickly ready to be turned into Italian Rum Cake (see p. 213) and layers of Yellow Butter Cake (see p. 212) are the beginnings of an elegant Charlotte Portugaise (see p. 211). The fruit syrup for Oranges Orientale (see

p. 225) kept in the refrigerator in a jar, will last almost indefinitely; pour it over any cut-up fresh fruit, and the sweet course is ready.

More than almost any other foods, desserts have shape and style. Specific equipment is needed for preparing and serving them. Soufflé dishes, flan rings, cake pans and tart pans, *barquette* molds, and mousse cups are all available in department stores and gourmet shops. Nice serving extras to have are special dessert plates, a nest of glass or crystal bowls, pot-de-crème pots, parfait glasses, and a chocolate-roll board.

For final flourishes, depend on the pastry bag and star tube (see p. 11). With these and a little whipped cream, the simplest dessert can be turned into a creation—one that can be accented with candied violets, a sprinkling of praline powder (see p. 209), grated nuts, or chocolate curls.

BEIGNETS WITH RASPBERRY SAUCE

½ cup unsalted butter	*2 cups vegetable shortening*
1 cup flour	*½ cup confectioners' sugar*
3 to 4 eggs	*Raspberry Sauce (recipe fol-*
1 tablespoon framboise	*lows)*

1. Put butter and 1 cup of cold water into a saucepan and bring to a boil.

2. As soon as the butter has melted, and with mixture still boiling, dump in the flour—all at once—and stir vigorously over high heat until mixture leaves the sides of the pan.

3. Remove from heat, and beat in 3 eggs, one at a time, beating each in thoroughly before adding the next, and the framboise. If the mixture does not fall lightly from the spoon when it is lifted, add another egg, ½ of it at a time, beaten enough to mix.

4. Heat shortening to 375° in a heavy saucepan—one about 3 inches deep. Check temperature with a fat thermometer, or test it with a bread cube, which will brown nicely in 1 minute if the temperature is right.

5. Drop the batter from a teaspoon directly into the hot fat. Fry about 6 teaspoonfuls, 6 beignets, for 1 to 1½ minutes on each side, or until both sides are browned.

• Allow fat to return to 375° before frying more beignets.
• Mixture makes about 24 beignets.

6. Remove beignets from fat with a slotted spoon, drain them on brown paper or paper towels; and to keep them warm while you fry the remaining beignets, put them on a cake rack lined with brown paper, set the rack on a baking sheet, and place it in a low (250°) oven.

7. When all the beignets are fried, heap them on a serving platter and sift confectioners' sugar over them. Serve immediately, with Raspberry Sauce.

• Beignets may be made ahead and left at room temperature for up to 6 hours and reheated by placing them on a baking sheet in a 250° oven for about 10 minutes or until heated through.

Raspberry Sauce

2 10-oz. pkgs. frozen rasp-
    berries
½ *cup confectioners' sugar*
2 *tablespoons framboise*

1 *teaspoon arrowroot*
½ *cup red currant jelly*
3 *tablespoons lime juice*

1. Thaw raspberries—reserve 1 tablespoon of the juice—and place berries and remaining juice in a blender, and purée them. Strain into a saucepan.
2. Stir in confectioners' sugar and framboise.
3. Mix arrowroot with a little cold raspberry juice and stir it into saucepan.
4. Add currant jelly and lime juice and heat, stirring constantly, about 5 minutes or until slightly thickened. *Makes 6 to 8 servings.*

CRÊPES À LA JULIE

For this unusual dessert, stuff plain crêpes with Pastry Cream mixed with candied pineapple, roll the crêpes, coat them with cooky crumbs, and fry in deep fat.

½ *cup chopped candied pine-*
    apple
½ *cup rum*
1 *recipe Pastry Cream (recipe*
    follows) made without addi-
    tional egg whites or heavy
    cream

8 *5-inch crêpes (see p. 158)*
    made a little thicker than
    usual
2 *lightly beaten egg whites*
¾ *cup crumbed vanilla wafers*
2 *cups vegetable shortening*

1. Marinate the candied pineapple in rum for 1 hour.

• Instead of rum, cognac or Madeira can be used. Instead of candied pineapple, orange peel, marinated in Grand Marnier.

2. Drain the pineapple and fold it into the Pastry Cream.
3. Lay out the crêpes, light side up, and spoon pineapple and Pastry Cream onto each one.

4. Roll the crêpes, folding in the edges to enclose the filling—work fast, for the cooled Pastry Cream will be close to setting—and place them, seam side down, on a baking sheet.

• For a lighter version of this dessert use warm crêpes and after filling them, flame and serve.

5. Dip the rolled crêpes in lightly beaten egg whites, then coat with cooky crumbs.

• The crêpes can be prepared a day ahead up to this point, then refrigerated. They're really better if they stay in the refrigerator overnight. Don't freeze them.

6. Heat fat to 375° in a heavy saucepan or a deep-fat fryer. Check temperature with a fat thermometer, or test it with a bread cube, which will brown nicely in 1 minute if the temperature is right.

7. Fry crêpes, 2 at a time, in the hot fat. Fry just until brown and crispy—about 3 minutes.

• Allow fat to return to 375° before frying each pair of crêpes.

8. Drain on paper towels and serve immediately. *Makes 8 servings.*

Pastry Cream

Pastry Cream is a delicious filling for cakes and hollow pastries. The classic recipe is thickened with eggs and flour, but I've found that the addition of gelatin makes success more certain. For an extra-luscious filling, Pastry Cream can be enriched with egg whites or heavy cream, or both.

2 eggs
2 egg yolks
½ cup flour
½ cup sugar
2 tablespoons (2 envelopes)
  unflavored gelatin

2 cups milk
2 egg whites, optional
1½ cups heavy cream, op-
  tional

1. Put eggs, egg yolks, flour, and sugar in a heavy saucepan—not an aluminum one—and beat with a whisk until well mixed.

2. Stir in gelatin, straight from the envelopes.

• The eggs serve as the cold liquid necessary to soften gelatin before dissolving it.

3. Add milk, place the pan over high heat, and constantly moving the whisk all over the pan (this prevents lumping), cook until the mixture is thick and creamy.

4. Remove from heat and allow to cool.

5. For enriched Pastry Cream, fold stiffly beaten egg whites or heavy cream whipped to the same consistency as the Pastry Cream, or both, into the cooled Pastry Cream.

• Pastry Cream can be made ahead and refrigerated. Cover it tightly with plastic wrap until ready to use it. It should not be frozen, but it will keep in a refrigerator for 2 to 3 days. *Makes enough to fill 1 cake or 8 crêpes or tartlets.*

DESSERT CRÊPES FLAMBÉES

With prepared crêpes in your freezer, you always have the makings of a glamorous dessert. Here are some suggestions for elegant flaming desserts that call for only last-minute preparation. Each of the recipes below calls for 1 recipe basic crêpes (see p. 158) and makes 8 7-inch or 12 5-inch crêpes. The crêpes should be warmed before filling.

Apricot Crêpes Flambées

Fold ½ cup of chopped walnuts or almonds into 1 cup of apricot jam or jelly. Fill and roll crêpes and put them seam-side down in a flame-proof serving dish. Sprinkle with ¼ cup melted butter and 3 tablespoons sugar and heat for about 10 minutes in a preheated 350° oven. Flame the crêpes with 2 tablespoons of rum and bring them to the table flaming.

Jam Crêpes Flambées

Fill crêpes with 1 cup of strawberry or raspberry jam. Sprinkle them with ¼ cup melted butter and 3 tablespoons sugar and heat in a preheated 350° oven for 10 minutes. Flame with 2 tablespoons framboise.

Banana Crêpes Flambées

Slice 3 bananas. Melt 2 tablespoons of butter in a skillet, stir in 2 tablespoons of brown sugar and ¼ teaspoon of cinnamon. Heat bananas in mixture over high heat for about 5 minutes or until they are caramelized. Roll bananas in crêpes, sprinkle with ¼ cup melted butter and 3 tablespoons sugar, and flame with rum. *Makes 8 to 12 servings.*

CHOCOLATE CRÊPES

6 *tablespoons flour*	⅓ *cup milk*
2 *tablespoons cocoa*	2 *cups heavy cream*
¼ *teaspoon salt*	¼ *cup confectioners' sugar*
2 *eggs*	3 *tablespoons instant coffee*
2 *egg yolks*	1 *recipe Chocolate Fudge*
1 *tablespoon sugar*	*Sauce (see p. 233)*
¼ *cup vegetable oil*	

1. Make batter by putting flour, cocoa, salt, eggs, egg yolks, sugar, oil, and milk into a blender jar and blending at medium speed until smooth.
2. Refrigerate the batter for 1 hour to allow flavor to blend.

• The batter should have a consistency between that of light and that of heavy cream. If it comes out too thick, thin it with a little milk.

3. Fry the batter, following the directions for crêpes (see p. 158) and using a 5-inch crêpe pan. Makes 12 crêpes.
4. Whisk heavy cream in a large bowl over ice. When cream mounds softly, add confectioners' sugar and instant coffee. Continue whisking until cream will stand in peaks when the whisk is lifted.
5. Put a big spoonful of the cream mixture on each crêpe and roll it up. Arrange 2 rolled crêpes on each of 6 individual serving dishes and top with Chocolate Fudge Sauce. *Makes 6 servings.*

LEMON CURD

Lemon Curd is an English lemon butter, which can be stored, in covered jars, in a refrigerator for about 1 week. Its uses are legion. It can be spread on toast at teatime; it is a delectable filling for pâte brisée shells (see p. 36), cakes, and sponge cake roll (see recipe for Marron Roll, p. 217); or it can be served, as here, in individual soufflé cups, dressed up with whipped cream and candied violets.

4 large lemons	*2 tablespoons confectioners'*
2 cups sugar	*sugar*
2 cups unsalted butter	*12 to 14 candied violets*
6 beaten eggs	*(available in gourmet*
⅛ teaspoon salt	*shops)*
1 cup heavy cream	

1. Grate the peel from all 4 lemons, squeeze out the juice, and put peel and juice, sugar, butter, beaten eggs, and salt into the top part of a large double boiler.

2. Cook the mixture over boiling water—do not let the water touch the bottom of the inset pan—stirring constantly with a wooden spatula for about ½ hour, or until the mixture has the consistency of thick cream sauce.

3. Pour the mixture into individual soufflé cups and put them into a refrigerator for several hours, until they are firm and cold.

4. Whip the cream with the confectioners' sugar over ice until it stands in peaks, then spoon it into a pastry bag fitted with a star tube and pipe a fat rosette on each soufflé cup. Decorate each with a candied violet. *Makes 12 to 14 servings.*

PRALINE FLAN

1 cup blanched or un-	*2 tablespoons (2 envelopes)*
blanched almonds	*unflavored gelatin*
¼ teaspoon cream of tartar	*1½ cups light cream*
1½ cups sugar	*5 egg whites*
Butter to grease baking sheet	*1½ cups heavy cream*
2 tablespoons vegetable oil	*2 tablespoons confectioners'*
5 egg yolks whisked with 5	*sugar*
tablespoons sugar	*2 tablespoons rum*

1. Put almonds, cream of tartar, and 1½ cups sugar in a heavy saucepan or skillet and stir constantly, with a wooden spatula, over medium heat until the sugar melts and the mixture turns a dark caramel color. This will take about 15 minutes, and when the mixture is ready, it will give off a slight puff of smoke and boil up with lots of bubbles. Remove from heat immediately.

2. Immediately pour the caramel mixture onto a buttered baking sheet. Let it get hard, then break it into pieces and either put it into a blender and blend it to a powder or roll it to a powder with a rolling pin (or pound it with a mallet). Set aside.

• This powder—called praline powder—can be kept on a pantry shelf in a covered jar, for a month.

3. Lightly oil a 9-inch round cake pan, one with a removable bottom, and set it on a baking sheet.

4. Soften the gelatin by sprinkling it in the egg-yolk mixture.

5. In a saucepan, not an aluminum one, scald the light cream—that is, heat the cream until little bubbles form around the edges of the pan.

6. Pour the scalded cream into the bowl with the egg-yolk mixture in a thin stream, stirring constantly. Then pour the contents of the bowl back into the saucepan, return it to low heat, and cook, stirring constantly, for 10 to 15 minutes, or until the mixture will coat the back of a spoon.

7. Remove from heat, cover the saucepan with plastic wrap or foil, and put in a refrigerator to chill 10 minutes or until syrupy, on the verge of setting.

• Instead of refrigerating the mixture can be stirred over ice to hasten the cooling.

8. Whisk the egg whites until they form stiff peaks, then—very gently —fold them into the cooled yolk mixture.

9. Whip ¾ cup of the heavy cream with 1 tablespoon of the confectioners' sugar, and when this mixture is the same consistency as the egg mixture, add the rum and ¾ cup of the set-aside powder to it, gently fold it into the egg mixture, and pour into the oiled pan.

10. Put the pan in a refrigerator for at least 2 hours, or until the mixture sets.

• This can be done the day before the flan is to be served.

11. Whip the remaining ¾ cup of heavy cream with the remaining 1 tablespoon of confectioners' sugar, and when mixture is fairly stiff put it into a pastry bag fitted with a star tube.

12. Remove mixture from refrigerator, run a knife around the edge of the pan to loosen the flan, then turn the pan over on a serving dish and lift off, first, the rim, then the removable bottom.

13. Decorate the top of the flan with rosettes of whipped cream and sprinkle it with the remaining praline powder. *Makes 8 servings.*

COFFEE POT DE CRÈME

4 cups heavy cream
1 cup strong black coffee
5 tablespoons sugar
10 egg yolks
¼ cup coffee essence

1 teaspoon powdered chicory
2 tablespoons instant coffee
or ¼ cup candied coffee
beans, optional

1. Put the cream in a heavy saucepan, scald it—that is, heat it until little bubbles appear around the edges of the pan—then stir in coffee and sugar and stir over high heat until sugar is dissolved.

2. Beat egg yolks at medium speed in the large bowl of an electric mixer, and when they are light and fluffy, pour coffee mixture over them in a thin stream, stirring to keep the yolks from curdling.

3. Stir in coffee essence and chicory.

• Look in gourmet food stores for coffee essence, a concentrated coffee flavoring, for powdered chicory, which is ground from the root of the chicory plant and sometimes used to flavor coffee, and for candied coffee beans.

4. Pour the cream mixture into 10 small pot-de-crème pots, set them in a pan of boiling water, and bake in a preheated 350° oven for about 25 minutes, or until mixture is barely set.

5. Remove from oven and chill 1 to 2 hours in a refrigerator.

6. Before serving, garnish, if desired, either with instant coffee or with candied coffee beans. *Makes 10 servings.*

BISCUIT TORTONI

¾ cup sugar
5 egg yolks
¼ cup dry or cream sherry

2 cups heavy cream
2 tablespoons ground
blanched almonds

1. Put sugar and ¼ cup of water in a small saucepan, bring to a boil, stirring to dissolve the sugar, then cook, uncovered, over high heat for 5 minutes to make syrup.

2. In the large bowl of an electric mixer, beat egg yolks at medium speed until they are fluffy.

3. Continue beating while adding syrup in a thin steady stream.

4. Transfer the mixture to the top of a double boiler and stir it over hot—not boiling—water until it is very thick.

5. Remove from heat and add sherry.

• Instead of sherry, sweet Marsala can be used.

6. Strain mixture through a fine sieve into a bowl. Cool completely.

7. Whip the cream until stiff and fold into the cooled custard.

8. Pour into 12 small paper soufflé cases, sprinkle top of each with about ½ teaspoon of ground almonds, and set in a freezer for at least 3 hours.

• Tortoni can be poured into parfait glasses instead of paper cups if desired.

• Instead of sprinkling almonds on top, the ground almonds can be folded into the custard after step 7.

9. Before serving, let stand at room temperature about 1 minute (Tortoni starts to soften almost immediately). *Makes 12 servings.*

CHARLOTTE PORTUGAISE

This is a meringue-frosted cake that is steeped in liqueur and crème anglaise. Make it in the morning of the day it is to be served, or make it the day before, or bake and fill the cake the day before and pipe on the meringue just before serving.

2 9-inch layers Yellow But- ter Cake (recipe follows)	1½ cups sugar
	2 cups half-and-half
10 tablespoons Grand Mar- nier or other orange liqueur	Grated peel of 1 orange
	6 egg whites
4 egg yolks	¾ cup sliced or slivered blanched almonds

1. Prick top of cake layers lightly in many places with a fork, then sprinkle each layer with liqueur, using about 3 tablespoons for each.

2. Make crème anglaise by whisking the egg yolks in a bowl, adding ½ cup of sugar, and whisking until thick and lemony in color.

3. Heat the half-and-half to the boiling point in a stainless-steel-lined or an enamel-on-iron pan.

• An egg mixture—one is to be added here—tends to discolor when cooked in aluminum.

4. Gradually pour hot half-and-half into egg mixture, whisking constantly. Then pour the egg–half-and-half mixture into the saucepan and cook over high heat, stirring with whisk, until it thickens slightly.

• The mixture will be thin, but it should coat the back of a spoon—that is, it should film the back of the spoon enough so that a line can be drawn in the film with your finger.

5. Stir orange peel and the remaining ¼ cup of liqueur into the mixture.

6. Put a layer of cake on a stainless-steel tray or an ovenproof platter or serving dish and spoon warm crème anglaise over it. Let the crème anglaise soak in.

7. Stack the second layer on top and soak it with the crème anglaise. Prick the cake with a fork so that the crème will soak in.

8. Make the meringue by beating the egg whites until foamy in an electric mixer, adding the remaining 1 cup of sugar, 1 tablespoon at a time (if the sugar is added too fast, the meringue will get watery), and beating until the mixture looks like marshmallow. This will take a lot of beating. Rub a bit of the mixture between your fingers, and if it feels granular, beat it longer. When it is smooth, it's ready to use.

9. Put meringue in a large pastry bag fitted with a star tube and pipe meringue up and down to cover the sides of the cake, extending it over the top edge. Cover the top with rosettes. The cake should be completely covered.

10. Throw almonds against top and sides of cake so they stick to the meringue.

11. Bake in a preheated 400° oven for 5 to 6 minutes, or until meringue is set, then place cake in refrigerator to chill. *Makes 12 servings.*

YELLOW BUTTER CAKE

Before starting to make this cake have all ingredients at room temperature.

1 cup unsalted butter, plus butter to grease cake pan or pans
3 cups sifted cake flour, plus flour to shake into pan or pans

2 cups superfine sugar
4 separated eggs
1 tablespoon vanilla extract
1 tablespoon baking powder
1 cup milk

1. Prepare 2 9-inch layer-cake pans or 1 deep 10-inch pan by buttering generously, then shaking in flour and tapping out the excess flour.

2. In an electric mixer bowl, cream remaining 1 cup of butter and gradually add sugar. Beat until very light and fluffy.

3. Beat in egg yolks, one at a time, and continue beating until well mixed.

4. Beat in vanilla.

5. Sift baking powder and 3 cups of flour together, then make batter by adding them to the butter-egg-yolk mixture alternately with milk. Begin and end with flour and beat well after each addition.

6. In another bowl, beat egg whites until they stand in stiff peaks.

• Be certain beaters are completely clean.

7. Stir a spoonful of the whites into the batter to lighten it, then fold in the remaining whites.

8. Pour mixture into the prepared cake pan or pans—divide it evenly if 2 pans are used—and put in a preheated 350° oven for 25 to 30 minutes, or until a cake tester is clean when inserted and removed.

• An oven rack should be placed so the top of the cake pan (or the tops of the 2 pans) will be in the middle of the oven, with the pan sides not touching the oven walls, and if 2 pans are used, not touching each other. This will allow heat to circulate freely around the pan or pans and help the batter to bake evenly.

9. Set the pan or pans on a cake rack to cool for about 10 minutes, then run a knife around the edges to loosen the cake, and turn it out to cool completely.

• This cake can be frozen if it's wrapped well in plastic wrap or foil. *Makes 2 9-inch layers.*

ITALIAN RUM CAKE

A wildly magnificent rococo cake, elaborately decorated. Although it takes some time, little real skill is needed to make it.

1 cup mixed candied fruits
½ cup rum, about
1 10-inch Sponge Cake (recipe follows)
3 lbs. ricotta cheese
1½ cups confectioners' sugar
2 tablespoons crème de cacao
1 cup shaved dark sweet chocolate
3 cups heavy cream
8 candied cherries
16 tiny pieces candied angelica (available in gourmet shops)
¼ cup chopped green pistachios

1. Soak the mixed candied fruits in 6 tablespoons of rum for 1 hour, then drain and reserve the rum. Set fruits aside.

2. Cut the sponge cake—not while it's warm—into 3 layers either with a serrated knife or by sawing it through with a thread.

• To make the layers even, mark the cuts all around the cake with toothpicks.

3. Sprinkle the layers with rum, using the reserved rum plus enough additional rum (6 tablespoons in all) to get 2 tablespoons on each layer. Let it soak in.

4. In the big bowl of an electric mixer, beat ricotta cheese at medium speed until fluffy. Beat in 1 cup of confectioners' sugar and continue beating until very fluffy. Beat in crème de cacao.

5. Transfer ⅓ of the cheese mixture to another bowl and fold ½ cup of the shaved chocolate into it.

6. Fold the set-aside candied fruits into the remaining cheese mixture.

7. Place the bottom layer of the cake, cut side up, on a serving platter and cover the top of this layer with ½ the candied-fruit-cheese mixture. Then put the next layer in place and cover the top of it with the chocolate-cheese mixture. Finally, put the top layer in place and cover it and the sides of the cake with remaining candied-fruit–cheese mixture.

8. Whip the cream at medium speed in a large bowl of an electric mixer, adding the remaining ½ cup of confectioners' sugar gradually and beating until stiff.

• For best results, bowl, beaters, and cream should all be chilled. Watch carefully when the cream starts to get stiff. There's a very fine line between stiffly whipped cream and butter. Cream should be stiff enough to stand in peaks when beater blades are lifted.

9. Stir in the remaining 2 tablespoons of rum.

10. Use about ¼ of whipped cream and frost the cake all over, smoothing it with a spatula. Try to get the top very smooth.

11. Fill a large pastry bag, fitted with a star tube, with the remaining whipped cream and pipe it up and down to cover the sides and the top edge of the cake. Leave the top smooth.

12. Soak angelica for about 20 minutes in warm water to soften it, then cut it into 8 leaf shapes.

13. Decorate the top of the cake by spacing candied cherries around the edge, placing the angelica leaves beside the cherries, then sprinkling on chopped pistachios and the remaining shaved chocolate.

14. Put cake in a refrigerator to allow the flavors to blend for 24 hours before serving. *Makes 12 servings.*

SPONGE CAKE

6 separated eggs	1½ cups sugar
1 tablespoon grated orange peel	¼ teaspoon salt
	1⅓ cups sifted cake flour
½ cup orange juice	1 teaspoon cream of tartar

1. In an electric-mixer bowl, beat egg yolks at high speed for 5 minutes.

2. Add orange peel and juice and continue beating.

3. Beat in 1 cup of sugar and salt, 1 tablespoon at a time, and continue beating until the mixture will "form the ribbon"—that is, until some will fall from the beaters and look like a ribbon on the surface of the rest.

4. Fold flour into mixture and set aside.

• To sift and measure cake flour, place measuring cups on waxed paper, sift flour directly into cups, and level off the tops with a spatula.

5. In another bowl, and with clean beaters, beat egg whites until they begin to foam, then add cream of tartar, beat until the mixture forms soft peaks, add the remaining ½ cup of sugar, 1 tablespoon at a time, and beat until the mixture forms stiff peaks.

• It is important that bowl and beaters be absolutely clean—with no fat or grease and not the tiniest trace of egg yolk; otherwise the egg whites will not beat properly.

6. Gently, with a rubber spatula, fold the egg-white mixture into the egg-yolk mixture.

7. Pour folded mixture into an ungreased 10-inch tube pan with a removable bottom and place in a preheated 325° oven for 55 minutes, or until a cake tester, inserted in cake, comes out clean.

8. Place cake upside down on a bottle (if cake pan hasn't legs) to cool for about 1 hour.

9. When cake is completely cooled, loosen it from the sides of the pan with a knife, using an up-and-down motion, and turn it out.

• Sponge cake can be frozen for up to 1 month. *Makes 1 10-inch cake.*

Hazelnut Roll with Whipped-Cream Filling

Ground nuts replace flour in this unusual cake roll.

Oil to grease baking pan and
paper
7 separated eggs
1 cup sugar
2 teaspoons baking powder
1¼ cup ground hazelnuts

2 tablespoons confectioners'
sugar, plus confectioners'
sugar to dust on cake
1½ cups heavy cream
1 tablespoon rum

1. Oil an 11-by-17-inch jelly-roll pan or baking tray, line it with waxed paper, letting the paper extend about 3 inches over the ends, and oil again. Set aside.

2. In an electric mixer bowl, beat egg yolks at medium speed. Gradually add sugar and beat 5 to 7 minutes until the mixture is thick and will "form the ribbon"—that is, until part of it will fall from the beaters and look like a ribbon on the surface of the rest.

3. Mix baking powder with ground hazelnuts and add to egg mixture. Beat at low speed just enough to mix.

• Hazlenuts can be bought ground. If you grind your own in a blender, spread them out on a baking sheet overnight to dry.

4. In another bowl, with clean beaters, beat egg whites until they form soft peaks. Egg whites should not be dry.

5. Stir ¼ of the egg whites into the nut mixture to lighten it, then gently fold in the remaining whites.

• To fold, cut down through the center of the bowl with a big rubber spatula, then cut across the bottom, up a side, over to the center, down again, and so on. Keep turning the bowl as you fold. And do not overfold: flecks of white should still be visible when the mixture is turned into the baking pan.

6. Spread mixture in the prepared baking pan and bake in a preheated 350° oven for 15 minutes.

7. Let cake cool for a few minutes with paper towels spread over it to prevent crust from forming. Remove towels, loosen cake from edge of pan, and dust generously with confectioners' sugar.

8. Lay 2 strips of waxed paper, overlapping lengthwise, on a table or counter, dust the waxed paper with confectioners' sugar, turn the baking pan over onto the paper, then lift the pan off the cake and peel away the paper lining.

9. In a bowl set over ice, whip heavy cream, with a whisk, sweetening it with 2 tablespoons of confectioners' sugar. Stir in rum.

10. Spread whipped cream on the cake, then roll up the cake like a jelly roll, starting on the long side. Use waxed paper strips to help you roll the cake and transfer it to a long serving board. Remove all waxed paper.

• The roll can be put in a plastic bag or wrapped in plastic wrap or foil and frozen. Defrost it in a refrigerator.

11. Sift confectioners' sugar over the cake before serving. **Makes 8 to 10 servings.**

MARRON ROLL

One of my favorite desserts—maybe because it's indestructible. The sponge roll can be filled with jelly or with strawberries mixed with sour cream, or with Lemon Curd (see p. 207). This version, filled with preserved marrons (chestnuts packed in syrup) and whipped cream, can be completely finished, including the decorations, and frozen for use later on.

5 separated eggs
¼ cup sugar
¼ cup flour
2 tablespoons vanilla extract
   or rum
Vegetable oil to grease baking
   pan and paper

2 cups heavy cream
¼ cup confectioners' sugar
¾ cup preserved chopped
   chestnuts, drained
4 whole preserved chestnuts

1. Beat egg yolks with an electric mixer at medium speed until light and fluffy.

2. Add sugar and continue beating until the mixture is thick and lemon-colored.

3. Stir in flour and 1 tablespoon of vanilla (or rum) and set aside.

4. In another bowl, with clean, dry beaters, beat egg whites until stiff but not dry. They should make soft peaks.

5. Fold whites into egg-yolk mixture to make sponge-roll batter.

6. Oil an 11-by-17-inch jelly-roll pan, line it with waxed paper, oil the waxed paper, and pour batter on the paper. Spread evenly.

7. Bake in a preheated 400° oven for 12 minutes, when cake should be golden.

8. Loosen the edges of the cake, turn it out on 2 overlapping sheets of waxed paper or on a tea towel, roll it up lengthwise in the waxed paper or the towel, and chill 20 minutes.

9. Whip cream by beating it in a bowl set over ice. Beat in 2 tablespoons of confectioners' sugar and 1 tablespoon of vanilla (or rum). Cream should be firm enough to hold a definite shape, but take care not to overbeat it, for it can turn to butter very quickly.

• Cream whipped over ice (and sweetened with confectioners' sugar instead of granulated sugar) is less likely than other cream to get watery or separate later.

10. Into ¾ of the whipped cream—reserve the rest for decoration—fold chopped chestnuts. Unroll the cake, spread filling on it, then roll it up again and place it on a long wooden board (this is called a chocolate-roll board) or a narrow silver platter.

11. Decorate the top of the roll with 4 rosettes of whipped cream made with a pastry bag and a large star tube.

12. Place a whole preserved chestnut on each rosette, sift confectioners' sugar over the decorated roll, and refrigerate until serving time.

• If the roll is to be frozen, wrap it loosely in plastic wrap or foil. Defrost in refrigerator. *Makes 10 servings.*

REHRÜCKEN

(Mock Saddle of Venison Cake)

This Viennese almond cake is baked in a rectangular ribbed mold that supposedly resembles the back of a deer.

1 tablespoon butter	*6 tablespoons sugar*
½ cup bread crumbs (see p. 7)	*½ cup ground blanched almonds*
3 egg yolks	*¼ teaspoon ground cinnamon*

3 tablespoons very finely
chopped citron (available
in gourmet shops)
⅓ cup grated bittersweet
chocolate
4 egg whites
¼ teaspoon cream of tartar

Chocolate Glaze (recipe follows)
½ cup halved or slivered
blanched almonds
1 cup heavy cream
2 tablespoons confectioners'
sugar

1. Butter—use 1 tablespoon of butter—a 1-quart Rehrücken mold measuring approximately 4 inches by 12 inches. Dust it with ¼ cup of bread crumbs and turn it upside down to knock out the excess crumbs.

2. In the large bowl of the electric mixer, beat egg yolks at medium speed until thick and light in color.

3. Gradually beat in ¼ cup of sugar at high speed and beat until the mixture will "form the ribbon"—that is, until part of it will fall from the lifted beaters and look like a ribbon on the surface of the rest. This will take about 5 minutes of beating.

4. Slow the mixer to medium speed and add ground almonds, cinnamon, citron, chocolate, and the remaining ¼ cup of bread crumbs. Beat to form a dense, moist mass. Set aside.

5. In another bowl, with clean beaters, beat egg whites and cream of tartar at medium speed until foamy.

6. Add the remaining 2 tablespoons of sugar, 1 tablespoon at a time, and beat until egg whites form soft peaks.

7. Fold ¼ of the egg-white mixture into the egg-yolk mixture to lighten it, then gently fold the lightened egg-yolk mixture into the remaining egg-white mixture, folding just until all trace of egg white disappears.

8. Pour mixture into the prepared mold and put it in a preheated 375° oven for 40 minutes, or until the cake is golden brown and springs back when touched lightly.

9. Cool the cake in the mold for 2 to 3 minutes, then turn it out on a cake rack to cool completely, about 30 minutes.

10. When the cake is cool, set the rack on waxed paper (which will catch any drippings) and spoon slightly cooled Chocolate Glaze evenly over it.

11. Toast the almond halves or slivers by spreading them on a shallow pan and putting them in a preheated 300° oven for about 15 minutes, or until they're lightly browned. Toss them around a couple of times as they brown.

12. Stick the toasted almonds, like porcupine quills, into the glaze in even rows along the ribs of the cake (see illustration, p. 220).

13. Whip the heavy cream with confectioners' sugar until it will hold a definite shape. Serve separately with the cake.

Chocolate Glaze

⅓ cup heavy cream
3 tablespoons butter
½ cup cocoa

¾ cup sugar
½ teaspoon vanilla

1. Put all ingredients except vanilla into a saucepan, set over medium heat, and cook, stirring constantly, for 3 to 4 minutes.

2. Remove pan from heat and stir in vanilla.

• Glaze should be smooth, thick, and shiny. ***Makes 8 servings.***

VIENNESE ALMOND BALLS

1 cup butter
½ cup confectioners' sugar, about
¼ teaspoon salt
1 cup ground blanched almonds

1½ cups flour, about, plus flour to dust on baking sheet
¼ cup rum

1. Beat butter with an electric mixer at medium speed until light and fluffy, then add 6 tablespoons confectioners' sugar, 1 tablespoon at a time, add salt, and continue beating until well mixed. Scrape sides and bottom of mixing bowl when necessary, using a rubber spatula.

2. Add ground almonds and beat well.

3. Gradually add flour—a little more than 1½ cups if necessary—to make a stiff batter.

4. Mix in rum. Chill the batter 20 minutes.

5. Roll the batter into balls the size of marbles, place the balls on a lightly floured baking sheet, and bake in a preheated 350° oven for about 15 minutes, or until the balls are light brown in color.

6. Cool the balls slightly, then roll them in about 2 tablespoons confectioners' sugar—twice if necessary—to coat generously. *Makes about 24 balls.*

Oeufs à la Neige

This is a spectacular dessert—a pyramid of poached meringue "eggs" floating in custard and decorated (if desired) with spun caramel.

1 quart milk	*6 separated eggs*
¾ cup sugar, plus ½ cup sugar, optional (for caramel)	*¼ teaspoon salt*
	⅛ teaspoon cream of tartar
1 2-inch piece of vanilla bean or 2 teaspoons vanilla extract	*1 teaspoon cornstarch*
	1 tablespoon rum

1. Prepare poaching mixture by bringing milk to a boil in a skillet, then stirring in 6 tablespoons of sugar and vanilla bean or extract, and reducing heat to simmer.

• To flavor milk with vanilla bean: split the pod, scrape out the seeds, and drop both seeds and pod into the sugar-milk mixture.

2. While the milk simmers, make meringue mixture in a mixer bowl by beating egg whites at high speed until foamy, and adding salt and cream of tartar. Continue beating, adding 6 tablespoons of sugar, 1 tablespoon at a time, then adding cornstarch. Beat until the mixture looks like marshmallow.

• It's almost impossible to overbeat. The mixture must be very, very stiff. The classic recipe does not call for the addition of starch, but this holds up the egg whites during poaching.

3. To shape the meringue mixture dip 2 serving spoons in a bowl of hot water, scoop up a mound of the mixture in one spoon, and round it off—it should be egg-shaped—with the other spoon.

4. Slide the shaped mixture from the spoon into the simmering milk, repeat step 3 once or twice more (depending on the size of the skillet), slide the 1 or 2 more "eggs" into the milk, and poach about 30 seconds on each side (turn the "eggs" over with 2 forks).

5. Drain the poached "eggs" on paper towels.

6. Keep repeating steps 3, 4, and 5 until the rest of the meringue mixture has been used up, then strain the milk.

7. Make custard, by beating the egg yolks until foamy, then gradually pouring on the strained milk, stirring with a whisk. Pour the mixture into a saucepan (not an aluminum one) and cook at medium high heat, stirring constantly, until it is the consistency of heavy cream and will coat the back of a spoon so that a line can be drawn on the film with your finger. Flavor with rum and strain into a shallow glass serving dish.

8. Pile the meringue "eggs" in a pyramid on the custard and then, if desired, make caramel to be spun over them.

9. Make caramel by putting ½ cup of sugar and ¼ cup of water into a small heavy saucepan and cooking over high heat, stirring, until the sugar is dissolved. Do not stir any more, but keep tilting the pan back and forth over heat to keep the syrup moving, for about 15 minutes.

• Caramelizing sugar is touchy but it is interesting to do. It is imperative to watch it closely, as it turns from white to butterscotch to dark amber. I like it almost burned. If you don't, take it off the heat before it gets too dark.

• Just before the syrup is ready it gives off a little puff of smoke and boils up with lots of big bubbles.

• Another test, if you have tough fingers and are careful (the hot syrup can burn badly): pinch a drop of syrup between thumb and forefinger and pull apart; if there is a thread, the caramel is ready.

10. Take caramel off heat. Stop the cooking by setting the saucepan in cold water or over ice. Dip into the caramel with a fork, lift the fork,

and use it to spin threads of caramel round and round the pyramid of "eggs."

• Instead of spun caramel, the "eggs" can be garnished with shaved chocolate, or Raspberry Sauce (see p. 204) can be poured over them.
• Refrigerate the "eggs" uncovered if you're not ready to serve. But they won't hold for more than 2 or 3 hours; then the meringue "eggs" begin to weep—that is, they begin to give off liquid. *Makes 6 servings.*

PFANNKUCHEN

(German Apple Pancake)

¼ cup flour
7 teaspoons sugar, plus sugar to sprinkle on pancake
¼ teaspoon salt
2 eggs
⅔ cup milk
¼ cup butter

2½ cups peeled, cored, and thinly sliced apples
1 teaspoon cinnamon, plus cinnamon to sprinkle on pancake
½ cup dairy sour cream

1. Make batter by putting flour, 1 teaspoon of sugar, salt, eggs, and milk in a blender jar and blending until smooth.
2. Refrigerate the batter for 1 hour.
3. Melt 2 tablespoons of butter and sauté the apple slices in it, stirring, until they begin to look transparent.
4. Add 2 tablespoons sugar and 1 teaspoon of cinnamon and cook over high heat until the apple slices are soft and caramelized. This will take about 10 minutes. Set aside.
5. When ready to bake the pancake, melt the remaining 2 tablespoons of butter in a 10-inch skillet.

• A good pan to use for this is one lined with Teflon.

6. When the butter is sizzling, pour on ¾ of the batter. Let it set for 2 seconds, then spread the apple mixture over it, patting the apple mixture out to cover the batter.
7. Pour the remaining batter over the apple mixture, then tip the pan back and forth over high heat to allow the uncooked batter to run underneath the pancake. If the pan is hot enough, this will take only about 5 minutes.
8. Shake the pan smartly to loosen the pancake. Tip the pan to aid in rolling the pancake like an omelette and turn it out on a warm serving platter.
9. Sprinkle it generously with a mixture of sugar and cinnamon, and serve with sour cream on the side. *Makes 2 servings.*

BANANAS VIEUX CARRÉ

This is a New Orleans specialty that's simple to make and nice to do for company. The bananas can be readied for baking before dinner, baked while you eat, then flamed at the table.

½ cup butter	*½ teaspoon cinnamon*
6 bananas	*¼ cup honey*
Grated peel of 2 oranges	*⅓ cup light rum*
½ cup orange juice	*Crème Fraîche, optional*
3 tablespoons lime juice	*(recipe follows)*

1. Melt ¼ cup of the butter in an ovenproof dish that can be taken to the table (an oval au gratin dish is ideal).
2. Peel the bananas, split them lengthwise, and roll the halves in the melted butter. Coat well.
3. Dot the remaining ¼ cup of butter on the banana halves, sprinkle them with grated orange peel, orange and lime juice, cinnamon, and honey, and bake them for 15 minutes in a preheated 375° oven.
4. Flame with rum by warming rum in a small pan and igniting and spooning the flaming sauce over the bananas until the flames die down and serve with the rum sauce and also, if desired, with Crème Fraîche.

Crème Fraîche

There is nothing in the United States like the French Crème Fraîche, a naturally thick cream with a flavor all its own, usually served in a crock with a wooden spoon. This is how I make a pseudo Crème Fraîche to serve either with Bananas Vieux Carré or over berries.

3 oz. cream cheese	*1 cup heavy cream*
½ cup dairy sour cream	

1. Bring all ingredients to room temperature.
2. Soften the cream cheese and beat it with sour cream, using a whisk or an electric mixer.
3. Combine with heavy cream, barely whipped.
4. Let the mixture stand at room temperature for an hour before serving (don't refrigerate it, or the cheese will set), preferably in a tall crock with a wooden spoon. *Makes 6 servings.*

CHERRY FRITTERS

1 lb. Bing cherries, with stems	1 tablespoon melted butter
2 separated eggs	½ teaspoon baking powder
⅔ cup milk	1 tablespoon kirsch
1 tablespoon sugar	2 cups vegetable shortening
1 cup flour	½ cup confectioners' sugar
¼ teaspoon salt	

1. Wash and dry cherries. Leave the stems on and the pits in (pits help the fritters stay warm).

2. Beat egg yolks and stir in milk, sugar, flour, salt, butter, baking powder, and kirsch. Beat until smooth.

3. Beat egg whites until they form soft peaks, then fold them into the yolk mixture.

4. Heat the shortening to 375° in a heavy saucepan. Check the temperature with a fat thermometer, or test it with a bread cube, which will brown nicely in 1 minute if the temperature of the fat is right.

5. Hold a cherry by the stem, dip it into fritter batter, then drop it into the hot shortening. Dip and drop in about 5 more cherries (fry no more than 6 fritters at a time, or the fat will cool too much for the fritters to brown properly), fry for about 2 minutes or until the fritters are golden brown and crusty, then remove the fritters with a slotted spoon and drain them on brown paper or paper towels.

6. Return the shortening to 375° (check the temperature again), then repeat step 5; repeat as many times as necessary to use up all the cherries.

7. Heap the fritters in a pyramid on a serving plate and sift confectioners' sugar over them.

• The most efficient way to do this is to put the sugar in a sieve and stir it with a spoon. *Makes 4 to 6 servings.*

ORANGES ORIENTALE

8 large navel oranges	1 tablespoon grenadine or a
2 cups sugar	few drops of red food color-
¼ teaspoon cream of tartar	ing
½ cup Cointreau or any other	8 candied violets (available in
orange liqueur	gourmet shops)

1. Make orange-peel syrup by peeling the oranges as thinly as possible with a potato peeler, removing the orange-colored covering but

not the bitter white part. Setting the oranges aside, lay the peel on a chopping board, and with a chef's knife, cut it into the finest shreds or slivers possible.

2. Put the slivers into a saucepan with 2 cups of water, sugar, and cream of tartar (cream of tartar keeps syrups from crystallizing), bring to a boil, then reduce heat to simmer, and cook until thick and syrupy—about 25 to 30 minutes.

3. Remove from heat, stir in liqueur, then add grenadine or enough red food coloring to tint the syrup a pretty orange color. Chill.

4. Finish peeling the oranges, cutting off all the white part. Leave the oranges whole and pile them in a pyramid in a glass bowl. Refrigerate them for 2 hours.

5. Before serving, spoon chilled syrup over the oranges, spooning as much as possible of the shredded peel over the top of the oranges, and garnish each orange with a candied violet. *Makes 8 servings.*

POIRES AU VIN ROUGE

The pears used for this recipe should be either green winter pears or brown Boscs, and they should be firm but not hard. If they're not ripe enough when you buy them, leave them overnight in a closed brown paper bag at room temperature.

8 pears	*1 cup red currant jelly*
1 tablespoon lemon juice	*½ teaspoon red food coloring*
1 cup sugar	*1 cinnamon stick, optional*
2 cups port wine	*8 fresh mint leaves*

1. Leaving the stems on, peel the pears with a vegetable peeler, cut a little slice off the bottom of each pear so it will stand upright, and immediately drop each into a bowl containing 1 quart of water mixed with 1 tablespoon of lemon juice. (This will keep the pears from turning dark.)

2. In a saucepan big enough to hold all the pears, boil together the sugar, wine, jelly, red food coloring, and if you like cinnamon, the cinnamon stick, for 5 minutes.

3. Put pears into the mixture, return to a boil and then lower heat to a simmer. Poach the pears in this mixture, spooning it over them or turning them in it to get them an even red color. After 15 minutes begin to test with a fork for tenderness.

4. When the pears are tender, remove them from syrup with a slotted spoon and place them upright on a cake rack set on a tray and put them in a refrigerator to chill for 1 hour.

5. Boil the liquid in which the pears cooked until it thickens slightly; and when the pears are chilled, take them out of the refrigerator, spoon some of the hot liquid over each, collect the drippings in the tray, and return them to the saucepan. Put the pears in the refrigerator for 1 hour to chill again. Repeat this glazing-chilling process 2 more times, or until the pears are very shiny and a deep red color.

• The liquid clings best when it's hot and the pears are cold.

6. Before serving, decorate the stem of each pear with a mint leaf.

• Serve plain or with sour cream. **Makes 8 servings.**

Pears Hélène

6 *Bartlett pears*
1 *cup sugar*
1 *tablespoon vanilla extract*
6 *slices Sponge Cake (see p. 215)*
1 *pint vanilla ice cream*
2 *cups Chocolate Fudge Sauce (see p. 233)*

1 *cup heavy cream*
2 *tablespoons confectioners' sugar*
6 *candied violets (available in gourmet shops)*

1. Peel and core the pears, leaving them whole.
2. Combine sugar and 1 quart of water in a saucepan, bring to a boil, then add the pears, reduce heat, and simmer, uncovered, for 10 minutes, or until the pears are tender. Turn the pears occasionally so they cook evenly.

• The cooking time will depend on the ripeness of the pears. Test them with the tip of a paring knife; if it goes in easily the pears are done.

3. Remove pan from heat, add vanilla, and let the pears cool in the liquid, spooning it over them a couple of times while they're cooling.
4. Cut the cake slices in rounds, place them on individual serving dishes, and top each round with a slice of ice cream.
5. Stand a drained pear on each slice of ice cream and coat with chocolate fudge sauce.
6. Whip cream with confectioners' sugar until stiff, put it into a pastry bag fitted with a star tube, and pipe a rosette of whipped cream on each chocolate-covered pear.
7. Decorate each rosette with a candied violet. **Makes 6 servings.**

Apricot Mousse with Chocolate Cornets

Vegetable oil to grease collar
  of soufflé dish
1½ 12-oz. pkgs. dried apricots
  2 tablespoons (2 envelopes)
  unflavored gelatin
⅓ cup cognac
  7 egg whites
¼ teaspoon salt

18 tablespoons (1 cup plus 2
  tablespoons) sugar
3 tablespoons Grand Marnier
2 cups heavy cream
2 tablespoons confectioners'
  sugar
2 Chocolate Cornets (recipe
  follows)

1. Prepare a 4-cup soufflé dish with a paper collar: fold a strip of waxed paper about 2 feet long in half lengthwise to make a strip about 7 inches wide, oil the collar, place it around the outside of the dish and extending 4 to 5 inches above it, then tie a string around it.

2. Soak the apricots in cold water to cover for 2 hours.

3. Drain the apricots, put them in a saucepan, cover with fresh water, and bring to a boil. Cover, reduce heat, and simmer for 20 to 25 minutes or until soft.

4. Drain off all but ¼ cup of liquid from the apricots and purée them in a blender. There must be 2 cups of purée.

5. Put cognac in a glass measuring cup, sprinkle gelatin over it, let it stand about 5 minutes while the gelatin softens, then set it in a pan of boiling water and stir until the gelatin dissolves.

6. Stir the dissolved gelatin mixture into the apricot purée. Mix well.

7. In large mixer bowl, beat egg whites, adding salt when they begin to foam.

8. Add sugar, 1 tablespoon at a time, and continue beating until the mixture looks like marshmallow. Pinch a bit of it between your fingers; if it feels smooth, it's ready.

9. Beat in the apricot purée and 2 tablespoons of Grand Marnier.

10. In another bowl, whip 1 cup of cream to the same consistency as the apricot mixture.

11. Fold the cream into the apricot mixture, pile into the prepared soufflé dish, and put in a refrigerator for several hours to set.

• This can be done the day before the mousse is to be served.

12. Whip the remaining 1 cup of cream with confectioners' sugar until stiff and mix in the remaining 1 tablespoon of Grand Marnier.

13. Put the cream into a pastry bag with a star tube, and after carefully removing the waxed-paper collar from the soufflé dish, pipe whipped-cream rosettes around the top of the mousse.

14. Pipe cream into 2 chocolate cornets and place them in the center of the mousse, facing in opposite directions. ***Makes 12 generous servings.***

Chocolate Cornets

To get 2 cornets, it's wise to make 4, allowing for breakage.

¼ lb. dark sweet chocolate

1. Melt the chocolate—just enough to make it spreadable—in a heat-proof glass dish set over a saucepan of simmering water in such a way that steam won't rise around the dish and touch the chocolate.

• Melting chocolate directly over heat or getting a drop of water in it will cause it to separate.

2. Make 4 waxed-paper cones by cutting triangles of waxed paper 6 by 6 by 8½ inches, twisting them into cone shapes and fastening them with bits of tape.

3. Place the waxed-paper cones inside 4 cornucopia molds or 4 cone-shaped paper drinking cups, then coat them *inside* with chocolate, using a tiny spatula or demitasse spoon.

4. Stand the molds in flat-bottomed paper cups and put in a refrigerator for about 1 hour, or until set.

• Don't put the molds in a freezer, or the chocolate will turn gray.

5. Remove the waxed-paper cones from the molds or cups and very carefully peel the waxed paper from the chocolate. *Makes 4 cones.*

BUTTERSCOTCH-RUM PARFAIT

The true parfait has a boiled sugar syrup added to an egg-yolk base, and it is sinfully rich. If butterscotch isn't your favorite, use this same technique to make chocolate or fresh fruit parfaits.

¾ cup brown sugar	*⅛ teaspoon salt*
¼ cup butter	*2 cups whipped heavy cream*
3 egg yolks	*3 tablespoons crushed*
1 tablespoon rum	*blanched almonds*

1. In a small saucepan, make syrup by bringing brown sugar, butter, and ¾ cup of water to a boil, stirring to dissolve the sugar, then boiling hard for 3 minutes. Set aside.

• For flavor changes, make the syrup with granulated sugar instead of brown sugar, flavor the egg yolks (step 4) with 1 tablespoon of vanilla extract instead of with rum, and fold in ½ cup of melted chocolate, or chocolate and coffee-flavored liqueur, or fresh berries, or peaches along with the whipped cream (step 6). Or invent your own parfait.

2. In a small electric mixer bowl, beat egg yolks at medium speed until light and fluffy.

3. Gradually pour in the set-aside syrup, in a thin stream, beating all the while.

4. Beat in rum and salt, then place the mixture in a saucepan and whisk over high heat until it is as thick as heavy cream.

5. Set mixing bowl over ice, and whisk about 10 minutes or until cool.

6. Fold in whipped cream, pour into parfait glasses, and set in a freezer for at least 1 hour.

• The cream should be whipped to the same consistency as the parfait base but not as thick as cream whipped for decorating.

• The longer the parfait stays in the freezer, the more solid it becomes. I like to make it the day before I plan to serve it.

7. Three hours before serving, remove parfaits from freezer and place in refrigerator.

• When served, parfaits should be the consistency of frozen custard.

8. Sprinkle tops with crushed almonds. *Makes 6 servings.*

TARTE AUX PÊCHES

1 *wholly baked 9-inch pâte brisée shell (see p. 36)*	5 *tablespoons confectioners sugar*
2 *tablespoons bread crumbs (see p. 7)*	1 to 2 *1-pound cans snow peach halves*
1½ *cups heavy cream*	½ *cup apricot jam or jelly*
2 *tablespoons framboise*	¼ *cup natural pistachio nuts*

1. Sprinkle the bottom of the pâte brisée shell with bread crumbs to prevent filling from soaking into the shell.

2. Whip the cream by hand in a large bowl set over ice until it will stand in stiff peaks. Beat in framboise and 3 tablespoons of the confectioners' sugar.

• Cream whipped over ice and sweetened with confectioners' sugar doesn't tend to separate on standing. This allows you to assemble the tart in the morning, for dinner that night.

3. Spread cream into the pâte brisée shell.

4. Drain and dry 1 can of peach halves and arrange them, rounded sides up, over the cream. If more peaches are needed to fill the tart (the number of peaches in a can varies), open the other can.

5. Make glaze by putting the jam or jelly into a small pan with 1 tablespoon of cold water, stirring over high heat until the jam or jelly melts, bringing it to a boil, then straining.

• Apricot glaze, which can be kept in a small jar in the refrigerator, can be used on any light-colored fruit.

6. With a pastry brush, paint the peach halves with glaze. Take care that none drips onto the whipped cream.

• For other fruit tarts: white grapes, cherries, large strawberries, or other berries can be substituted. Arrange over cream and follow directions for glazing, except that for red fruits or berries—cherries, strawberries, raspberries—make glaze with red currant jelly rather than with apricot jam or jelly. If using berries, omit nuts (step 7); if using grapes, substitute blanched almonds for pistachios.

• For fruit tartlets, an assortment of which makes an excellent dessert, bake pâte brisée in individual tart shells or barquette molds.

7. Put the pistachios between 2 sheets of waxed paper, crush them with a rolling pin or mallet, then sprinkle them over the peach halves.

8. Before serving, sift the remaining 2 tablespoons of confectioners' sugar around the edge of the tart. ***Makes 6 servings.***

CASSIS SHERBET

4 cups light cream	*1 cup sugar*
⅔ cup black currant jam	*⅔ cup cassis liqueur*
6 egg yolks	*3 cups heavy cream*

1. Scald the light cream in a saucepan—that is, heat the cream in the pan until bubbles appear around the edges.

2. Add jam to the scalded cream and stir over high heat until the jam dissolves.

3. Beat egg yolks until light and fluffy.

4. Gradually beat in sugar and continue beating until the mixture will "form the ribbon"—that is, until some will fall from the lifted beaters and look like a ribbon on the surface of the rest.

5. Slowly pour the cream mixture into the egg-yolk mixture, stirring with a whisk.

6. Whisk well, pour into the saucepan used for the cream, place over heat, and cook over high heat, stirring constantly, until the mixture will coat the back of a spoon enough so that a line can be drawn in the film with your finger.

7. Chill in a freezer about 10 minutes, then stir in cassis and refrigerate until cold.

8. Whip the heavy cream and fold it into the cassis mixture.

9. Pour into the can of an ice-cream freezer and freeze according to manufacturer's directions, or pour into ice-cube trays, freeze about 1 hour or until mushy, remove from trays, beat with an electric mixer, return to the trays, and freeze about 2 hours or until firm. ***Makes 8 to 10 servings.***

MERINGUE SHELLS

Filled with fruit and whipped cream or filled with ice cream and topped with a favorite sauce these shells make delicious desserts. They can be kept in a plastic bag or air-tight container on your pantry shelf for 1 month.

6 *egg whites*	1 *teaspoon white vinegar*
2 *cups sugar*	1 *teaspoon vanilla*

1. Put egg whites in a large electric mixer bowl and beat until foamy; then, beating all the while, add 1 cup of sugar, 1 tablespoon at a time, add vinegar and vanilla, and add the remaining 1 cup of sugar, 1 tablespoon at a time.

2. Continue beating for 5 to 10 minutes, or until the mixture looks like marshmallow and is smooth, not granular, when you pinch a bit of it between thumb and forefinger.

3. Put mixture into a large pastry bag fitted with a plain round tube

and pipe out solid circles—there should be 10 to 12 of them—from 3 to 4 inches in diameter by starting in the center of each circle and spiraling out; then build up the sides of each shell to the desired depth by piping the mixture around the edge of each circle, 1 ring on top of another.

4. Set the formed shells aside for several hours to dry out; then place them either on baking sheets lined with baking parchment or brown paper or on Teflon-coated baking sheets and bake them in a preheated 250° oven for about 45 minutes, or until they are hard to the touch. They should be white or creamy white; never brown.

5. Turn off the oven and let the shells stand in it with the door closed until they're cool. *Makes 10 to 12 shells.*

CHOCOLATE FUDGE SAUCE

This is the best fudge sauce I know. Serve it hot or cold, on cakes, ice cream brownies, puddings—you name it.

½ *cup cocoa*	3 *tablespoons butter*
1 *cup sugar*	¼ *teaspoon salt*
1 *cup light corn syrup*	1 *teaspoon vanilla*
½ *cup light cream*	

1. Put all ingredients except vanilla into a small saucepan, bring to a boil, and boil 5 minutes.

2. Remove from heat and stir in vanilla. *Makes almost 2 cups.*

NOTES ON SOUFFLÉS

The reputation hot soufflés have for being tricky dates back to the days of ovens without heat controls. Today fabulous high-rising soufflés can be produced every time. But one word of caution: guests must wait for soufflés; soufflés will not wait for guests.

To serve a soufflé, open it with a serving spoon and fork held back to back; don't plunge into it with a spoon, or it will deflate immediately. For each serving, lift out some of the crusty part first, then some from the center, which should be moist, almost like a sauce.

Egg whites make soufflés rise. The recipes in this book say to beat them (sometimes with cream of tartar, which helps to stabilize them) in an unlined copper bowl, using a piano-wire balloon whisk, for egg whites beaten this way mound higher—and thus make higher soufflés —than do those beaten in an electric mixer.

Before using the bowl, clean it with 1 tablespoon of coarse salt and 1 tablespoon of vinegar, rub it out with paper towels, and rinse it with *hot* water; dry it thoroughly. Before using the whisk, make sure it, too, is clean—completely free of grease, that is, and without a speck of egg yolk, which is fatty, which will keep the whites from mounding properly. If you don't own an unlined copper bowl or a piano-wire balloon whisk, use an electric mixer or a rotary beater, making sure the beaters and whatever bowl is used are thoroughly clean.

Eggs are easiest to separate when they're cold from a refrigerator, but eggs whites that are to be beaten should be at room temperature. For the best results, don't try to beat more than 8 whites at a time; and, keeping the tip of the whisk always in the bowl, swing the whisk round and round—use wrist muscles, not shoulder muscles—to beat as much air as is possible into the whites.

Stirring a big spoonful of egg whites into the base mixture lightens it, making it easier to blend the mixture completely.

When adding the remaining egg whites to the mixture—folding them in, that is—work quickly and lightly. Use a big rubber spatula and cut down through the center of the mixture and to the bottom of the bowl, then move across the bottom and up a side, over to the center, down again, and so on. Keep turning the bowl as you fold. And do not overmix: it's better to leave a few fluffs of white showing than to risk deflating the egg whites.

For a crustier-than-usual outside, bake the soufflé on the bottom shelf of the oven; for a softer outside, stand the soufflé in a pan of hot water and bake it 15 minutes longer than recipes state.

Some experts say you can prepare a soufflé ahead and keep it under an inverted bowl for ½ hour before baking it, but I don't recommend you try this. Soufflés can't be prepared in advance; I don't care what anyone says. Do the base mixture far ahead; then excuse yourself from your guests, beat the egg whites, fold the soufflé together, and put it in the oven—it doesn't take long, and the results are well worth the wait.

VANILLA SOUFFLÉ

For this recipe use either a 6-cup soufflé dish or a 4-cup soufflé dish fitted with a paper collar made by folding a 2-foot strip of waxed paper in half lengthwise, wrapping it around the top of the dish so it extends 4 to 5 inches above the dish, and tying it around the dish with string; it is not necessary to butter the dish, but if a collar is used, butter the inside of it. Or use 6 or 8 individual soufflé cups, ¾- or 1-cup size.

3 *tablespoons butter*	5 *egg yolks*
3 *tablespoons flour*	2 *tablespoons vanilla*
1 *cup milk*	7 *egg whites*
⅓ *cup sugar*	¼ *teaspoon cream of tartar*

1. Melt butter in a non-aluminum saucepan over high heat and stir in flour with a wooden spatula.

• For a hot lemon soufflé, use ¼ cup of butter and ¼ cup of flour here, and in step 5, eliminate the vanilla and use ½ cup of lemon juice and 1 tablespoon of grated lemon rind instead.

2. Cook the flour, stirring constantly, for a few minutes. Do not let it brown.

3. Remove from heat and add milk, whisking vigorously, then return to high heat, add sugar, and cook, stirring constantly, until the mixture comes to a boil and is thick and smooth. Set aside to cool slightly before adding egg yolks.

4. Beat in egg yolks 1 at a time, or beat the yolks together enough to mix them and then beat them into the mixture with a whisk.

5. Add vanilla. Mixture should be the consistency of mayonnaise. If it's too thin, set the pan over low heat and cook, whisking vigorously, until thickened. Cool slightly.

• Soufflé can be made ahead to this point and refrigerated for several hours.

• For a Grand Marnier soufflé, substitute 2 tablespoons of Grand Marnier for the vanilla and add 1 tablespoon of grated orange peel.

6. Beat egg whites in an unlined copper bowl, using a piano-wire balloon whisk. When whites foam slightly, add cream of tartar. Continue beating until the mixture is stiff but not dry.

• Egg whites are ready when most of them can be scooped onto the whisk.

7. Stir about ⅛ of the egg whites into the egg-yolk mixture to lighten it, then fold in the remaining egg white.

8. Either pour the mixture into a single soufflé dish and place it on the bottom shelf of a preheated 375° oven and bake for 30 minutes, or pour it into individual cups, rounding it a little (but don't make the cups too full), and bake for 15 minutes. Serve immediately.

• For a vanilla soufflé with macaroons: soak 12 macaroons for 10 minutes in ½ cup of Grand Marnier; pour ½ the soufflé mixture into a single dish and sprinkle on ½ the soaked macaroon crumbs; pour in the remaining soufflé mixture and sprinkle the remaining crumbs around the edge; then bake. For a soufflé with ladyfingers: dip 6 ladyfingers in liqueur, place them in half-filled soufflé dish; fill the dish with mixture; and bake. *Makes 6 to 8 servings.*

Frozen Lemon Soufflé

For this recipe use an 8-cup soufflé dish with a paper collar made from a length of waxed paper long enough to go around the dish with some overlap. Fold the paper in half lengthwise and brush the inside edge with vegetable oil, then tie it around the top of the dish, extending 4 to 5 inches above it.

10 *separated eggs*
2 *cups sugar*
Grated peel of 4 lemons
1 *cup lemon juice*
¼ *teaspoon salt*
2 *tablespoons (2 envelopes) unflavored gelatin*

½ *cup light or dark rum*
3 *cups heavy cream*
2 *tablespoons confectioners' sugar*
½ *cup ground almonds*
Candied violets (available in gourmet shops)

1. In an electric mixer bowl, beat egg yolks until light and fluffy.

2. Gradually add 1 cup of sugar and continue beating until the mixture will "form the ribbon"—that is, until some of it will fall from the beaters and look like a ribbon on the surface of the rest.

3. Add grated lemon peel, lemon juice, and salt.

• Use a small hand grater on the lemons. Grate off just the thin yellow layer of peel; don't dig into the bitter white part.

• Lemons keep best when they are wrapped in plastic bags and stored in the vegetable drawer of a refrigerator.

• For a Frozen Daiquiri Soufflé, use the grated peel of 2 lemons and 2 limes with ½ cup of lemon juice and ½ cup of lime juice here; use ground pistachios in step 12; and if desired, decorate the center of the soufflé with a slice of lime dipped in crystallized sugar.

4. Blend thoroughly, then transfer the mixture to a heavy pan (not aluminum) and stir it over low heat, constantly, until it thickens enough to coat the back of a spoon—to film the spoon, that is, enough so that a line can be drawn in the film with your finger. The mixture must not curdle; if it seems to be getting too hot, take the pan off heat for 1 or 2 seconds.

5. Sprinkle the gelatin over rum to soften it, then stir the rum-gelatin mixture into the egg-and-lemon mixture. Stir until the gelatin is completely dissolved, then remove mixture from heat, pour it into a large bowl, and let it cool, stirring occasionally.

6. In another bowl and with clean beaters, beat egg whites until foamy. Gradually add the remaining 1 cup of sugar, 1 tablespoon at a time, and beat until the mixture looks like marshmallow. Feel it between thumb and forefinger; if it feels smooth, it's ready.

7. In a chilled bowl, beat 2 cups of the heavy cream until it mounds nicely but isn't too stiff.

8. Fold egg-white mixture into the egg-and-lemon mixture thoroughly. Then fold in the whipped cream.

9. Pour the mixture into the prepared soufflé dish and put it in a refrigerator to set for at least 3 hours. It's better to refrigerate the mixture longer so that flavors have time to blend.

10. Before serving, whip the remaining 1 cup of cream with confec-

tioners' sugar until stiff, then put it into a pastry bag fitted with a star tube.

11. Carefully remove collar from soufflé.

• When the collar is put on with the fold at the bottom (and the open edges at the top), a warmed table knife can be run between the pieces of waxed paper to loosen it.

12. Decorate the sides of the soufflé extending above the dish with ground nuts by holding the dish with one hand (hold it over a pan or a piece of waxed paper), and scooping up nuts and pressing them against the soufflé with the other hand.

13. Pipe rosettes of whipped cream around the top of the soufflé and put a candied violet on each.

• If desired, put some candied lemon peel dipped in crystallized sugar in the center. *Makes 12 to 14 servings.*

STOCK AND SAUCES

STOCK

There are three basic types of stock: beef (see p. 240), chicken (see p. 241), and fish (see p. 242). The technique used for each is the same, and it is easy. Although preparing stock takes several hours, the flavor that homemade stock adds to recipes makes the time spent simmering meat (or poultry or fish), bones, vegetables, herbs, and water together in a large kettle well worth it.

It isn't necessary to watch stock closely while it cooks, and it is virtually impossible to ruin it. Stock can be stored in wide-mouth jars or plastic containers in a refrigerator for up to a week if it is brought to a boil each day to destroy any foreign organisms, or it can be frozen (I like to freeze it in measured amounts) for up to 2 months. Many cooks store bones and scraps of meat, poultry, or fish in their freezers until they've collected enough for a large quantity of stock; then they make enough at one time to serve their cooking needs for 1 or 2 months.

Stock is often called the building block of the kitchen, for the uses for it are almost endless. It serves as the liquid for braising meats or for poaching poultry or fish. It is also used to cook hearty vegetables, to flavor rice dishes, and to provide the traditional base for classic sauces

—from light Brown Sauce (see p. 248) to rich Velouté (see p. 246)—and for homemade soups. Moreover, when clarified, stock is an instantly elegant consommé (see p. 243); jellied, it becomes a tasty and decorative aspic (see p. 243); and concentrated, it is meat glaze (see p. 244), which provides a wonderful lift for the sauce or gravy that is missing "something."

Stock should certainly be in the repertoire of any aspiring cook. Take the time to learn about it, and the recipes will remain among the most frequently used in your collection.

BEEF STOCK

2 *lbs. cubed lean beef brisket or shin*	1 *medium clove mashed garlic*
2 *lbs. raw beef bones*	½ *teaspoon dried thyme*
1 *veal knuckle*	1 *bay leaf*
1 *cup sliced carrots*	3 *sprigs parsley*
2 *medium peeled onions*	2 *tablespoons tomato paste*
4 *whole cloves*	1 *tablespoon salt*
1 *cup sliced celery ribs, with leaves*	½ *teaspoon freshly cracked black pepper*
1 *cup dry white wine*	

1. Put beef, beef bones, veal knuckle, carrots, celery, and onions stuck with cloves all together into a roasting pan and place in a preheated 450° oven for about 30 minutes, or until the beef is thoroughly browned. To make sure the vegetables do not scorch, take the pan from the oven occasionally and stir them with a wooden spatula; remove them as soon as they are brown.

2. Put the browned vegetables and meat and the bones in a deep kettle or stock pot. Then pour 1 cup of cold water into the roasting pan and scrape up the brown bits. Pour the water and brown bits into the kettle or stock pot, add enough cold water to make 4 quarts in all, add wine, garlic, thyme, bay leaf, parsley, tomato paste, salt, and pepper, and bring to a boil very slowly. Skim off all scum that rises to the top.

3. Reduce heat, partially cover the kettle or pot, and simmer gently for 4 hours. Skim occasionally.

4. Strain through a sieve lined with a double thickness of cheesecloth wrung out in cold water.

• Taste for seasoning, if desired. But note, stock should be underseasoned, for many times it is used in reduced or concentrated sauces, which too highly seasoned stock may ruin.

• If recipe calls for extra-strength stock, boil ordinary stock, uncovered, over moderately high heat until it is reduced by one third. *Makes 2 to 3 quarts.*

CHICKEN STOCK

Do not confuse chicken stock with chicken soup, which contains many more ingredients, but for sublime chicken soup, first make chicken stock, then use the stock to cook chicken for the soup.

4 *lbs. chicken backs, wings, necks, and giblets or a 4-lb. whole chicken*
1 *cup sliced carrots*
1 *cup sliced celery ribs, with leaves*
2 *medium peeled onions*
4 *whole cloves*
1 *cup dry white wine*
1 *medium clove mashed garlic*
½ *teaspoon dried thyme*
1 *bay leaf*
3 *sprigs parsley*
2 *tablespoons tomato paste*
1 *tablespoon salt*
½ *teaspoon freshly cracked black pepper*

1. Place all ingredients and 4 quarts of cold water in a deep kettle or stock pot, sticking 2 whole cloves into each onion, and bring to a boil slowly. Skim off any scum that rises to the top.

• Chicken parts to be used for stock can be stored in a freezer as you collect them and stock made when the collection is large enough.

2. Reduce heat, partially cover the kettle or pot, and simmer gently for 1½ hours.

3. Remove the chicken, strip the meat from the bones, return the bones to the kettle or pot, and simmer for another 2½ hours.

• The stripped meat can be used in salads or sandwiches, or in any recipe calling for cooked chicken.

4. Strain through a sieve lined with a double thickness of cheesecloth wrung out in cold water.

• Taste for seasoning if desired. But note, stock is often used in reduced or concentrated sauces, and if it's already seasoned to taste, intensification may ruin the sauce.

• If recipe calls for extra-strength stock, boil ordinary stock, uncovered, over moderately high heat until it is reduced by one third. *Makes 2 to 3 quarts.*

Veal Stock

Follow the recipe for chicken stock, substituting veal and veal bones for the chicken.

FISH STOCK

1 cup sliced onion	1 cup dry white wine
½ cup sliced celery rib	Bouquet garni (see p. 7)
½ cup sliced carrot	1 teaspoon salt
2 lbs. fish bones and trim-	½ teaspoon freshly cracked
mings, all from lean fish	white pepper

1. Put all ingredients and 1 quart of cold water into a kettle or stock pot and bring to a boil. Skim off any scum that rises to the top.
2. Reduce heat, partially cover the kettle or pot, and simmer ½ hour. Skim if necessary.
3. Strain through a fine sieve.

• For stronger stock, boil to reduce.
• Fish stock can be frozen in plastic containers or wide-mouth jars. **Makes 3 to 4 cups.**

COURT BOUILLON

(Short Broth)

Court bouillon, unlike fish stock, contains no fish trimmings and takes only about 10 minutes to prepare. It can be used for poaching or boiling any fish or shellfish, but never, never drop fish or shellfish into boiling Court Bouillon—it will toughen the fish.

2 cups dry vermouth or other	2 teaspoons salt
dry white wine or 2 cups	8 peppercorns
cider vinegar	3 sprigs parsley
½ cup roughly chopped onion	1 bay leaf
½ cup roughly chopped carrot	1 clove
½ cup roughly chopped celery	¼ teaspoon dried thyme
rib	

1. Put all ingredients and 2 quarts of cold water into a large saucepan or kettle, bring to a boil, and boil rapidly for ½ hour.
2. Strain bouillon and cool. **Makes 9 to 10 cups.**

BEEF AND CHICKEN CONSOMMÉS

3 quarts beef stock (see
   p. 240) or chicken stock (see
   p. 241)
½ cup sliced carrot
2 tablespoons sliced leek,
   white part only

½ cup small sliced onion
½ cup sliced celery rib
1 tablespoon tomato paste
3 egg whites

1. Degrease stock—thoroughly—by putting it in a refrigerator to chill, then lifting off the fat that comes to the top and solidifies.

2. Put cold stock in a kettle, add remaining ingredients, and bring to a boil, whisking constantly to make the egg whites foamy. The whites will then attract floating particles in the stock, thus clarifying it.

• The flavor of beef consommé can be intensified by adding small pieces of raw beef.

3. Reduce heat and simmer gently for ½ hour. As the stock simmers, the egg whites and particles attracted to them will coagulate and form an island; don't disturb this island.

4. Strain through a sieve lined with a double thickness of cheesecloth wrung out in cold water, pouring carefully so as not to disturb the island, which should not be squeezed or pushed through the cheesecloth. Do not let the sieve touch the clear broth that has dripped through it, or the consommé will be cloudy. *Makes 2½ quarts.*

ASPIC

2 cups strong chicken stock
   (see p. 241), fish stock (see
   p. 242), or veal stock (see
   p. 242)
½ cup tomato juice
2 envelopes unflavored gelatin

1 crushed eggshell
2 lightly beaten egg whites
2 tablespoons cognac, brandy,
   Madeira, or white wine
1 teaspoon salt
½ teaspoon freshly cracked
   black pepper

1. Combine all ingredients in a saucepan and bring slowly to a boil, whisking constantly.

2. Remove from heat and let stand 5 minutes.

3. Strain into a bowl through a strainer lined with a double thickness of wet cheesecloth. Do not force it through, just let it drip through by itself. Keep the strainer well above level of the aspic. If not clear, pour it through the strainer again.

4. Place in a refrigerator for 1 hour to set.

• Aspic can be made a day ahead and kept refrigerated but it should not be frozen. *Makes about 2 cups.*

MEAT GLAZE
(Glace de Viande)

Meat glaze, which is nothing more than strained beef stock reduced to a syrup, can be bought, but it's easy to make and store—in a covered jar in the refrigerator. Use it whenever a concentrated beef flavor is desired (particularly good for seasoning sauces).

> *3 quarts beef stock (see*
> *p. 240)*

1. Boil stock, in a large kettle for ½ hour, or until it's reduced to about 1 quart.
2. Strain the reduced stock into a small saucepan and boil ½ hour, or until it is further reduced, to about 1½ cups.

• Watch it carefully near the end, so it doesn't burn.

3. Cool about 1 hour.

• Always use a clean spoon to dip into meat glaze. *Makes about 1½ cups.*

Sauces

It would take an entire cookbook to describe the hundreds of different sauces that can be used to complete or to enhance meat dishes, fish, poultry, eggs, vegetables, and salads. This section is not designed as a definitive sauce-book, but rather as a basic primer of sauces. Every one of the classic sauces, no matter how complicated, is just a variation of one of the basic or mother sauces. After you have mastered the preparation of the sauces in this section, no other sauce recipe will be difficult for you—it will only be a variation of a technique with which you are already familiar.

There are five basic warm sauces: three of them, Béchamel (see p. 245), Velouté (see p. 246), and Hollandaise (see p. 246) are light-colored; two,

Demiglace (see p. 248) and Tomato (see p. 250), are dark. Cold sauces stem from two basic roots, Mayonnaise (see p. 251) and Vinaigrette (see p. 252), both of which are light-colored. Finally there are all of the butter-based sauces, which may be served hot or cold and are either light or dark in color.

I've included recipes for some of my own favorite variations of the basic sauce groups, but I do hope that you will experiment with your own favorite herbs and additions to develop personal variations.

BÉCHAMEL SAUCE

This white sauce can be made thin, medium, or thick. It is used as a base for soufflés and I make it when I want a cream sauce for vegetables.

> *2 cups milk*
> *¾ cup chopped onion*
> *1 small bay leaf*
> *½ teaspoon salt*
> *¼ teaspoon freshly cracked*
> *white pepper*
>
> *⅛ teaspoon freshly grated*
> *nutmeg*
> *1 to 3 tablespoons butter*
> *1 to 3 tablespoons flour*

1. Put milk, onion, bay leaf, salt, pepper, and nutmeg into a saucepan and simmer, uncovered, for 15 minutes.
2. Strain. There should be 1 cup of seasoned milk.
3. Melt butter in a saucepan—for thin Béchamel use 1 tablespoon, for medium use 2 tablespoons, and for thick use 3. Then make a roux by stirring in flour—1 tablespoon for thin Béchamel, 2 tablespoons for medium, and 3 tablespoons for thick—with a wooden spatula and cooking, over high heat, stirring, for at least 2 minutes.
4. Remove from heat and add the seasoned milk, beating vigorously with a wire whisk for 5 minutes.
5. Return to heat and cook, stirring constantly, until smooth and thick. *Makes 2 cups.*

Mornay Sauce

Stir ½ cup grated Parmesan or Swiss cheese into 2 cups hot Béchamel Sauce in step 5. Use over cauliflower or crêpes.

Duxelles Sauce

Stir 1 recipe Duxelles (see p. 130) into 2 cups hot Béchamel Sauce. Great over poached poultry or sautéed veal.

Aurore Sauce

Stir ½ cup tomato paste or puree and 2 tablespoons sherry into 2 cups hot Béchamel Sauce. Serve over vegetables or eggs.

VELOUTÉ SAUCE

Velouté is a white sauce made with stock. For chicken dishes, use chicken stock; for fish, fish stock; for veal, veal stock.

¼ cup butter	*p. 241), fish stock (see*
¼ cup flour	*p. 242) or veal stock (see*
2½ cups chicken stock (see	*p. 242)*

1. Melt butter in a saucepan and stir in flour with a wooden spatula. Cook over high heat, stirring constantly, for at least 2 minutes. Do not let the flour brown.

• The quick way to save any mixture that's suddenly getting too hot is to lift the pan off the heat. It's as simple as that. Don't waste time turning a knob or pushing a button.

2. Take the pan off heat and add stock all at once, beating vigorously with a wire whisk for 3 minutes.
3. Return the pan to high heat and cook, stirring, until the mixture thickens and comes to a boil. Boil 1 minute. *Makes 2 cups.*

Sauce Bonne Femme

Add ¼ cup heavy cream and 2 tablespoons lemon juice to 2 cups Velouté. Use on broiled or sautéed foods.

Sauce Suprême

Fold ¼ cup whipped cream and 2 tablespoons butter into 2 cups Velouté. Serve with green vegetables or poached chicken.

Sauce Bercy

Simmer 1 cup finely minced onions in ¾ cups dry white wine until all of the liquid is absorbed. Then stir onions into 2 cups hot Velouté Sauce. Serve over sautéed liver, poached chicken, or seafood casseroles.

HOLLANDAISE SAUCE

Hollandaise is an easy sauce to make. I prefer to use the direct heat method, which is faster and yields slightly more sauce than do the other methods.

½ cup butter
3 egg yolks
2 tablespoons lemon juice

¼ teaspoon salt
¼ teaspoon freshly cracked
white pepper

1. Melt butter, which should be very hot when you are ready for it.
2. Put egg yolks and 3 tablespoons of cold water in a small non-aluminum pan and whisk them together over high heat, raising and lowering the pan over heat as you whisk. The outside of the pan must not get too hot to touch or the sauce will curdle. If it starts to get hot, take the pan completely off the heat for a moment, but don't stop whisking. Whisk about 10 minutes, or until the mixture starts to mound and is the consistency of heavy cream.

• For blender Hollandaise, blend egg yolks, lemon juice, salt, and pepper 1 minute, then with the blender on high speed, pour in very hot melted butter (use the opening in the top of the blender) in a thin stream. Sauce will thicken by itself.

3. Take the pan off heat, whisk in ¼ cup of the hot melted butter, 1 tablespoon at a time, then return the pan to high heat, and still whisking, add the remaining butter in a thin stream. Whisk about 5 minutes until the mixture is thick and creamy, and snatch the pan off the heat for a moment—but don't stop whisking—if it starts to get too hot.
4. Add lemon juice, salt, and pepper, and if necessary to hold the sauce until serving time, stand the pan in warm water (Hollandaise should not be served hot, just warm, on hot food) and whisk occasionally.

• If the sauce isn't thick enough, put it back on heat and whisk until it thickens.
• If it curdles because of overcooking, it can be brought back by whisking in 1 tablespoon of cold water or 1 tablespoon of boiling water or by first whisking a fresh egg yolk, then very slowly whisking the sauce into it.

Minted Hollandaise

Add 1 tablespoon of fresh chopped mint leaves to Hollandaise sauce before serving. Serve with lamb.

Sauce Maltaise

Omit lemon juice and before serving season Hollandaise with the juice of ½ orange and 2 teaspoons of freshly grated orange rind.

• Maltaise is especially good on vegetables.

BÉARNAISE SAUCE

This sauce is part of the Hollandaise family and is especially good with steak. I also like it with lamb and over green vegetables.

½ cup butter
1 tablespoon chopped shallot
½ cup tarragon vinegar
1 tablespoon dried tarragon or 3 tablespoons finely chopped fresh tarragon

3 egg yolks
¼ teaspoon salt
¼ teaspoon freshly cracked white pepper
2 tablespoons chopped parsley, optional

1. Melt butter, which should be very hot when you are ready for it.
2. Put shallot, vinegar, and tarragon in a small heavy pan and cook, stirring with a wooden spatula, over moderately high heat about 5 minutes, or until all liquid evaporates. Do not let the mixture burn.
3. Take the pan off the heat, add egg yolks and 2 tablespoons of cold water and whisk together until well blended.
4. Return the pan to heat and whisk the egg-yolk mixture, raising and lowering the pan over heat (to keep it from getting too hot), until the mixture is the consistency of heavy cream.
5. Take the pan off heat, whisk in ¼ cup of the hot butter, 1 tablespoon at a time, then return the pan to heat, and still whisking, add the remaining butter in a thin stream. Whisk, raising and lowering the pan over heat, until the mixture is thick.

• Strain sauce, if desired, before adding parsley.

6. Season with salt and pepper.

• Stir in parsley if desired. *Makes ¾ to 1 cup.*

BASIC BROWN SAUCE

(Demiglace)

Purists insist that Brown Sauce must cook for several days, but I doubt that many people have palates sensitive enough to tell the difference between a purist's Brown Sauce and mine, which is a quick one.

3 tablespoons butter
¾ cup finely minced onion
½ cup diced carrot
4½ teaspoons flour

2 cups beef stock (see p. 240)
1 tablespoon minced shallot
2 medium cloves minced garlic

Bouquet garni (see p. 7)
2 teaspoons tomato paste
¼ teaspoon freshly cracked
black pepper

½ teaspoon meat glaze (see
p. 244)

1. Melt butter in a small pan, and when it is hot and foaming, add onion and carrot and cook over high heat for 5 minutes, stirring with a wooden spatula.

2. Blend in flour, stirring with the wooden spatula, to make a roux.

3. Cook the roux, stirring constantly, about 10 minutes, or until it turns brown.

• The browned roux gives the sauce its characteristic flavor.

4. Remove pan from heat and add beef stock, beating vigorously with a wire whisk.

5. Add shallot, garlic, bouquet garni, tomato paste, pepper, and meat glaze, then return pan to heat, bring mixture to a boil, reduce heat, cover the pan, and cook mixture *very* slowly for ½ hour, or if there is time, longer (I prefer to cook about 2 hours in all) to intensify flavor.

6. Strain through a fine sieve, then taste for, and if necessary, adjust seasoning.

• Brown sauce freezes well (I like to store measured cupfuls in the freezer); in a refrigerator it will keep for 1 week. *Makes 1 cup.*

Sauce Robert

A hearty, spicy sauce—very good with pork.

2 tablespoons butter
¾ cup very finely chopped
onion
¼ cup wine vinegar
1 cup Basic Brown Sauce (see
p. 248)

¼ cup chopped gherkins
1 teaspoon Dijon mustard
1 tablespoon chopped parsley

1. Melt butter in a small saucepan, add onion, and cook, stirring, until mixture is transparent. Do not let it brown.

2. Add vinegar and cook over moderately high heat until vinegar is reduced by one half.

3. Add Basic Brown Sauce, bring to a boil, and reduce heat.

4. Simmer for 15 minutes, then stir in gherkins, mustard, and parsley, and bring to a boil again.

Sauce Périgourdine

A truly elegant sauce to serve with good beef.

1 cup Basic Brown Sauce (see p. 248)
½ cup dry Madeira

2 tablespoons chopped truffle
Reserved pan drippings

1. Strain Basic Brown Sauce, then boil it until it is reduced by one third.

2. Stir in Madeira and chopped truffle and add the pan drippings reserved from the beef. Taste for seasoning and, if desired, add salt and pepper. Serve warm.

Madeira Sauce

Good on beef, excellent on sweetbreads.

1 recipe of Basic Brown Sauce (see p. 248)
2 tablespoons minced shallots

9 tablespoons Madeira
1 tablespoon cognac

1. Cook shallots and ½ cup of the Madeira in a saucepan over medium heat until mixture is reduced to 1 tablespoon. Take care that it doesn't burn.

2. Strain Brown Sauce and whisk it into the pan. Mix well. Return pan to heat. Heat contents, but do not let them boil.

3. Remove pan from heat, stir in cognac, and the remaining 1 tablespoon of Madeira.

TOMATO SAUCE

1 cup chopped onion
½ cup chopped carrot
½ cup chopped celery
2 medium cloves chopped garlic
¼ cup butter
3 tablespoons flour
1 cup strong beef stock (see p. 240) or chicken stock (see p. 241)

4 cups diced fresh tomatoes or 4 cups canned Italian plum tomatoes, squeezed through your fingers
2 teaspoons salt
¼ teaspoon freshly cracked black pepper
Bouquet garni (see p. 7)

1. Simmer the onion, carrot, celery, and garlic in butter for 20 minutes, in a covered skillet.

2. Stir in the flour and cook without browning for 3 minutes.

3. Add remaining ingredients and cook for 3 hours to develop flavor and reduce some of the liquid. Half-cover the kettle. Stir the mixture frequently. If it gets too thick, add more stock.

4. Remove bouquet garni, and puree the mixture through a food mill, using the finest blade. Taste the sauce and adjust seasoning. Use, or freeze for later use. *Makes about 4 cups.*

Sauce Italienne

Add ½ teaspoon oregano and ½ teaspoon basil in step 3. Wonderful on pasta.

Sauce Portugaise

Combine an equal amount of Tomato Sauce and Brown Sauce and serve over fish, poultry, or meat.

Sauce Provençale

Add 1 medium clove chopped garlic to 4 cups Tomato Sauce. Serve with fish, poultry, or eggs.

MAYONNAISE

½ teaspoon salt	*¼ teaspoon freshly cracked*
1 tablespoon tarragon, red- or	*black or white pepper*
white-wine, or cider vinegar	*1 cup olive or vegetable oil*
or 1 tablespoon lemon juice	*or a mixture of the two*
1 egg yolk	

1. Put salt, vinegar (or lemon juice), pepper, and egg yolk into a small (about 1-quart) bowl and whisk well.

• For blender mayonnaise, blend salt, vinegar (or lemon juice), pepper, 2 egg yolks, and 2 tablespoons of oil for a few seconds to mix, then with the blender on high speed, pour in the remaining oil in a thin stream.

2. Whisk in ¼ cup of oil, 1 tablespoon at a time (whisk thoroughly after the addition of each spoonful), then pour in the remaining oil in a thin stream (use a measuring cup with a pouring lip), whisking constantly about 5 minutes, or until mixture is thick and smooth.

• If the oil is added too quickly, the mixture will curdle. If it does, whisk a fresh egg yolk in another bowl, and whisking constantly, add the curdled mixture to it, 1 teaspoon at a time.

• I like to season mayonnaise by adding either 1 teaspoon of Dijon mustard or 1 tablespoon of chopped fresh herbs. *Makes 1 cup.*

Green Mayonnaise

Cover 4 or 5 spinach leaves with boiling water, boil 1 minute, then drain, squeeze out excess water, chop as fine as possible, and stir into 1 cup mayonnaise. Use on cold fish.

Tartar Sauce

Add 1 small dill pickle, finely chopped, 2 tablespoons of drained capers, and 2 tablespoons of finely chopped parsley to mayonnaise. Serve with fish.

Aioli

Stir 4 or more finely mashed cloves garlic into 1 cup mayonnaise. Wonderful as a dip with raw vegetables.

VINAIGRETTE SAUCE

True French vinaigrette is made with salt, pepper, vinegar, and oil in varying proportions, depending on what it's to be used for. To Americanize the vinaigrette, try the following, which is particularly good with artichokes (see p. 163) and asparagus (see p. 163) and in the hollows of pitted ripe avocado halves.

1 tablespoon vinegar
½ teaspoon salt
¼ teaspoon freshly cracked black pepper
2 tablespoons lemon juice
6 tablespoons olive oil
½ teaspoon dry mustard
1 chopped hard-cooked egg
1 tablespoon chopped parsley

1 teaspoon dried tarragon or 1 tablespoon fresh
2 tablespoons washed and dried capers
1 tablespoon chopped scallion, white part only
½ teaspoon chopped shallot
1 tablespoon chopped fresh chives, if available

Put all ingredients into a bowl and stir with a fork to mix. *Makes ¾ cup.*

Maître d'Hôtel Butter

Pack this butter in little containers and store them in a refrigerator or freezer. Brush this butter over hot steak or chops at the table.

½ cup butter
1 tablespoon lemon juice
½ teaspoon salt
¼ teaspoon freshly cracked
black pepper
1 tablespoon finely chopped
parsley

1 teaspoon finely chopped
shallot, optional
¼ teaspoon finely chopped
garlic, optional

1. Cream butter in an electric mixer (use the flat whip if the mixer is a heavy-duty one).
2. Beat in lemon juice, salt, pepper, parsley, and if you like (I do, since otherwise I find Maître d'Hôtel Butter a little bland), shallot and garlic. *Makes ½ cup.*

Lemon Butter

Stir 2 tablespoons lemon juice and 1 tablespoon chopped parsley into ½ cup hot melted butter. Serve over vegetables or fish.

Beurre Noir

Melt ¼ lb. of butter over *very* low heat; take about 15 minutes to do this so that the butter toasts but does not burn. This sauce is especially good on cauliflower or any green vegetable, fried eggs, or sautéed fish.

Truffle Butter

Add 1 tablespoon finely chopped truffle to ½ cup hot melted butter. This very elegant sauce is served with beef or poached chicken.

CREATIVE COOKING SCHOOL MENUS

BRUNCH, LUNCH, OR LIGHT SUPPER

Hors d'Oeuvre Variés
French Omelettes
Hot French bread, pot of unsalted butter
Tarte aux Pêches

Quiche
Potage Paysanne
Beefsteak Tomato and Onion Salad
Poires au Vin Rouge

Shrimp Pâté
Crêpes Stuffed with Cheese Soufflé
Watercress and Mushroom Salad
Coffee Pot de Crème

Pâté Maison
Minestrone alla Milanese

Italian bread
French Green Salad
Gorgonzola cheese and fresh fruit

Roulade of Salmon
Raw Mushroom Salad
Fresh fruit and cheese

Garlic Soup
Salade Niçoise
Poires au Vin Rouge

Mushroom Soup Royale
Parmesan Sticks
Egg Mousse with Cucumber or Cold Lobster Mousse
Oranges Orientale

Ring Mold of Flounder Stuffed with Salmon Mousse
Minted Cucumbers
Lemon sherbet served with half fresh lemon

Senegalese
Flounder en Papillote
Lemon Curd

Poached Striped Bass with Sauce Gribiche

Broccoli Soufflé
Pears Hélène

Whitebait with Caper Mayonnaise
Minted Cucumbers
Lemon Curd

Cold Curried Avocado Soup
Lamb Chops in Mint Aspic
French Potato Salad
Meringue Shells filled with Cassis Sherbet

DINNER

Pyramid of Cheese Balls
Chicken Breasts Duxelles with White Wine Sauce
Rice Pilaf
French Green Salad
Cassis Sherbet (pass bottle of cassis)
Viennese Almond Balls

Mushroom Soup Royale
Flounder with Champagne Sauce
Filet de Boeuf en Croûte with Sauce Périgourdine
French Green Salad
Roquefort Mousse with toasted crackers
Oranges Orientale

Manhattan Clam Chowder
Baked Lobster Nicholas
Waffled Potatoes
Romaine Salad
Frozen Lemon Soufflé

Billi-Bi
Roast Fillet of Beef
Braised Belgian Endive

Potatoes Anna
Oeufs à la Neige

Pumpkin Soup
Truffled Turkey Flambé
Braised Brussels Sprouts
Chestnut Croquettes
Belgian Endive Salad
Rehrücken

Oysters Bienville
Roast Goose
Celery Sticks
Carrot Ring
Marron Roll

Lobster Bisque
Roast Veal
Potatoes Savoyard
Raw Spinach Salad
Beignets with Raspberry Sauce

Chestnut Soup
Canard aux Pêches
Seven-Minute Green Beans
Crêpes Flambées

Hungarian Chicken Paprika
Spaetzle
French Green Salad or Raw Spinach Salad
Vanilla Soufflé (Fudge Sauce, optional)

Mussels Marinara
Petti di Pollo
Sautéed Mushroom Caps and Pine Nuts
Romaine Salad or Zucchini Salad
Italian Rum Cake

Crudités with Skordalia
Ham en Croûte
Gâteau de Haricots Verts
Charlotte Portugaise

Stuffed Ham with Champagne Sauce and Frosted White Grapes
Mushroom Roll
Belgian Endive Salad
Frozen Daiquiri Soufflé

Piroshki
Shrimp à la Kiev
Onions à la Grecque
Butterscotch-Rum Parfait

Braised Boned Leg of Lamb
Soissons
French Green Salad
Marron Roll or Apricot Mousse

Blanquette de Veau or Veal Casserole
Rice Timbales or Rice Ring
Romaine Salad
Chocolate Crêpes

Crème de Crécy
Gigot d'Agneau Persillé

Cauliflower Mousse
Fresh pears

Selle d'Agneau
Potatoes Sarlandaise
Sautéed Cherry Tomatoes
Praline Flan

Rib Roast of Beef
Potatoes Dauphinoise
Carrots Vichy
Hazelnut Roll with Whipped-Cream Filling

Liptauer Cheese
Hungarian Goulash
Spaetzle
Pfannkuchen
(German apple pancake)

Pâté
Vitello Tonnato
Roman Tomatoes
Cherry Fritters

Mushrooms à la Grecque
Curried Shrimp with Condiments
Saffron Rice
Cucumber Salad with Yoghurt
Frozen Lemon Soufflé

Ham Slice with Madeira
Cabbage Stuffed with Cabbage
Cherry Fritters

Melon and Prosciutto
Veal Piccata
Italian Gnocchi
Zucchini Provençal or Raw Mushroom Salad
Biscuit Tortoni

Pork with Pistachios
Braised Boston Lettuce

Whipped Carrots
Crêpes à la Julie

Crudités with Skordalia—Pâté
   Maison
Cioppino
French Green Salad
Italian bread
Italian Rum Cake

French Pot Roast
Gâteau de Haricots Verts
Potatoes Dauphinoise
French Green Salad
Bananas Vieux Carré with Crème
   Fraîche

Steak au Poivre or Noisettes of
   Lamb
Noodle Nests filled with Pea Puree
Belgian Endive and Citrus Salad
Apricot Mousse with Chocolate
   Cornets

Parsley Soup
Barbecued Spareribs
Potatoes Savoyard
Beefsteak Tomato and Red Onion
   Salad
Fresh fruit or vanilla ice cream
   with Fudge Sauce

Trout Meunière
Rack of Lamb
Pommes Pailles
Flageolets
Oranges Orientale

Lobster Flambé or Steak Diane
Pommes Pailles
Artichokes Vinaigrette
Charlotte Portugaise

Pot Roast in Beer
Whipped Carrots
French Green Salad
Fruit and cheese

MEASURES

COMMONLY USED MEASURES

3 teaspoons = 1 tablespoon
4 tablespoons = ¼ cup
5⅓ tablespoons = ⅓ cup
8 tablespoons = ½ cup
10⅔ tablespoons = ⅔ cup
12 tablespoons = ¾ cup
16 tablespoons = 1 cup
2 cups liquid = 1 pint
4 cups liquid = 1 quart

Miscellaneous Equivalents

Bread: 1 slice = ½ cup cubes or crumbs
Butter: 1 pound = 2 cups or 32 tablespoons
      ¼ pound stick = ½ cup or 8 tablespoons
Carrots: 1 medium = ½ cup chopped
Celery: 1 medium rib = ½ cup chopped

Cheese: ¼ pound = 1 cup grated
Garlic: 1 medium clove = 1 teaspoon chopped
Gelatin: 1 envelope = 1 tablespoon
Herbs: 1 teaspoon dried = 1 tablespoon fresh
Lemon juice: Juice of 1 medium lemon = 3 tablespoons
Mushrooms: ¼ pound = 1 cup sliced
Onions: 1 medium = ¾ cup chopped
Potatoes: 1 medium = 1 cup chopped
Shallots: 1 medium = 1 tablespoon chopped
Tomatoes: 1 medium = ¾ cup chopped
Yeast: 1 package dry = ¼ ounce

Index